THE CURRICULUM: THEORY AND PRACTICE

(SECOND EDITION)

THE CURRICULUM:
THEORY AND PRACTICE
(SECOND EDITION)

A. V. KELLY

Harper & Row, Publishers
London

Cambridge San Francisco
Hagerstown Mexico City
Philadelphia Sao Paulo
New York Sydney

Harper & Row Ltd
28 Tavistock Street
London WC2E 7PN

British Library Cataloguing in Publication Data

Kelly, A.V.
  Curriculum: theory and practice – 2nd ed.
  1. Education – Curricula
  I. Title
  375   LB1570

  ISBN 0-06-318217-3
  ISBN 0-06-318218-1 Pbk

Typeset by Inforum Ltd, Portsmouth
Printed and bound by the Pitman Press, Bath

About the author

Vic Kelly is Dean of the School of Education at Goldsmiths' College and thus has overall responsibility for all of the work of that college in the field of Education, in both the initial and continuing education of teachers. He is conscious of the need to maintain, and, if possible, extend, the distinguished record of that institution in this sphere. His own particular interest is in the teaching of Curriculum Studies at both undergraduate and postgraduate levels.

His career in the education service spans almost thirty years of teaching in secondary modern and comprehensive schools and in teacher-education. His professional ambition is to encourage teachers to a greater recognition of the importance of thinking at a professional level about their educational practice, to raise the level of that thinking and thus to contribute to the development of an education system conducted by people who really understand what they are about. He is of the opinion that there are still too few of these at all levels of the present system and, further, that their number is in inverse ratio to the age of their pupils and thus to the form and length of their professional preparation.

The quality of the teacher's theory and practice is closely related to the kind of education he or she has enjoyed both before and subsequent to entering the profession, and current trends encourage little optimism in this area. Every attempt must continue to be made, however, to persuade teachers of the need to reflect about their work and to assist them to do this in a productive way. It is to this end that all of his publications, including this book, have been directed.

CONTENTS

Acknowledgements

There is an important sense in which one's awareness and understanding of curriculum issues are enhanced by every kind of contact with students, teachers and colleagues. Thus there is a wide range of people whose influence on the thinking behind this book must be acknowledged.

Particular mention must be made, however, of the contribution of those – largely anonymous – people who reviewed my first draft. They will quickly recognize in what follows the degree to which this final version reflects my appreciation of their highly perceptive and cogent comments.

I must also express my gratitude to Geva Blenkin, co-author with me of *The Primary Curriculum*, for permitting me to make extensive use of some of the material we used there in Chapter 4 of the present book. And, finally, I must declare my indebtedness to Jill Thorn, whose typing and editorial skills not only enabled me to come uncharacteristically close to meeting the publisher's deadlines, but also provided me with the kind of clean copy of my outpourings which made my own revisions easier and more effective.

Vic Kelly

'The teacher, like the artist, the philosopher, and the man of letters, can only perform his work adequately if he feels himself to be an individual directed by an inner creative impulse, not dominated and fettered by an outside authority.'

Bertrand Russell, *Unpopular Essays* (1950), p. 159.

Foreword

The first edition of *The Curriculum: Theory and Practice* attempted, amongst other things, to draw attention to and to commend the evolutionary nature of curriculum theory and curriculum practice. Indeed, the careful reader will have detected elements of that evolutionary nature even within the book itself. For that process of evolution accelerated while the book was in preparation and its final chapter on 'A Common Curriculum' represented an attempt to catch, in a rapid review and before the work became ossified by the printing of it, some features of the new developments that were already in train. Those developments have gathered massive momentum since that time.

In the five years since the publication of that first edition there have been major changes of scene. The background constraints on curriculum planning have moved closer to the foreground; concern with curriculum evaluation has grown into demands for teacher accountability; the role of the teacher in curriculum development, whose centrality that book was designed to stress, has been rapidly eroded; and in general the 'secret garden' of the curriculum has been thrown open to the public – an event which, as in many other stately homes, has led not only to proper forms of preservation but also to some trampling on the flower-beds.

The curriculum scene, then, is not only one of continuous change, it is also one in which that change has in recent years been dramatic in nature. This second edition of *The Curriculum: Theory and Practice*, therefore, in attempting the same kind of overview that was attempted by its forerunner, finds itself surveying a very different scene, one whose major features and whose focuses of interest have been transformed. Its publication, however, is still predicated on the belief that such an overview is necessary, a belief which is strengthened rather than weakened by the awareness that a broad understanding of the theory and practice of the curriculum is now needed not only by teachers but by all others who wish to contribute to the curriculum debate.

Introduction

For perhaps too long the assumption has been made by many teachers that education theory is for those who wish to talk about education, but of little value to those who wish to practise it. The gap between the theory and the practice of education has long been a yawning chasm and the rejection of theoretical considerations by many teachers has been total. This state of affairs has illustrated two things, each of them equally harmful to educational advance. For, in the first place, it represents what must be conceded as 'fair comment' on a good deal of what teachers have been offered under the heading of 'Education Theory' – by Departments of Education everywhere and by much of the literature. But, secondly, it also reflects an unwillingness on the part of teachers to modify or change their practices, since such modification and change, if it is not to be a mere slavish following of fashions or joining of bandwaggons, requires the kind of conscious reflection that only a theoretical perspective can provide. There is no doubt that intuition, in teaching as much as elsewhere, can lead, and often has led, to good, even superb, practice, but it will not suffice when deliberate planning for change is undertaken, whether by teachers themselves or by others.

It is the advent of the need for this kind of deliberate planning of curriculum change that is currently leading many teachers to a change of heart on this issue. For the process of change and planned curriculum development which might be said to have begun in the United Kingdom, certainly for the primary sector of education, with the publication of the Hadow Reports (Board of Education 1926, 1931) and which has been a major feature of education at all levels during the last two decades, has accelerated of late in response to increased external pressures upon schools.

Whatever else the 'Great Debate' did or did not do to forward educational progress, it did establish in the minds of both teachers and laymen the fact that it is necessary to engage in some theorizing about the curriculum before one can plan changes in educational practice.

As a result, it is becoming clear to teachers that they need to learn how to articulate their curricular practices in order to be able to modify and change them, and it is, or should be, even more apparent to them that they need to be able to do this in order to meet, to evaluate and to respond appropriately to, the demands that are increasingly being made of them from outside. For that same 'Great Debate', while rightly suggesting that society and all its members have a right to know about and to comment on what goes on in schools, also, unfortunately, because of the low level at which it was itself conducted, concealed the fact that to analyse curricular practices is a highly complex intellectual task and thus encouraged the belief that anyone can rush into it, no matter how untutored.

There are thus some dangers to be avoided in this search for a proper theoretical underpinning to curriculum planning. To begin with, it is as true here as in any other sphere of human activity that a little knowledge can often be more dangerous than no knowledge at all. And it is clear that often the knowledge upon which some teachers, even among those who rejoice in grand titles like 'Director of Studies' and have specific responsibility for the development of the curriculum of their schools, continue to base their forward planning is very slender indeed. Even more serious is the level of knowledge revealed by many local authority advisers in their attempts to influence and even to exercise control over what goes on in whole clutches of schools. For example, little has been more disturbing in recent educational practice than to observe the bland, even pretentious, manner in which many such advisers have been demanding from schools and teachers statements of their curriculum objectives, or records of their achievements framed in terms of such objectives, in apparent ignorance of the problematic nature of that approach to curriculum planning. In short, a failure to appreciate the intellectual level at which the curriculum debate must be conducted is not confined to people outside the teaching profession.

Secondly, there are dangers in going to the other extreme and indulging in debate at a level or of a kind that has little relevance for practice. It was this kind of spurious academicism that led many teachers to reject Education Theory in the first instance. Theorizing about the curriculum must achieve a proper linking of theoretical and practical considerations, and the question of what constitutes such a proper linking itself needs much careful thought. It must also be said that we are unlikely to attain such a proper linking if we continue to permit ourselves to be restricted by the conventions of the so-called 'contributory disciplines'. Philosophy, psychology, sociology and history will not of themselves provide us with a useful perspective on curriculum practices; indeed, they will often provide us with conflicting perspectives and they will certainly tempt us into their own levels of abstraction. What is needed is an amalgam of them, whose focus and organizing rationale is the practice of education itself. Furthermore, we must not deprive ourselves of what other disciplines may have to offer – disciplines such as anthropology, economics and political science.

A third danger is that much of the debate about the curriculum will continue to be conducted within subject areas rather than against the wider backcloth of the total educational experience offered to pupils. Much of the curriculum development that has taken place has been of this kind. Most of the work of the Schools Council, even in the primary field, has been devoted to curriculum development within particular school subjects, and the organizational structure of schools, certainly in the secondary sector, along with the forms of training provided for intending teachers, has also been such as to reinforce this approach. The unbalanced forms of curriculum that this can lead to have become all too apparent of late, not least as a result of the recent survey of secondary schools carried out by HM Inspectorate (DES 1979). If this danger is to be avoided, a wider perspective must be adopted by teachers and, indeed, by all who are concerned with the advancement of education.

Teachers, then, need an understanding of the theoretical bases of their work that will enable them to undertake deliberately planned curriculum change, to respond appropriately to suggestions and pressures from outside as to the form such change should take and, indeed, to articulate their practices in order to defend them against what they may regard as unwarranted pressures upon them to change. To enable them to do these things, their understanding must display a proper intellectual rigour, but it must at the same time reveal a practical relevance and it must embrace a breadth of knowledge across many relevant disciplines and across all the areas of the curriculum. Only this kind of theoretical understanding will provide a genuine underpinning for curricular practice which is educationally valid.

The purpose of this book, like that of its predecessor, is to assist teachers to develop this kind of theoretical perspective on their work as a basis for improved practice, for clarity of thinking and of purpose in their planning and for sound evaluation of external pressures. To achieve this purpose it attempts not to speak from the point of view of one traditional discipline, not to deal with one specific aspect of Curriculum Theory and not to argue one particular case, but rather to offer the kind of overview which has just been described. This it seeks to do by considering many of the theories that are offered in this area in order to provide the reader with the understanding he needs to weigh them against each other, and in order to help him to develop the kind of theoretical understanding he needs if his practical provision is to have real effect and if the gap between theory and practice is to be bridged.

If the book does argue a specific case – and it could hardly avoid doing so – that case has two main features. The first is a concern with education as a process that goes beyond the mere provision of pupils with useful information and skills and embraces also that enrichment of life that enhanced intellectual awareness can and must bring. In recent times the focus of the educational debate has shifted from educational ideals to political and economic realities. It is important to ensure that the acknowledgement of those realities does not lead to the complete loss of those ideals and thus to a lowering of the quality of life both for the individual and the community.

The second specific case this book argues is the centrality of the teacher's role in the process of education and in the whole process of curriculum development. For the book is written in the belief, and it attempts to establish the thesis, that control of curriculum development and of the quality of educational provision will always effectively rest in the hands of the teacher in the classroom, and that we would do better to direct our efforts towards attempting to support him in meeting that responsibility than towards endeavouring to take it from him and place the control in the hands of others who are in no position to exercise it effectively. In short, a main purpose of this book is to emphasize the vital importance of the initial and the continuing, in-service education of teachers as curriculum developers.

Finally, the book itself is offered as a contribution to that task of helping teachers to develop the expertise they need to fulfil a function for society which they, and they alone, can fulfil adequately.

CHAPTER 1

CURRICULUM DEVELOPMENT

It is stating the obvious to assert that education has changed drastically in the last twenty or thirty years. Both in the United Kingdom and elsewhere many important modifications have been made to all aspects of the education system. Nor is it surprising that the nature and structure of our education system should have been changing so extensively at a time when we have been experiencing social change of an equally dramatic kind, much of it prompted by rapid technological advance. The education system is a social institution which should be expected to change along with other such institutions. It would be more surprising, not to say disturbing, if the education system were to stand still while all else changed and it is this that renders incomprehensible the efforts of those who wish to see educational change arrested or even advocate a return to former systems, the suitability of which even to the times that spawned them is often difficult to discern.

Amidst all of this change, nothing has been more significant nor as fundamental as the major modifications that have been made to the curriculum. The significance of this lies in the fact that it has manifested itself at all levels of educational activity, from the nursery school through to the university, from the education of the least able pupils to that of the most educationally gifted. Its fundamental nature derives from the fact that the curriculum is the very foundation of any education system, and no amount of tinkering with the structure of the system, the organization of schools or the selection procedures to be used will have more than a peripheral effect unless accompanied by a rethinking of the real substance of education – the curriculum itself.

And so, changes to the structure of the school system, such as the introduction of comprehensive schools and of mixed-ability classes, have been followed by attempts to make corresponding modifications to the curriculum, since it has become clear that, in order to meet the demands of society, whether they be for more highly skilled and qualified technologists or for the provision of greater educational opportunities for all, close attention must be given to the curriculum itself. Indeed, without curriculum change, modifications to the structure of the system make little sense and have little point, since, as has become apparent from the attempts to promote equality of educational opportunity, in themselves they have but little effect. It is this awareness that has led to the increased attention that has been directed towards the school curriculum since the mid-1970s, both from within and from outside the teaching profession.

One feature that has characterized the curriculum change of recent years, and which must be realized at the outset of this discussion, is the increased incidence of planning and preparation in curriculum development. Most of the curriculum change that we have seen in the past has been of a kind best described as unplanned 'drift' (Hoyle 1969a) and a good deal of this still goes on. Recently, however, educationists have begun to see the need for planned innovation, to recognize that if educational change is to keep pace with and match changes in society, it must be deliberately managed rather than merely left to happen. To recognize this is not, of course, to be committed to a totally revolutionary approach to curriculum development. The advantages of evolution over revolution are at least as evident in education as elsewhere. It is, however, to acknowledge that the process of evolution can be smoother, quicker and more effective, if it is not left to chance but implemented according to carefully thought-out strategies. It is this that makes the kind of understanding of curriculum development that can come from a deep study of Curriculum Theory the most essential item in the armoury of the modern teacher.

It is the aim of this chapter to identify what is involved in this, to outline some of the essential ingredients both of the study of Curriculum Theory and the practice of curriculum planning. Almost all of these points will be examined in greater detail in the chapters that follow, but an overall framework, a rationale, a cognitive map offered at the outset may help to establish and maintain the interrelationship of the many factors involved in curriculum development. For a major problem facing the teacher as he recognizes his responsibility for curriculum planning is the range of interconnected factors that he must constantly keep in balance. Like a juggler he must not only keep many balls in the air at the same time, he must also maintain the proper relationships between them if disaster is not to ensue.

What is the curriculum?

The first need is to achieve some clarity over what we are to understand by the term 'curriculum'. It is a term which is used with several meanings and a number of different definitions of it have been offered, so it is important that we establish at the beginning what it should be taken to signify throughout this book.

To begin with, it will be helpful if we distinguish the use of the word to denote the content of a particular subject or area of study from the use of it to refer to the total programme of an educational institution. Many people still equate a curriculum with a syllabus and thus limit their planning to a consideration of the content or the body of knowledge they wish to transmit. It is also because this view of curriculum has been adopted that many teachers in primary schools have regarded issues of curriculum as of no concern to them, since they have not regarded their task as being to transmit bodies of knowledge in this manner. It will be clear, then, that this kind of definition of curriculum is limiting in more than one way and that it is likely to hamper rather than to assist the planning of curriculum change and development. Indeed, as was suggested in the Introduction, some of the inadequacies of previous attempts at curriculum planning can be attributed to the fact that it has tended to proceed in a rather piecemeal way within subjects rather than according to some overall rationale, so that the curriculum can be seen as 'the amorphous product of generations of tinkering' (Taba 1962, p. 8).

Both of these dimensions of curriculum development are, of course, important, but it is the rationale of the total curriculum that must have priority. 'Schools should plan their curriculum as a whole. The curriculum offered by a school, and the curriculum received by individual pupils, should not be simply a collection of separate subjects' (DES 1981, p. 12). At the very least, the total curriculum must be accorded prior consideration, and the main task that currently faces curriculum planners is to work out a basis on which some total scheme can be built.

Since it seems that this should be the main concern, this will be the focus of our discussion in this book and we will understand by the term 'curriculum' this overall rationale for the educational programme of an institution, and these general features of curriculum change and development, although much of what is said about curriculum development in this sense will, of course, be of relevance to the problems of developments within individual subject areas.

A further question that needs to be resolved is whether we are to place any limit on the kinds of school activity that we will allow to count as part of the curriculum. Again, the word can be found in use in a number of different contexts and again we need to distinguish these clearly.

For example, some educationists speak of the 'hidden curriculum', by which they mean those things which pupils learn at school because of the way in which the work of the school is planned and organized but which are not in themselves overtly included in the planning or even in the consciousness of those responsible for the school arrangements. Social roles, for example, are learnt, it is claimed, in this way, as are sex roles and attitudes to many other aspects of living. Implicit in any set of arrangements are the attitudes and values of those who create them, and these will be communicated to pupils in this accidental and perhaps even sinister way.

Some would argue that the values implicit in the arrangements made by schools for their pupils are quite clearly in the consciousness of some teachers and planners and are equally clearly accepted by them as part of what pupils should learn in school, even though they are not overtly recognized by the pupils themselves. In other words, teachers deliberately plan the school's 'expressive culture'. In such instances, therefore, the curriculum is 'hidden' only to or from the pupils. If or where this is so, the values to be learnt clearly form a part of what the teachers plan for their pupils and must, therefore, be accepted as fully a part of the curriculum.

Others, however, take a less definite and perhaps less cynical line on this but wish nevertheless to insist that teachers do have a responsibility here. They accept that the values and attitudes learnt via the hidden curriculum are not directly intended by teachers, but believe that, since these things are being learnt as a by-product of what is planned, teachers should be aware of and accept responsibility for what is going on, for what their pupils are learning in this unplanned way (Barnes 1976).

There is no doubting the importance of this notion of the hidden curriculum nor the need for curriculum planners and teachers to keep its implications constantly before them. Some, however, would argue that to use the term 'curriculum' to denote such kinds of learning is to render the planning of a total curriculum impossible since the term is being used here expressly to denote experiences that by definition have not been deliberately planned, and which cannot be so, at least without ceasing to be 'hidden' in the sense used. They prefer, therefore, to confine the use of the word 'curriculum' to those activities that are planned or are the result of some intentionality on the part of teachers and planners, and to deal with these other kinds of learning as the hidden results or by-products of the curriculum rather than as part of the curriculum itself.

Much the same point emerges when we consider the distinction that has sometimes been made between the official curriculum and the actual curriculum. By the official curriculum is meant what is laid down in syllabuses, prospectuses and so on, the actual curriculum being what is covered in the practice of the school. The difference between them may be conscious or unconscious, the cause of any mismatch being either a deliberate attempt by the teachers or others to deceive, to make what they offer appear more attractive than it really is, or merely the fact that, since teachers and pupils are human, the realities of any course will never fully match up to the hopes and intentions of those who have planned it.

Both of these distinctions are important and we would be foolish to go very far in our examination of the curriculum without acknowledging both the gaps that must inevitably exist between theory and practice and the predilection of some teachers for elaborate 'packaging' of their wares. Furthermore, we must not lose sight of the fact that curriculum study must ultimately be concerned with the relationship between these two views of the curriculum, between intention and reality, if it is to succeed in linking the theory and the practice of the curriculum (Stenhouse 1975).

Lastly, we must also recognize the distinction that is often drawn between the 'formal' curriculum and the 'informal' curriculum, between the formal activities for which the timetable of the school allocates specific periods of teaching time or which, as in the case of the primary school, are included in the programme of work to be covered in normal school hours, and those many informal activities that go on, usually on a voluntary basis, at lunchtimes, after school hours, at weekends or during holidays. These latter activities – sports, clubs, societies, school journeys and the like – are often called 'extracurricular' activities and this suggests that they should be seen as separate from, as over and above the curriculum itself.

The reasons for this, however, are difficult to discern unless they are those that derive from the time of the day or week when they take place or the nature of the voluntary participation that usually characterizes them.

For activities of this kind are usually seen to have as much educational validity and point as any of the formal arrangements of the school. Indeed, some would even argue that in certain cases they have more point than many such arrangements. It was for this reason that the Newsom Report (Central Advisory Council for Education 1963) recommended that they 'ought to be recognized as an integral part of the total educational programme' (§ 135) and that to this end they be included in the formal timetable of an extended day. It is also for this reason that educationists such as Charity James have suggested that they be regarded and planned as one element of the curriculum (James 1968). The inclusion of this kind of activity in the formal provision made by the school is also a major feature of the philosophy of many of those concerned with the present development of community schools (Cooksey 1972, 1976a, 1976b).

Again, it would seem that, if we are concerned with curriculum planning, it would be foolish to omit by our definition of the curriculum a whole range of activities which teachers plan and execute with deliberate reasons and intentions. In looking at curriculum planning, therefore, there would appear to be nothing to be gained from leaving out of consideration any planned activity. It is for this reason that John Kerr had defined the curriculum as 'all the learning which is planned and guided by the school, whether it is carried on in groups or individually, inside or outside the school' (Kerr 1968, p. 16). Such a definition provides us with a reasonably secure basis for planning all the organized activities of a school.

However, there are real difficulties in attempting to operate with a definition of curriculum which excludes from consideration the unplanned effects of teacher activity, as the notions of the 'hidden' and the 'actual' curriculum indicate. There are more aspects to curriculum than are dreamed of in the philosophy of most teachers, and a definition of curriculum which confines its scope to what teachers actually plan will omit many important dimensions of curriculum study. We need a definition which will take us 'beyond curriculum' (Holly 1973). On the other hand, a definition which is too broad will not only tend to make the term 'curriculum' co-extensive with education itself, it will also encourage the view that everyone is an expert in this sphere with a contribution to make to curriculum planning and development.

The problems of definition are thus serious and complex and it may be that they are best avoided by not attempting to define it too closely. The chapters which follow will reveal that in planning for curriculum change and development we need to be aware of all aspects and dimensions of the educational experiences which pupils have during any period of formal education. And so, with the proviso that the expert is the person who can keep all or most of those dimensions in view rather than concentrating on one or two of them, we might accept that as the kind of loose definition we need.

Such a loose definition will remind us that the term 'curriculum' embraces rather more than the school timetable or even a set of subject syllabuses, that it is not 'simply a collection of separate subjects' (DES 1981, p. 12) and that it must embrace also considerations of the purposes, procedures and principles of education. The importance of this kind of definition will become immediately apparent when we look at the problems of curriculum planning and at some of the planning models which have been offered.

Planning models

It has been suggested (Tyler 1949) that the curriculum has to be seen as consisting of four elements and curriculum planning, therefore, as having four dimensions: objectives, content or subject matter, methods or procedures and evaluation. In short, we must distinguish in our curriculum planning what we are hoping to achieve, the ground we are planning to cover in order to achieve it, the kinds of activity and methods that we consider likely to be most effective in helping us towards our goals and the devices we will use to evaluate what we have done. Tyler's own way of putting this point is to suggest that there are 'four fundamental questions which must be answered in developing any curriculum and plan of instruction' (op. cit., p. i). These he lists as:

1. What educational purposes should the school seek to attain?
2. What educational experiences can be provided that are likely to attain these purposes?
3. How can these educational experiences be effectively organized?
4. How can we determine whether these purposes are being attained? (ibid.)

This analysis, then, if taken just as it stands, would give us a very simple model for curriculum planning, a linear model which requires us to specify our objectives, to plan the content and the methods which will lead us towards them and, finally, to endeavour to measure the extent of our success. It is, however, too simple a model for many reasons, most of which will become apparent when we consider the problems of prespecified objectives in Chapter 4.

One reason why it will not suffice, which must be mentioned here, is that it does not make sufficient allowance for the interrelatedness of the separate elements. At the very least we must allow for the fact that the results of our evaluation processes may be used to modify our planning. Thus it has been suggested that we should employ a cyclical rather than a linear model and link up evaluation with the framing of objectives to create a continuous cycle (Wheeler 1967).

This would seem to be a step in the right direction but many would claim that the influence of evaluation on curriculum planning should be a continuous process rather than being delayed until the exercise is over and, if we accept that, then we must expect such continuous evaluation to result in regular modifications of our planning. In fact, we must go further than this and acknowledge the interrelationship of all four elements, since the practical experience of most teachers suggests that every one of these four elements is constantly being modified by every other and that the whole business of curriculum planning must be seen as one of constant interaction between the elements. A more suitable model might therefore be derived from the idea of a permutated entry on a football pool with every possible kind of combination allowed for, or the physicist's notion of 'dynamic equilibrium' where stable progress is made possible by the balanced interaction of a variety of forces.

What these models of curriculum planning have in common, however, is their acceptance that curriculum planning must begin with a statement of its objectives and, indeed, it has been argued (Hirst 1969) that this is necessary if it is to qualify as a rational activity, since, it is argued, what characterizes a rational activity is that it is directed at some clear goal or set of purposes. This view, however, is by no means universally accepted and, as we shall see when we come to examine it in detail in Chapter 4, there are some very compelling arguments against adopting this kind of model for educational planning.

The alternative models that are available lay stress on other elements of Tyler's fourfold analysis of curriculum. One approach to curriculum planning has placed the emphasis on the content of education. This, as Paul Hirst

(1969) suggests, has been the main characteristic of the traditional approach to educational planning, and it might be argued that this form of curriculum continues to predominate in secondary schools (and, indeed, in institutions of further and higher education). To plan a curriculum on this model is to state what subjects are to be studied and perhaps what aspects of them are to be studied and to answer questions about the point or purpose of their study in terms of some intrinsic value they are deemed to possess rather than of the extrinsic ends they are held to serve. This is a planning model that has perhaps been too readily reviled and rejected in recent years in favour of some form of objectives model.

A further planning model, and one whose attractions appear to be becoming increasingly acknowledged, is that which emphasizes that element of Tyler's analysis of curriculum which is usually referred to as 'procedures', although not in quite the sense in which most people have understood it. Paul Hirst (1969) associates this approach with 'progressive' education and the form of curriculum which has been seen in some primary schools. The view he takes of this model is that its main concern is with methods of learning, with such things as project work, enquiry methods and discovery learning generally, and he criticizes it for not paying adequate attention either to the purposes of these activities or to the content of what is learnt by them.

However, that is a highly simplistic interpretation of a form of education which needs to be analysed at a rather more sophisticated level. For this approach to curriculum planning is predicated on the view that education is centrally concerned with certain processes of intellectual or cognitive development, that what is crucial to it, therefore, is not the bodies of knowledge that are assimilated nor is it the behavioural objectives that are attained or the behavioural changes that are brought about, but the processes of development that are promoted (Blenkin and Kelly 1981). In short, it is based on the belief that to have been educated is to have been helped to develop certain intellectual capacities rather than to have acquired factual knowledge or to have had one's behaviour modified in certain ways. On this view, then, curriculum planning must start with a clear statement of the processes it is concerned to promote and thus the procedural principles upon which the teacher's day-to-day decisions and judgements are to be based. Indeed, it might be argued that such principles are a prerequisite of the other models too, since some criteria of this kind are a necessary basis both for the initial selection of objectives or content and for the continuing modification of these in the light of subsequent evaluations.

From this kind of thinking, then, and as a reaction to those models which emphasize either content or objectives as the central elements in curriculum planning, there has emerged a 'process' model which, although it may be difficult to implement, nevertheless seems to many people to reflect more adequately than the other models available what the process of education is essentially concerned with.

Thus Tyler's analysis of the logic of curriculum planning, useful and interesting as it has been, does not offer us the clear-cut definition of curriculum planning that some have seen in it, but rather opens up a number of conflicting possibilities and has thus given rise to the appearance of several different models.

None of these models, however, in itself resolves for us those value questions that are integral to education and none of them offers us any basis or set of criteria upon which we can make a selection of our objectives or our content or decide upon the processes we should endeavour to promote. It is to meet this problem that some of the more sophisticated models for curriculum planning that we are offered have been designed. Some of them are so highly complex that it is difficult to imagine their being of any practical use to a teacher or a planner of real curricula. However, we must note the point that they do draw our attention to, namely that curriculum planning must be concerned with decisions about what is of educational value as well as with the choice of blueprints.

The model that Denis Lawton (1973) offers us is an attempt to provide a workable scheme that will help us also to deal with these difficult questions of value. It is also a model that can perhaps be seen as an attempted compromise between the three main kinds of emphasis we have noted in the other models we have considered.

For he suggests that in planning a curriculum we should frame our objectives and decide on appropriate content and procedures by reference to three main kinds of consideration. Firstly, we must take note of those considerations that derive from the nature of knowledge itself. It has been suggested that certain questions about the curriculum can be answered for us by an analysis of what knowledge is, the different forms of knowledge and the different kinds of logic that are said to exist (Hirst 1965). This is a view which is highly problematic and to which we must later give closer consideration, but it is enough if we acknowledge here the claim that the curriculum planner must pay due regard to this kind of argument. Secondly, he claims, we must take full account of the nature of the child or of the individual children for whom the curriculum is being planned. Some programmes have been put together without any reference to anything other than what knowledge was thought to be. Indeed, it was this feature of 'traditional' education that led some thinkers to that emphasis on the child himself that has characterized the 'progressive' or 'child-centred' movement in education. No adequate curriculum plan can emerge unless due regard is paid to what we know about cognitive growth and child development generally. Thirdly, Lawton suggests that our curriculum must take full account of the social situation, the pressures and the needs of the society of which the school is a part. It is this kind of consideration that has led to recent demands for relevance in the curriculum and, although the concept of relevance needs careful elucidation and analysis, few would wish to deny that a curriculum planned without reference to society would have little hope of achieving success, no matter how success was to be gauged.

Such a model, then, has the merit of recognizing that choices and selection have to be made and of suggesting some of the factors that we will need to keep in mind when we come to make these choices. But that is as far as it takes us and, indeed, it is as far as any model can take us. It leaves the most fundamental question of all unanswered. For it offers us a series of factors some of which will be in conflict with each other. Among the many kinds of consideration it draws our attention to we must decide which are to have priority and we need some basis for balancing and evaluating the inevitably competing claims that we will discover, for example, between the demands of the individual child and those of society.

In engaging in curriculum planning, therefore, we need to be clear about the logic of the process and we need to take full account of all those other factors that appear to have some relevance to our enterprise, but we also need some basis upon which we can make the necessary choices and selection, a set of criteria, a framework of values within which to work. This, as we shall see in subsequent chapters, will be far from easy to attain.

The model that Denis Lawton offers us confuses some of the distinctions we suggested earlier were important, as any attempt at a compromise solution must inevitably do, and it also pre-empts some of the issues we saw they raised and which need much more detailed examination. However, it has one merit to which attention must be drawn. For it recognizes that curriculum planning cannot go on in an intellectual vacuum, cut off from contact with the society and the culture in which it is being practised, that the curriculum planner must be aware not only of the logical constraints of the activity in which he is engaged but also of the social pressures to which he and the curriculum development he is trying to foster are subject. Indeed, we shall see in later chapters that these pressures play an important part in influencing the kinds of planning model that are available to him, particularly by forcing him towards the adoption of the simpler forms.

These pressures take a number of forms and it is as well to be aware at the outset of the more influential of them, so that we are not misled into believing that curriculum planning is merely a matter of the application of rationality and logic.

Pressures on curriculum planning

It is perhaps worth noting first of all that the factors we are about to consider will have their impact on curriculum development whether we like it or not. Indeed, it is these factors that were at work in the past and still are at work in situations where curriculum change is the result of the kind of unplanned 'drift' we have already referred to. If teachers and others do not plan their curriculum, these are the forces that will control the direction and form of curriculum change. On the other hand, if curricula are to be planned realistically and planned change effected smoothly, these factors must be taken into account in the planning process. Again, evolution is to be preferred to revolution, which is often not only painful but also ineffective.

The curriculum, then, is subject to a great many pressures. These pressures are often subtle and it is not always easy to justify what they may lead to, but their presence and their influence must be recognized and acknowledged.

First, we must note the force of tradition which is at least as strong in education as anywhere else. The main thrust of tradition, of course, is not towards change but towards stability and, some might say, ossification. Nevertheless, and all the more so, its existence and its effects must be recognized. There are two particular ways in which tradition exercises its influence on the curriculum. The first is through an inevitable tendency of teachers to cling to those forms of teaching they were trained in, have in some cases practised for years and thus have come to feel at home with and confident in. This is a point we will return to later when we consider the role of the teacher in curriculum change and development.

There is a second aspect of the influence of tradition on the curriculum, however, which we must consider here. It is possible for certain kinds of teaching, certain subjects, certain approaches to education to become enshrined in respectability and thus to attain an unquestioned acceptability merely because they appear to form part of what has traditionally come to be regarded as education. Thus few parents would be likely to question the fact that their children might be studying mathematics or science or even, one suspects, Latin or Greek, regardless of the appropriateness of such an educational diet, in the way that they might if they found that a good deal of their offspring's time was being devoted to, say, Craft, Design and Technology. The danger here is that, since the place of these activities in the school curriculum appears to be so well established, not only does no one question them but also, as a result, no one asks what the continued point or relevance of them is. It is here that the threat of ossification looms large, for without this kind of continuous questioning of the point and purpose of certain kinds of teaching, much of that point and purpose can be lost.

The influence of tradition on the curriculum, then, is an important one and its dangers must be borne in mind. However, it is not necessarily to be resented, since it is a factor which ensures that curriculum change will be evolutionary rather than revolutionary in character and it does act as an important counterbalance to the many other pressures whose thrust may be towards rapid change.

First in importance among these are those pressures on the curriculum which derive from economic sources. There is no way in which we can or should ignore the economic function of the education system. As the Crowther Report (Central Advisory Council for Education 1959) reminded us, education has to be seen, at least in part, as a national investment from which society is entitled to expect some return. For the most part, that return will take the form of the output of a sufficient number of young people who have acquired the knowledge and skills that society needs to maintain and extend its development.

It is, of course, this kind of pressure that has prompted that recent increase of external interest in the curriculum which we have already noted on several occasions. From this source will come pressures for the introduction of certain kinds of subject into the curriculum, such as reading, mathematics, sciences and technological subjects, and perhaps for important changes in the way in which we approach all or most of what we teach. A good example of this is the transmutation of handicraft into Craft, Design and Technology which recent years have witnessed, a development which has been in part prompted by and is one instance of the wave of interest in and enthusiasm for the development of creative technology that followed the launching by the Russians of Sputnik I, the first space probe, in 1957. Technological change, especially on the scale we have witnessed in recent years, must have very serious consequences for the planning of the curriculum, for it results in major changes in the kinds of knowledge that society wants its children to be given. Indeed, the whole of the development of state-provided education can be seen as the result of exactly this kind of economic pressure.

It also results, however, in demands for changes of a more fundamental kind, changes in the manner in which we encourage children to learn as well as the content of that learning. For one of the clearest lessons of the technological change of recent years, again well brought out by the Crowther Report and its notion of 'general mechanical ability', is that if the citizen of the future is to be able to adapt to the changes he will continue to experience, his education must provide him with the flexibility of mind necessary for this. The emphasis will therefore need to be on the development of understanding rather than on the acquisition of knowledge in any lesser sense, and the consequences of that for curriculum planners are far-reaching. This is a point that has not always been appreciated by contributors to the educational debate of recent times.

A similar point emerges when we consider a second, and perhaps more important, consequence of technological change – the social changes that it brings in its train. For technological change leads to changes in the values and norms of a society and thus to another source of pressure on the curriculum. As man discovers that he can do more, that he can influence more and exercise more control over his physical and social environment in the widest sense of those terms, he also realizes that there are important questions to be asked about what he *ought* to do, how he *ought* to influence his environment. Technological change raises new moral problems over such issues as birth control, abortion, organ transplantation, pollution and the ecological balance of nature.

The rapid technological change of recent years has therefore been accompanied by equally dramatic changes in the very fabric of society and these social and moral changes also have their impact on the development of the curriculum, as will quickly be apparent from an examination of what has been happening within religious education in recent years and the advent and development of such areas as moral education and social education. It is for this reason that the most recent publication on curriculum of the

Department of Education and Science in the United Kingdom, to which reference has already been made, gives as examples of the new claims which are being made on the curriculum 'the development of economic understanding, environmental education, preparation for parenthood, education for international understanding, political and social education, and consumer affairs' (DES 1981, p. 4).

Again, too, the very fact of such continuous change creates demands for changes in the manner of learning, a fact which explains why we are increasingly concerned that pupils should learn to solve their own moral problems rather than to accept prepackaged solutions which are unlikely to be adequate when they come as adults to cope with moral issues that have not yet arisen and cannot yet be foreseen. Teachers cannot predict the sorts of problem with which pupils may be faced, so that they must educate them in such a way that they learn to work out their own solutions as and when it becomes necessary. The relationship between social change and curriculum change needs a good deal more careful analysis than it has as yet received, but that there are important considerations here for the curriculum planner cannot be doubted.

Lastly, we must note a point which leads on naturally from the one we have just considered. We must take full cognisance of the ideological influences to which the curriculum planner is subject. We must not ignore the political function of education. In sociological parlance, ideologies are rival value systems which influence the power structure within a society. The very fact that several such ideologies can be discerned in most contemporary societies, that they are pluralist and often, indeed, multicultural societies, has in itself implications for the way in which we plan a curriculum since it suggests that we should develop in children the ability to cope with competing systems rather than initiate them into any one such set of beliefs or values.

However, what is important here is that we recognize that such ideologies are and have always been a major influence on curriculum development from the days of the 'aristocratic' ideology, which perhaps lingers on in certain places, to more recent attempts to champion the cause of the 'lower orders' in education. A good many curriculum changes of recent years have been prompted by a concern over problems of social class differences, the social mobility function of education, and this continues to be a major source of pressure on curriculum planners, not least through the work of those sociologists who have recently come to recognize that one major source of social inequality is the differentiated access to knowledge accorded to subcultural groups within the curriculum itself (Young 1971).

These general influences make their impact on the curriculum not only through the effect they have on everyone's thinking but also more directly through several kinds of agency. Some of these are completely overt and attempt to exert a direct influence on the development of the curriculum. Organizations such as the Schools Council in the United Kingdom have been set up with the deliberate purpose of exploring certain aspects of the curriculum and of developing new schemes or projects that it is hoped will lead to improvements in the quality and relevance of what is offered to pupils at all levels and in all aspects of their work in schools. From time to time also Consultative Committees, Royal Commissions or other committees of inquiry are set up quite formally by a government to look into certain aspects of education and to advise on changes that might with profit be effected. Often, of course, the published reports of these committees are largely concerned with questions of organization and administration but seldom can they ignore curriculum issues completely, since any attempt to do so or any failure to achieve a full understanding of these issues will vitiate any recommendations they make concerning the organizational and administrative matters themselves, as the James Report on Teacher Education (DES 1972), for example, made apparent. Thus some of these reports have led to quite dramatic changes in certain areas of the curriculum in some schools. The changes, not all of them for the better, brought about in the provision made in secondary schools in the United Kingdom for the 'less able' pupil as a result of the recommendations of the Newsom Report (Central Advisory Council for Education 1963) should provide sufficient evidence of the degree of influence that such reports can exercise.

In considering overt attempts to contribute to curriculum change and development we must also remember the role that it is intended should be played by the Inspectorate at both central and local government levels. These bodies are explicitly employed to advise educational institutions on the development of their curricula and to disseminate experience and ideas between institutions. A good deal of this work is now done also by teachers' centres, some of which act not only as institutions for the in-service training of teachers in the new skills required of them by some curriculum changes but also as centres for the interchange of ideas between teachers from different schools.

In addition to these agencies that have been established with the express purposes of contributing to curriculum development, there are other agencies whose impact on curriculum change is less overt but none the less influential; indeed, they may well be more important because their influence is indirect. If we can ignore the influence of certain commercial agencies such as publishers, these would seem to fall into two main categories which we might call the political or financial and the academic.

In some countries political influence on the curriculum is quite direct and decisions about curriculum content, method and even balance of subjects and allocation of time are made centrally, leaving the individual school very little discretion. This kind of direct central control has not been a feature of the history of the development of education in the United Kingdom, but proposals for the reintroduction of such control in some areas of the curriculum are currently being made. At present, however, the only legal requirement that any school in England and Wales must adhere to in planning its curriculum is the inclusion of religious instruction and a daily act of worship in its programme. It would be naive, however, to assume that each school is completely free to make its own arrangements in all other areas. Managing or governing bodies have to be satisfied that the school is fulfilling its role in the community as they envisage it and these bodies consist largely of people with particular political interests. Parents too are becoming increasingly vociferous in making their feelings known about what goes on in the schools their children attend, and their right to play a greater part in the government of those schools has been recognized in the recommendations of the Taylor Report (DES 1977a) on school management.

Finance too is a crucial factor. The way in which the moneys allocated to a school are spent is a matter for the governing body to determine and the granting of additional money for specific projects is at the discretion of local government, so that, in the ultimate, whether a school can or cannot pursue any particular line of innovation is a decision that rests with those who hold the purse strings. This was a major factor in determining the curriculum in the era of 'payment by results' and it is a factor that has gained strength in recent years when economic recession has resulted in serious reductions in the amounts of public money available for education.

We must also note the effect of organizational and administrative influences generally (Davies 1980). Those falling roles which have been a feature of the educational scene in the United Kingdom and elsewhere in recent times have their own effects on the curriculum. A secondary school with

1500 pupils can clearly provide a wider curriculum than it can when its numbers have fallen to little more than 1000. What is perhaps more important is to note the influence on the curriculum of whatever solution the providing authority might decide upon to meet this kind of change, whether that solution takes the form of closures, amalgamations or attempts to maintain all institutions in spite of the fact that they are reducing in size.

The internal administrative structure of the school will also exercise its influence on what can and cannot be attempted or achieved in curriculum development. One of the reasons why, as we noted in the Introduction, most of the curriculum development in secondary schools has gone on within rather than between subjects is the departmental structure that is to be found in most schools at that level. Conversely, it has been argued (Blenkin and Kelly 1981) that one reason why some primary schools have progressed much further in the development of their curricula is to be found in the fact that they have been free of the constraints created and imposed by this kind of tight organizational structure. The importance of such internal influences must not be ignored or underestimated.

The second main source of indirect influence on curriculum planning is the academic influences exercised by universities and other institutions of higher education. There are several aspects to this.

In the first place, what is done in schools depends very much on what the teachers in the schools have been prepared for by their initial courses of training, so that the kind of course offered in programmes of initial teacher education and in in-service courses will have an important impact on curriculum development. The teachers themselves, of course, can exercise some control over the content of these courses through their involvement in the planning and constructing of them, although in the United Kingdom such involvement, which is the point and purpose of the Professional Committees established to replace the Area Training Organizations, continues to be slight.

Secondly, institutions of higher education will continue to exercise a degree of control over what is taught, at least in secondary schools, through the entry requirements they set for admission to their courses. It would be quite wrong of any school to ignore these in planning a programme for pupils who are likely to want to go on to courses in other institutions, whether of higher or further education.

Thirdly, this influence is felt most obviously through the control exercised by the universities over the content of examination syllabuses. Indeed, it is the public examination which is recognized by all teachers as the most obvious source of external control over the curriculum. More often than not they see its effect largely as an inhibiting one, preventing them from effecting changes that they might otherwise bring about to improve the quality of what they are offering pupils. That the public examination can also initiate change, however, and encourage teachers to develop their work in directions that they might of themselves not have envisaged, can be seen from work that has been done in a number of areas, and perhaps particularly through the changes already referred to that have been brought about in the very concept of craft teaching in secondary schools by the new syllabuses that the University of London has set up for Craft, Design and Technology at both 'O' and 'A' levels of the GCE (Hicks 1976).

Both of these aspects of the influence exercised by public examination syllabuses highlight the close interrelationship of examination and curriculum and the need for the planning of both to be done jointly. This in turn suggests that it is important that teachers be more closely involved in the planning and conduct of public examinations. Indeed, an acceptance of this point was part of the rationale for the introduction of the CSE examination in the United Kingdom as a result of the Beloe Report of 1960. The various modes of assessment made available to teachers by this examination and the real involvement of teachers in the examining processes have done much to show how teachers can be given increased control over this particular source of influence on curriculum development. The lead thus established has been followed by some GCE Boards in certain subject areas and, indeed, in some cases joint GCE and CSE syllabuses have been approved and established, thus paving the way for the introduction of a single public examination at 16+, now scheduled for 1987, a significant feature of which may well be more extensive teacher involvement (Schools Council 1971a).

Curriculum development and the teacher

This brief discussion of the influence of the public examination on curriculum development brings us to a consideration of what is emerging as the most crucial factor in curriculum development – the role of the individual teacher and the individual school. The last, but by no means the least important factors we must consider in our brief initial survey of curriculum planning and development are those that derive from the local considerations operating in any given school or classroom. These are the factors that will in the end determine what the outcome shall be, in terms of the actual curriculum of the individual school, of the influences and pressures that we have been listing. To be effective, any particular curriculum innovation must 'take' with the school and become fully institutionalized (Hoyle 1969b) and it is becoming very clear that the extent to which any project will 'take' will depend on a whole range of local factors within each individual school. Thus it is increasingly apparent that real and effective curriculum development must go on within individual schools rather than by the creation of projects or other innovations hatched out in some central place detached from the realities of any actual school situation. The theory and practice of curriculum development must go hand in hand from the outset of any piece of planning; they cannot effectively be married up at a point when each has developed too far to be readily adapted to the other.

Several factors within the school are likely to be important here; local industrial and employment conditions, the social origins and interests of the pupils and their parents, the expectations the community in general has of the school and so on. Quite the most significant of these factors, however, as has become apparent from a number of different sources in recent years, is the attitudes of the teachers within the school, since these will be crucial in determining the realities of what goes on at the level of the individual classroom, which, after all, is what ultimately decides the actual curriculum of the school.

The positive role of the individual teacher in curriculum development is still not clear and this needs to be given more attention than it has hitherto had and to be more thoroughly explored. That the individual teacher has a 'make or break' role in relation to the attempts of any outside body to bring about curriculum change, however, is now indisputable, nor is this surprising since, as we have just said, it is the individual teacher who has the task of bridging any gap that might exist between curriculum theory and curriculum practice.

It is clear that many teachers can and do sabotage attempts to introduce changes into the curriculum. Teachers are often accused of conservatism, of too great an attachment to tradition, to 'tried and trusted methods'. Such an attitude is understandable when one realizes that, as was suggested earlier, their standing often depends on the maintenance of those areas of knowledge and experience in which they have a recognized expertise. This emphasizes the need to improve in-service opportunities so as to enable teachers to become rather less dependent on the skills and expertise they acquire in their initial courses. While such opportunities do not exist, however, the traditionalism of some teachers will remain a factor that we ignore at our peril in attempting to change any aspect of the curriculum of any school.

The converse of this is equally important. The degree to which any change that we attempt to introduce into a school is likely to be effective will largely be determined by the extent to which individual teachers become committed to it. There is simply no point in a Schools Council project team, a headteacher or even an enthusiastic group of teachers attempting to introduce some new scheme into a school's programme unless it has the support at least of all those teachers who will need to be involved in the implementation of it and preferably a good many other teachers as well, since saboteurs can work from without as well as from within. In particular, of course, it is vital that a project has the support of the headteacher and other senior staff, such as heads of relevant departments, heads of sections within the school, such as year groups and so on.

Nor is it only necessary for teachers to be committed to particular forms of curriculum change; they also need to understand their purposes and their basic principles if they are to make them work properly. Teachers cannot be operated effectively by remote control. If any educational innovation is to be successful, the teachers must understand as well as believe in it.

Nowhere has the truth of this been so manifest as in the attempts of some secondary schools in the United Kingdom in recent years to introduce mixed-ability forms of grouping. This kind of innovation involves major changes of method and approach, so that its success hinges on the willingness of individual teachers to adapt their methods and approaches to the requirements of the new situation. Unless teachers are willing to undertake this, and in the first instance to do so with a good deal of enthusiasm, or at least tolerance of the initial difficulties that must inevitably be experienced, it is better not to attempt to make the change at all. The importance of the individual teacher to the success or failure of this particular innovation in primary schools was one of the most significant findings of the major research project undertaken by the National Foundation for Educational Research in this field (Barker-Lunn 1970).

It will be clear, then, that if the role of the teacher is as central as this to successful curriculum development, no attempt to establish innovations derived from outside agencies will be successful unless the teachers are 'won over' to them, unless there is a change in their ideology, and unless they

have the opportunity to develop the understanding and the expertise necessary for their implementation. The prime needs are that they should both
understand the reasons for and should be committed to the values of what is
proposed, so that in-service back-up and every kind of support that is
offered must be attuned to achieving both of these ends, and not merely to
providing them with the new skills and techniques that will be required of
them.

Finally, as we shall see in Chapter 5 when we examine some of the
strategies which have been adopted to bring about curriculum change, if we
have learnt anything in the last decade about how the curriculum changes it
is that the only effective change is that which results from grass-roots
initiatives within a school. It is this that explains the advent of the notion of
school-based curriculum development. And so teachers, not only as individuals but also, and perhaps more importantly, as members of the staff of a
particular and individual educational institution, must be prepared to
accept responsibility for the continued development of the curriculum of
that institution. They must learn to see themselves not as the implementers
of the ideas of others but as responsible for the very substance of the
curriculum.

It will be clear that if the role of the teacher in curriculum development is
as central as has been suggested here, then those attempts in recent years to
create agencies of remote control outside the school are based on a serious
misunderstanding concerning not only the realities of curriculum change
but also the nature of the educational process itself. The implications of this
are far-reaching and we will need to explore them fully in later chapters.

Summary and conclusions

We have considered in this opening chapter some definitions of the term
'curriculum', concluding that the most useful kind of definition we can
adopt is one which is loose enough and broad enough to embrace all the
learning that goes on in a school and all dimensions of the educational
process. We then looked at some models of curriculum planning that have
been offered, noting in particular that different kinds of model emerge
according to whether one emphasizes objectives, content or processes in
planning the curriculum, and the difficulty of devising any kind of model
that will help us to resolve the value questions that are integral to education.

We then considered briefly some of the other factors that exercise their influence on curriculum planning, recognizing that this is not an activity that can profitably be regarded as going on, as it were, in a vacuum, but one which must be considered in its social context. This in turn led us finally to acknowledge the central role of the teacher in curriculum planning and development.

All of this suggests that we need to know more about how the curriculum changes, about the strategies of 'curriculum change' (Hoyle 1969a, b), and that this is at least as important an area of exploration as, and perhaps even more important than, those considerations of a more theoretical kind about the logic of curriculum planning, about rational curriculum planning, that have hitherto tended to dominate the attention of curriculum theorists. Indeed, what is now happening is that we are being forced to recognize that curriculum development is a practical as much as, or more than, a theoretical activity and that here, as in all branches of the study of education, a linking of theory and practice is long overdue.

The main concern must be that teachers and all others who are involved in curriculum planning should be aware of all the factors involved. Curriculum development must be planned in such a way as to take full account of all relevant rational and logical considerations, but at the same time to take cognisance of those other pressures that are exerted directly and indirectly on such planning and to recognize those factors that are to be found within the situation for which the planning is being done. Only when these three elements have been considered together, balanced against each other and given their full weight in the planning process, can we hope to achieve curriculum development that is rational, relevant and effective. 'The heart of the matter is what each child takes away from the school. For each of them, what he or she takes away is the effective curriculum' (Schools Council 1981, p. 9).

This in turn suggests that all curriculum development must be seen as essentially a matter of making modifications and adjustments to existing curricula in a way that makes full allowance for the idiosyncrasies of the individual situation and leads to evolution rather than revolution. Difficulties must arise if we regard curriculum development as a process of devising major innovations or projects and attempting to graft them on to living situations, the realities of which have not been taken into account in the planning of the project.

This would also suggest the need for a continuous study of curriculum issues of a kind that takes full account of the many facets of these issues that we have attempted to identify in this chapter. We must recognize that the study of the curriculum, again like the study of any other area of education, calls for a genuinely interdisciplinary and integrated approach. As should now be apparent, it is a field of study that draws on many sources of knowledge – on philosophy, logic and epistemology, on psychology, child development and theories of cognitive growth, on sociology both descriptive and phenomenological, on organizational theory and organizational studies, on history, on economics, on comparative studies and above all on an understanding of the practicalities of the real school situation in which any curriculum planning must be implemented.

Finally, in any exploration of the curriculum, we must remember the kind of theory we are dealing with. We have already noted the unavoidable value-element in curriculum planning and have suggested the impossibility of resolving this kind of question in any final, hard and fast way. Questions about the curriculum, like all questions in education, must remain open-ended and any answers we offer to them must be acknowledged as being tentative, hypothetical and subject to continuous review. Curriculum theory, therefore, must recognize that curriculum development must be a continuing process of evolution and planning. Knowledge continues to develop; society evolves; people change; and the curriculum must keep pace with all of these.

It is in this spirit that subsequent chapters in this book will consider some of the issues involved in the particular aspects of curriculum planning that the present chapter has endeavoured to isolate and to identify.

CHAPTER 2

CURRICULUM CONTENT

We saw in Chapter 1 that there is a strong case for claiming that in curriculum planning and, indeed, in any debate about the curriculum, we must look beyond considerations of content alone and recognize that questions of the purposes or reasons for our decisions are logically prior to those about their substance. If we accept that curriculum planning must begin with statements about the purposes we hope to attain or the principles upon which our practice is to be based, all decisions about the content of our curriculum must be subsidiary to those prior choices. For, as Ralph Tyler said (1949, p. 1), such decisions will be answers to the question, 'What educational experiences can be provided that are likely to attain these purposes?'

However, we also noted that many people have not fully appreciated the force or the implications of that claim. For many, a curriculum is still a syllabus, and even among those who have discussed and even advocated a more sophisticated approach to planning there are those who continue, at least in the practical recommendations they make, to regard decisions of content as the starting point. We saw, for example, in Chapter 1 that Denis Lawton's model for curriculum planning (Lawton 1973) requires us to select our objectives by reference to the nature of the child, the nature of the society in which he lives and the nature of knowledge itself, and thus effectively, if inadvertently, makes decisions of content prior to those concerning purposes. Others too, such as Paul Hirst (1969), while recommending an approach to curriculum planning by way of prestated objectives, have continued to regard analyses of the nature of knowledge as fundamental to the educational debate. Indeed, there is a long tradition of viewing certain subjects or kinds of activity as having some kind of inalienable right to be included in the curriculum without reference to, and even to the deliberate exclusion of, any claims that they might contribute towards the attainment of certain goals. This is one reason why, as we shall see in Chapter 4, some statements of objectives are couched in terms of content, in terms that make it apparent that decisions about the value of certain subjects have been reached prior to the choice of the objectives themselves. Talk about the importance of purposes and/or procedures in curriculum planning has by no means banished the traditional emphasis on content in the minds of either practitioners or theorists.

This may well suggest that we are taking too simple a view in attempting to place in rank order the questions the curriculum planner must ask. Perhaps we should acknowledge that questions of purposes and principles are inextricably bound up with questions of content and that all must be considered together. Certainly, we must recognize that questions of value are central to educational planning, even though they are not an essential part of the planning of courses of instruction, so that the issue of the status of assertions of value must be examined if we are to provide a basis for any kind of educational decision, be it concerned with purposes, content or procedures.

Whatever view one takes of education, that view will be predicated on certain assumptions about the nature of knowledge and a particular set of values. Both of these need to be examined closely and it is to such an examination that this chapter will address itself.

A second reason for undertaking this kind of examination is that, even if we do agree that other questions must be asked and answered first by the curriculum planner, it remains the case that, in order to deal with questions of content when we reach them, we will need to understand the issues which are involved and to appreciate the different viewpoints, the different epistemological and educational stances, which can be taken up. Thus, if we regard a major purpose of education as being to initiate pupils into the cultural heritage of society or into what is best within it (Lawton 1973, 1975) or into activities which are intrinsically worthwhile (Peters 1965, 1966; White 1973; Thompson and White 1975) or into the several forms of understanding or rationality (Hirst 1965), we need to ask many questions about what might be meant by 'our cultural heritage', the basis on which we might select that which is best within it, the grounds for attributing intrinsic value to certain activities, what is meant by a 'form of understanding or rationality' and many other related questions. Similarly, if we take what might be seen as a contrary stance and assert that education should be concerned to develop the knowledge pupils bring into the school with them (Keddie 1971), or their needs or their interests (Wilson 1971), we must explore the epistemological assumptions underlying such claims and the issues which they raise.

Issues of content, then, must remain central to the curriculum debate even if they must not be permitted to continue to dominate it. It is to the issue of what knowledge, if any, must be included in the curriculum and the related issue of the bases upon which we are to make all those value choices which curriculum planning presents us with that we now turn.

Knowledge and the curriculum

The question 'What is knowledge?' can be interpreted in several ways. It can be taken as a psychological question about how people come to have knowledge, about the psychological and behavioural changes that occur when learning takes place. It can equally be interpreted as a philosophical, semantic question about what it means to know something, what kind of behavioural changes are to count as evidence of the acquisition of knowledge, rather than of, say, the development of habits or fixed responses to certain stimuli. It is in this sense that it is often argued that the term 'knowledge' can only properly be used of that kind of learning that involves understanding, that knowledge *that* something is the case must always be accompanied by knowledge *why* it is the case, since only if we insist on this can we distinguish knowledge from belief, opinion or mere guesswork.

It is this latter point that leads us on to the question that is central to our discussion of curriculum content. Once again we must note the interrelatedness of these questions, but the questions that are most relevant to our immediate concerns are not those about the knower but those about the nature of knowledge itself and, in particular, questions about what will constitute grounds for the claim that we know something to be the case rather than merely believe or guess it to be so. In other words, what is it by virtue of which we are justified in claiming knowledge? What are the criteria by which we can assess the validity of knowledge? Interpreted in this way, the question 'What is knowledge?' becomes almost synonymous with the question 'What is truth?', and its central relevance to decisions of curriculum content will be clear, since it will be impossible to justify the inclusion of certain areas of knowledge in the curriculum for their own sake unless evidence can be produced as to their truth content, objectivity or intrinsic value.

The history of education in the western world, from at least as far back as ancient Greece, reveals, for example, a concern to distinguish those areas of learning promoted by teachers in order to attain certain social goals from those aspects of learning that have seemed to have some independent and intrinsic right to inclusion in the curriculum and which, therefore, not only do not seek but positively eschew justification in instrumental terms. This was the point of the attraction felt and expressed in the ancient world for the idea of a liberal education, of the later concern with the education of the cultured gentleman and the resultant contrasting of liberal and vocational forms of education, a conflict which can still be discerned in the practice of the present day and which has led to some very clear and overt hierarchical distinctions between certain kinds of school subject. The same kind of thinking also expresses itself in modern theory through the differences that are now stressed between education as such, a term which it is suggested should and can only be appropriately applied to those activities that can be viewed and justified as intrinsically worthwhile, and other processes that also involve teaching and that schools also concern themselves with, such as socialization, training, instruction and the like (Peters 1965, 1966; Hirst and Peters 1970).

On the whole, such dispute as there has been over the inclusion of vocational or utilitarian learning in the curriculum has centred on the issue of whether this is an appropriate concern of schools at all or whether it should be their concern only in relation to the needs of those pupils who cannot cope with the intellectual demands of those subjects that have been felt to be intrinsically valuable (Bantock 1968, 1971). No one has felt it necessary to challenge their justification beyond that point, since if one accepts the ends to which they are instrumental it must follow that, other things being equal, one accepts the means to those ends.

There has been much disagreement, however, over the question of what is to be included in the curriculum for its own sake. Indeed, this question has been the focal point of educational debate since such debate began. It continues to be a highly controversial issue, since it is by no means a straightforward matter to identify those areas of knowledge that have value in their own right or that are to be seen as intrinsically worthwhile nor, indeed, even to demonstrate that there are areas of knowledge of which this is true.

This question has been a major concern of philosophers since the time of Plato. Indeed, it could be argued that this is the focal point of philosophy itself since all branches of philosophy – ethics, aesthetics, politics and so on – can be seen as centrally engaged in a search for what will constitute knowledge in each particular field. Inevitably a number of different theories about the nature and structure of knowledge have been offered, all or most of which are still in vogue, and it would be for many reasons desirable that we should consider these in great detail; firstly, because particular theories about the nature of knowledge are implicit in or assumed by all theories that are proposed as bases for curriculum development and planning and, secondly and more importantly, because the assumptions about the nature of knowledge that such theories make are often left unquestioned and accepted uncritically. In other words, the epistemological bases of the curriculum are too little understood by curriculum theorists and most theories about the curriculum need to be looked at very critically and rigorously from this point of view.

However, we must content ourselves here with a brief survey of the main issues, a procedure that may be more acceptable since it begins to appear to me that the most important point for curriculum theorists to understand is perhaps not the details of particular epistemological theories, although clearly they should grasp them if they intend to base their own theories on them, but rather the variety of theories that have been offered and the fact that each of them is inevitably tentative and hypothetical and fails to offer an account of knowledge that is generally acceptable.

Two main kinds of theory have emerged during the development of Western European philosophy, those rationalist views that take as their starting point the supremacy of the intellect over other human faculties and stress that true knowledge is that which is achieved by the mind in some way independently of the information provided by the senses, and those empiricist views which have taken a contrary stance and maintained that knowledge of the world about us can only be derived from the evidence that the world offers us through the use of our senses.

This dispute reflects a distinction that has characterized Western European philosophy from the beginning between the idea of the fallibility of the senses as sources of information and views that some have held of the infallibility of the intellect. Thus such philosophers as Plato, Descartes and Kant have offered various versions of a rationalist epistemology which have shared the basic conviction that the evidence of our senses is misleading but that the rational mind can attain true knowledge independently of the senses by apprehending what lies beyond those sense impressions or in some way introducing a rational structure to our understanding of them.

Such theories, seeing knowledge as essentially independent of the observations of our senses, inevitably lead to a view of knowledge as reified, as in some sense God-given, 'out-there' and independent of the knower, having a status that is untouched by and owes nothing to the human condition of the beings who possess the knowledge they are concerned with. Thus for Plato, and especially for Aristotle, the act of contemplation of the supreme forms of human knowledge is a godlike act, through which man transcends his human condition and achieves, albeit momentarily, the supreme bliss of the life of pure intellect perpetually enjoyed by God. For St Thomas Aquinas, and indeed for those Thomists who continue to adhere to his doctrine, true knowledge is in a quite literal sense God-given, being 'revealed' by God to man. And for Kant too, at a more mundane level, the task of establishing a critique of knowledge is essentially one of discovering those elements of knowledge which owe nothing to our nature as human beings, those which are derived from pure reason and have nothing to do with human feelings or passions.

It is this kind of epistemological belief that underlies the claims of some present-day philosophers of education for the inalienable right of certain subjects to be included in the curriculum. For Richard Peters' 'transcendental' argument (1966) for the intrinsic value of certain kinds of human activity is in all major respects a reassertion of the rationalist arguments of Immanuel Kant; and the view of John White (1973; Thompson and White 1975) that a significant distinction can be drawn between activities that one needs to engage in to understand and those that can be understood, as it were, from the outside, is an attempt to provide a simpler and more easily understood (whether from the inside or the outside) rationale for adopting what is essentially the same kind of epistemological stance.

The best way to recognize what others have found unsatisfactory in this kind of view is to look at the basic tenets of the other main kind of epistemological theory, empiricism. For empiricism is best seen as a reaction to the mysticism of these rationalist views. Its fundamental tenet is well expressed in the claim of John Locke, the founder of the empiricist movement, that no knowledge comes into the mind except through the gates of the senses. The mind of the newborn child is seen as a *tabula rasa*, a clean sheet, 'void of all characters, without any ideas'. Such knowledge as it acquires, it acquires through experience, through sensation and reflection, that is, by what its senses tell it and by its own reflective introspection and interpretation of its perceptions. For the empiricist, there is no other source of knowledge, since he denies the validity of all *a priori* knowledge, that is, all knowledge which does not derive ultimately from experience.

A basic position such as this leads inevitably to a less confident view of knowledge and to a greater awareness of the tentative nature of human knowledge, since it is agreed by everyone that the rationalists are right in claiming that the evidence of our senses is unreliable. Indeed, one of the earliest and most ardent exponents of the empiricist view of knowledge, David Hume, came to the conclusion that no knowledge was possible at all or, at least, that we could have little certainty in our knowledge of the world about us. 'If we believe that fire warms or water refreshes, 'tis only because it costs us too much pains to think otherwise.' It is not perhaps necessary to go as far to the other extreme as this, but it is necessary, if one takes such a view, to recognize at the very least the hypothetical nature of knowledge, as present-day empiricist theories do (Ayer 1936, 1946).

Thus a number of recent theories of knowledge and theories of education have begun from the conviction that human knowledge has to be treated in a far more tentative way than many who take a rationalist view would concede and that, in relation to curriculum planning, we are in no position to be dogmatic about its content. The whole pragmatist movement, as promoted by John Dewey, which has been highly influential in the recent development of educational practice, has been founded on a view of knowledge as hypothetical and therefore subject to constant change, modification and evolution. Such a view requires us to be hesitant about asserting the value of any body of knowledge or its right to inclusion in the curriculum and encourages us to accept that knowledge is to be equated rather with experience, so that what it means for a child to acquire knowledge is that he should have experiences which he can himself use as the basis for the framing of hypotheses to explain and gain control over the environment in which he lives. In other words, we cannot impose what is knowledge for us upon him; we must assist him to develop his own knowledge, his own hypotheses, which will be different from ours if the process of evolution is to go on.

This certainly results in a view of education as a much more personal activity than any rationalist could acknowledge. It may also suggest that knowledge itself is personal and subjective. Thus some have stressed the phenomenological or existentialist claim that all knowledge is personal and subjective, that every individual's knowledge is the result of his own completely unique perceptions of his own world. As a result of arguments of this kind, we have demands from people like Illich (1971), Freire (1972) and others that society should be deschooled and the process of education made less formal.

This, however, is not a view that Dewey himself subscribed to. He believed that the proper model for all knowledge is that of scientific knowledge, where hypotheses are framed and modified according to publicly agreed criteria, so that while such knowledge has no permanent status it is objective in so far as it at least enjoys current acceptance by everyone. Mary Warnock (1977) is making the same point (although she develops quite different conclusions from it) when she speaks of 'received bodies of knowledge'.

Others have disputed this, however, and have suggested that knowledge cannot be seen as having even a current universal acceptance. This is the main thrust of the recent developments in sociology towards the generation of a sociology of knowledge. For it has been argued here not only that knowledge is a human product but that it is the product of particular social groups, 'a product of the informal understandings negotiated among members of an organized intellectual collectivity' (Blum 1971). On this view, then, knowledge is socially constructed and, since socially constructed knowledge is ideology, any attempt to make decisions about the content of the curriculum that are based on some views of what kinds of knowledge are valuable has to be seen as an attempt to impose one particular ideology on children and thus to achieve some kind of social control over them either deliberately or merely as a by-product of one's practice. Debate about the content of the curriculum is thus seen as dispute between conflicting ideologies. It is for this reason, amongst others, that it has been suggested that we should endeavour to base the content of the curriculum on the 'common sense knowledge' of the pupil rather than the 'educational knowledge' of the teacher (Keddie 1971). In this way it is suggested we will avoid the alienation we referred to earlier which, it is claimed, is experienced by children who see no point or meaning in the content of what is presented to them. In addition, we will repudiate the charge that we are endeavouring to gain control of them by indoctrinating them with the values, the ideology, of one dominant section of the community.

It is this debate which bedevils not only any attempt to establish a firm philosophical or epistemological basis for curriculum planning but also, as we shall see in the next section, any attempt to base our decisions on the nature of society or on some notion of education as cultural transmission. For this also requires that we discover some criteria within the nature of knowledge itself which will enable us to choose between conflicting cultures or to make a selection from what might seem to be the common culture and this we have just seen we cannot do. There is no universally accepted theory of knowledge and the theories that appear to have the strongest claims on our acceptance are those that tell us that they cannot establish the kind of objective status for knowledge that we require in order to make decisions about the content of the curriculum entirely on the basis of this kind of consideration.

In fact, our brief survey of some of the major features of what philosophers and others have said about knowledge has suggested that epistemological considerations in themselves can provide no positive help to curriculum planners, since one can find no clear, hard and fast theory of knowledge upon which any firm choice of curriculum content can be based. Similarly, as we shall see later, they offer no clear-cut basis for the development of an objective framework of values within which such decisions can be made.

This also highlights a fundamental tension, or even a contradiction, in Denis Lawton's model of curriculum planning which we considered briefly in Chapter 1 (Lawton 1973). He is suggesting that in making decisions about the curriculum we look to both philosophical assertions about the nature of knowledge and to sociological considerations about such things as social and technological change and that we balance these against each other. It should now be apparent, however, that if those philosophical assertions are such as to promote a view of knowledge as having a 'God-given' status, then they must also require of us that we do not, or even cannot, modify or compromise this God-given status by reference to mundane sociological considerations of the here-and-now of particular societies. If, on the other hand, these philosophical considerations do not lead to this view of knowledge, then they must lead to a view of it as socially constructed in some way, so that they are not fundamentally different kinds of consideration from the sociological considerations themselves.

Again, therefore, either epistemological considerations of a purely philosophical kind must dominate curriculum planning, no matter how socially irrelevant the curriculum is that they lead to, or it must be accepted that they are of no real help in curriculum planning at all.

If epistemology is of any value to the curriculum planner, that value derives only from the fact that this kind of enquiry can illuminate and introduce some clarity into our discussions of the curriculum, since such excursions into the theory of knowledge do help to point up some of the difficulties that curriculum planners face in this area and to bring out the assumptions implicit in some theories about the curriculum. They also provide some negative evidence as to where solutions to these problems are not to be found and suggest, therefore, both that we look elsewhere for solutions and that there are real dangers in expecting these solutions ever to be so conclusive that we can be dogmatic about them. For they also reveal that some of the difficulties that we meet in curriculum planning are a direct result of the adoption of one particular theory of knowledge on the assumption that it can not only help to solve our problems but that it can in itself provide a final answer to them. In other words, too close an adherence to any one theory of what knowledge is or of what is knowledge is likely in itself to generate problems, some of which, such as the problems of curriculum integration that we shall consider in Chapter 3, might not otherwise have existed.

This same difficulty, as has just been suggested, bedevils also the attempt to base curriculum planning on an analysis of the nature of society and it is to an examination of this view that we now turn.

Culture and the curriculum

First, then, let us consider the case for basing decisions about the content of the curriculum on an analysis of the nature of society.

It must be recognized that schools exist in advanced or sophisticated societies as agencies for the handing on of the culture of the society, so that at least in part their purposes must be seen in terms of socialization or acculturation, attending to that induction of children into the ways of life of society which is achieved in more primitive societies by less formal methods. On this basis it has been argued that a good deal of what is to be taught in schools can be decided by reference to the culture of the society they are created to serve. This has been one of the root justifications of those who take a hard line on the question of curriculum content, since it has been argued that a major task of the school is to hand on to the next generation the 'common cultural heritage' of the society (Lawton 1973, 1975).

Even if one accepts the force of this claim in principle, in practice it creates more difficulties than it resolves. To begin with, difficulties arise because the term 'culture' has several different meanings. In particular, confusions are created by the fact that the term is used, by anthropologists for example, to denote in a purely descriptive sense all aspects of the ways of life of a particular society, as when we speak of the cultural patterns of a primitive community. On the other hand, it is also used to denote what is regarded as being best in the art and literature of any particular society. Thus a 'cultured gentleman' is not one who knows his way about the ways of life, the habits and beliefs of his society; he is a man who has been brought to appreciate those works of his fellows that are regarded as being among the finer achievements of the culture. When people talk then of basing the curriculum on the culture of the society, some of them are suggesting that we socialize the young, while others are encouraging us to frame the curriculum in terms of what is regarded as being best or most valuable among the intellectual and artistic achievements of the society. A leaning towards the latter interpretation, even when the problems of definition are recognized and a clear definition is offered, is likely to lead to a view of two or more cultures, a high and a low, or an upper-class and a folk culture (Eliot 1948; Bantock 1968, 1971), and this has serious implications for curriculum planning and the practice of education generally which we must later examine. In particular, problems of both a theoretical and a practical kind arise when the distinction becomes associated with social class differences (Kelly 1981).

A second problem arises from the difficulty of establishing what is or should be the relationship between schools and the society in which they function. We have spoken so far as if the function of the schools is to transmit the culture of society, but there are those who would wish to argue that they exist rather to transform that culture, to act as positive agents of change. Do schools change society or do they themselves change in response to prior changes in society? These are nice questions. Even nicer are the issues we raise if we ask whether schools ought to be attempting to change society or merely to adjust to social changes. In reality, and perhaps in ideal terms too, it may be sufficient to recognize that both are interlinked and subject to many of the same influences and constraints so that changes occur in both *pari passu*, and this perhaps is how things should be.

Whatever view one takes of this issue, a further difficulty arises for those who wish to base decisions about the content of the curriculum on considerations of the culture of the society when we attempt to state in specific terms what that culture is. For it is clear that in a modern advanced industrial society no one pattern of life that can be called the culture of that society can be identified. Most modern societies are pluralist in nature; that is, it is possible to discern in them many different, and sometimes incompatible, cultures or subcultures. It does not follow that we must regard such subcultures as hierarchically related to each other but it is necessary to recognize them as being different from each other. It is also important to appreciate that most individual members of a society will participate in more than one of these subcultures at different times or in different aspects of their lives. Thus not only do most modern societies contain different ethnic groups, each with its own traditions, habits, beliefs, customs and so on, but they also contain different religious groups, different social groups, artistic groups, groups held together by many different shared interests, each of which will have its own norms, its own 'culture'.

The question as to whether schools should endeavour to promote a common culture or help diverse groups to develop their own different cultures is a vexed one, not least in relation to those minority ethnic groups that are to be found in most societies. What concerns us more directly here, however, is the implication that even if we believe that the content of the curriculum should be based on the culture of the society, it will be impossible to assert with any real expectation of general acceptance what that culture is and therefore what the content of the curriculum should be. All that this line of argument will achieve is to remind us of the view of the curriculum as a battleground of competing ideologies and to bring us face to face with age-old issues concerning the appropriate educational provision for different social and ethnic groups, as we shall see when we come to consider the question of the common compulsory curriculum. In fact, it is a line of argument which in the last analysis leads to a recognition of the need for diversity rather than uniformity of educational provision, and thus to an awareness of the inadequacies of any form of curriculum planning that lays too great a stress on the consideration of curriculum content.

The problem is aggravated by the fact that most societies are far from static entities and this implies that one feature of their culture is that it is changing, evolving, developing. Furthermore, western cultures 'are characterized not only by rapid change but also by deliberate change' (Taba 1962, p. 54). Technological change, as we saw in Chapter 1, must also lead to changes in the norms, the values, the beliefs, the customs of a society; in other words, it must lead to a fluid culture. Moral change too is more difficult in many ways to handle. It is slower to take effect, since people shed or change their values more slowly and more reluctantly than they exchange their cars or their washing machines. Thus there is a time-lag between the technological changes and those that follow in the norms, customs and social institutions of the society (Taba 1962).

There are several aspects of this that have serious implications for education and the curriculum. Firstly, it emphasizes the impossibility of the task of deciding which aspects of the culture schools should initiate their pupils into. Secondly, it raises again the question of what the role of the school is or should be in relation to the culture of society, in particular whether it is there to transmit that culture or to transform it. Thirdly, it raises questions about what schools should be attempting to do for their pupils in a society that is subject to rapid change.

A recognition of the rapidity of social change and of the need for people to be equipped to cope with it and even to exercise some degree of control over it suggests that schools should in any case go beyond the notion of initiation of pupils into the culture of the society, beyond socialization and acculturation, to the idea of preparing pupils for the fact of social change itself, to adapt to and to initiate changes in the norms and values of the community. This requires that pupils be offered much more than a selection of the culture of the society as it exists at the time when they happen to be in schools, even if this could be identified and defined clearly enough for adequate educational practice. It also constitutes, as we have seen, a strong argument for planning the curriculum by reference to the capacities we are endeavouring to promote in pupils rather than the bodies of knowledge we are concerned to pass on to them.

Furthermore, if we are right to suggest that this is the only viable role the school can take in a rapidly changing society, if it can only equip pupils to take their place in such a society by developing in them the ability to think for themselves and make their own choices, then the question of whether the school is there to transmit or to transform the culture of society has already in part been answered. For the adoption of this kind of role takes the school well beyond the mere transmission of knowledge – a role that in a changing society would seem to be in any case untenable. If the school is not itself to transform the culture, it is certainly there to produce people who can and will transform it.

This is one source of a further problem that arises if we attempt to establish as the content of our curriculum those things which we regard as being the essential valuable elements of the culture. Recent practice has revealed very clearly that this can lead to the imposition on some pupils of a curriculum that is alien to them, which lacks relevance to their lives and to their experience outside the school and can ultimately bring about their alienation from and rejection of the education they are offered. This is probably the root cause of most of the problems that the educational system is facing today and it is certainly a real hazard if not an inevitable result of this kind of approach to curriculum planning.

These last points lead us on to a much more general weakness of this line of argument. For it will be apparent that even if we see it as the task of our schools to initiate pupils into the culture of the society, it will not be possible to offer them the whole of that culture, however it is defined. A selection will have to be made and, since this is so, any notion of the culture of the society, no matter how acceptable in definition or content, will in itself not provide us with appropriate criteria of selection. We will need to look elsewhere for justification of the selection we do make so that the arguments for a curriculum content based on the culture or cultures of society will not in themselves take us very far towards finding a solution to our problem.

This brings us lastly to the realization that attempts to base decisions about the content of the curriculum on a consideration of the nature of society are, if interpreted in this way, essentially utilitarian arguments; they seek a social or sociological justification for curriculum content and therefore imply that that justification is to be sought outside the activity or the knowledge or the content itself, a procedure which we have already suggested is incompatible with the notion of education as such.

This charge can only be avoided if they go further and argue that what is valuable in the culture is valuable not merely because it is part of the culture but because it has some intrinsic merit which justifies its place not only on the curriculum but also in society itself. Thus, as we have seen, some curriculum theorists, such as Paul Hirst, argue for the inclusion of certain areas of knowledge in the curriculum on the grounds that these are those forms of knowledge that constitute rationality itself, that they represent what it means to be rational, so that without them nothing that can be called 'education' is possible since education is seen as essentially concerned to develop the rational mind (Hirst 1965, 1969).

To this argument others, such as Richard Peters, add the claim that certain kinds of human activity and achievement have a value that is intrinsic rather than utilitarian (Peters 1965, 1966; Hirst and Peters 1970).

And there are many people who would wish to argue that there are certain elements in the culture of any advanced society which go beyond the particularities of that society and reflect certain values which are timeless and, indeed, transcendental in every sense. It is on grounds such as these that many would want to press the case for the introduction of pupils to literature, music, art and ideas that are felt to be 'great' and to constitute a cultural heritage which is the heritage of mankind in general rather than of one particular nation.

To take this view is, of course, to propound a completely different argument from that which seeks justification in the culture itself and it does bring us back to the whole issue of the nature of knowledge and the question of whether any body of knowledge has or can have an intrinsic, objective, absolute value or status. The focus of the matter, therefore, continues to be the nature of knowledge and any attempt to seek for a justification of curriculum content in terms that are not instrumental or utilitarian must start with an examination of what knowledge is. We have already seen, however, the problems which that raises.

Appeals to the nature of society, then, like analyses of the nature of knowledge, fail to provide us with unassailable criteria of choice in curriculum planning. They also reveal the problematic nature of any framework of values we may set up to enable us to make choices, whether among bodies of knowledge or among the cultures and subcultures of society. They thus highlight the problem created for curriculum planners by the lack of any firm basis of values, and we must now consider that problem in a little more detail, noting as we do so that it is a problem that must be faced whether we are making choices of content, objectives or principles in the process of curriculum planning.

Values and the curriculum

It is only relatively recently that doubts have been expressed about the validity of the claim that certain kinds of knowledge are inherently more valuable or more important than others. For Plato there was no doubt that there was a very clear hierarchy of knowledge with philosophy at its peak and this, along with so many of the fundamental assumptions of Platonism, went unquestioned up to the time when the empiricists offered the challenge of a completely new approach to the question of knowledge. The fundamental principle of that hierarchy was that the greater the level of abstraction the more status a particular kind of knowledge had. Thus, in addition to the claims we examined earlier for the superiority of intellectual knowledge over sense-experience of the phenomena of the physical world, Plato also asserts that gradations must be recognized within the realms of intellectual knowledge according to degrees of abstraction, with philosophy, or dialectic as he calls it at this point in his argument, as a form of knowledge that he sees as totally abstract and not hypothetical in any way, at the pinnacle or as the coping stone. It is also worth noting here that another of the arguments Plato uses to support his claim for the superiority of philosophy over all other forms of knowledge is that all philosophers believe this to be so and they are the only people who are in a position to know.

The influence of that kind of thinking on curriculum development, or non-development, over the years should not need to be spelled out to anyone who has spent any time teaching in our schools or colleges or universities.

A major consequence of taking this view of knowledge as being hierarchically structured is that it leads to an inevitable stratification of society. Thus, in Plato's ideal society, all those citizens who have not revealed the talent necessary to be educated as philosophers will be brought up to accept the superior knowledge and judgement of the 'philosopher-kings' and to obey them without question. In other words, this is a view which, as we suggested earlier, leads to the generation of two or three levels of culture, two or three kinds of curriculum and two or three classes of people within society.

It is also a view, therefore, which makes the attainment of educational equality impossible (Kelly 1980). For, once one accepts a definition of education in terms of certain 'high status' subjects or bodies of knowledge, once one adopts the belief that, for example, to be educated is to have studied Latin and/or Greek or, indeed, whatever subjects one selects to put at the top of one's hierarchy, then it must follow, as the night the day, and as Plato fully appreciated, that anyone who cannot cope with the bodies of knowledge so designated cannot by definition be educated, but must be content with involvement in lower-status activities and with what is literally a second-class form of upbringing.

We have already noted, however, that an empiricist view of knowledge destroys this reified 'out-there' status of knowledge and, once that has gone, there is no basis for any such hierarchy. It was as a result of the empiricist movement, therefore, that the existence of qualitative differences between knowledge and types of human activity came first to be challenged. The full implications of this became clear in the doctrine of Utilitarianism as developed by Jeremy Bentham.

Bentham's main concern was to establish a moral principle for legislation and he found that principle in the notion of social utility – the greatest good of the greatest number. Thus, in his *Theory of Legislation*, he tells us, 'the end and aim of a legislator should be the HAPPINESS of the people. In matters of legislation, GENERAL UTILITY should be his guiding principle,' and again, 'The *Principle of Utility*, accordingly, consists in taking as our starting point, in every process of ordered reasoning, the calculus of comparative estimate of pains and pleasures, and in not allowing any other idea to intervene.'

Such a comparative estimate of pleasures and pains, however, results in the greatest good being conceived in terms entirely of social utility and not by reference to some metaphysical notion of quality. The only kinds of difference that he will allow between pleasures and between pains are quantitative differences, those to be found in their degrees of purity, intensity, duration and so on; he does not see any basis upon which we can make qualitative distinctions by claiming that certain pleasures are 'better' or 'more worthwhile' than others or upon which we can distinguish between good and bad taste. Thus John Stuart Mill in his essay on Bentham quotes him as saying, 'quantity of pleasure being equal, push-pin is as good as poetry'.

The implications of this view for education are clearly serious and it was as much because of his concern to promote education as for any other reason that John Stuart Mill endevoured to reframe the whole doctrine of Utilitarianism in such a way as to introduce or reintroduce the notion of qualitative differences between kinds of pleasure and kinds of human activity (West 1965). There is of course a fundamental tension between Utilitarianism itself, which takes at root an instrumental view of value, and the notion of intrinsic value, so that inevitably this resulted in its becoming a totally different doctrine as a result of Mill's work. Nevertheless, this is the point of Mill's often-quoted assertion that 'It is better to be a human being dissatisfied than a pig satisfied; better to be a Socrates dissatisfied than a fool satisfied' (J.S. Mill, *Utilitarianism*, ch. II). However, the argument he produces to support this claim is remarkably weak for a case that is so crucial and also very reminiscent of Plato's argument for the superiority of philosophy. For he goes on to say, 'And if the fool, or the pig, are of a different opinion, it is because they only know their own side of the question. The other party to the comparison knows both sides' (ibid.).

This particular battle still rages, especially in relation to the curriculum (Wilson 1967; Peters 1967a), and clearly it is of crucial importance. It has resulted in a questioning of the content of education of a kind which at one time would have been unthinkable. For as long as the view of values as fixed and unchangeable held sway, the model of education that it gave rise to remained virtually unquestioned. That model is the Platonic model of the slow ascent of the individual up the ladder of knowledge towards greater degrees of abstraction or, to use his own simile, the gradual emergence from the dark cave of ignorance into the light of the sun and finally to the contemplation of the sun itself. This is a view that can still be detected today as much in the unquestioned assumptions of some people's thinking about education as in certain explicit statements about it. Even the metaphors are similar, the child being seen as the barbarian at the gates and education as the process of gradual admission to the citadel of civilization (Peters 1965). The arguments too have a familiar ring to them since the superiority of certain kinds of human activity is still argued, as we have seen, in terms of such things as cognitive content, seriousness and intrinsic value (Peters 1966). The means/end aspect of the Platonic model has been rightly criticized and rejected but all else remains fundamentally much the same.

However, the difficulties have been revealed of establishing the claim that any kind of activity has an intrinsic value over and above the value that individual human beings place on it or that value in some way inheres in certain kinds of activity. Values are not entities that have some kind of existence of their own even in some metaphysical sense. Valuing is an activity; it is something people do. Only confusion can result when we allow such activities to become reified because the vagaries of English grammar allow certain verbal functions to be performed by the use of nouns. This is a fallacy common to a number of philosophical problems. Valuing can only be an activity and, as with all activities, different people do it differently.

Furthermore, such a view of values as objective is based on a view of knowledge as 'out-there' and God-given, a view that we saw earlier is at the very least highly questionable. If knowledge is not seen as having this sort of objective status independent of the knower, it is difficult to know what basis there could be for claiming that some activities have an intrinsic value independent of the value placed on them by individual human beings, and even more difficult to establish what these activities are.

Several further points must be made which derive from this basic feature of values. In the first place, a view of values as deriving their validity from the actual choices made by individuals is an essential feature of a view of man as an active rather than as a passive being, a creature whose behaviour is the result of his own choices and purposes and not merely of the causal effects of external events. Such a view of values, therefore, follows naturally from the idea of the autonomy of the individual and must lead to the rejection of any study of education or planning of the curriculum that is based on a behaviourist model of man.

It is worth going further too and stressing again that it is this which makes it possible to distinguish education from other activities such as training or conditioning. We have noted already the claim that development of autonomy is an essential feature of any distinctive concept of education (Peters 1965, 1966). We are here faced with one of the implications of that claim. Such a concept of education must acknowledge that autonomy for the individual implies his right to do his own valuing and not merely to be brought to recognize certain values for which, in Platonic style, objective status is claimed.

On the other hand, the need to make choices in the absence of any criteria of choice presents us with the archetypal dilemma of the existentialist and is conducive to nothing so much as the nausea that Jean-Paul Sartre and others have spoken of.

We must recognize, however, that to be engaged in educating anybody is to be committed *ipso facto* to the belief that some human activities are of more value than others. A second aspect of the concept of education which Richard Peters (1965, 1966) rightly draws our attention to is its essential value-element. Education is, indeed, a matter of initiation into intrinsically worthwhile activities, even though he is wrong in claiming that we can objectively identify or determine what those intrinsically worthwhile activities are. To say that qualitative differences between kinds of knowledge and kinds of human activity cannot be demonstrated is not to say that we will accept them all as being of equal merit. Of course, we will all make distinctions of this kind. We must realize, however, that our basis for making such distinctions is insecure and shifting, and that the values we adhere to will represent our own favoured ideological position rather than our grasp on any eternal truths. This is the important thrust of those recent developments in the sociology of knowledge to which we have already referred (Young 1971).

It must follow from this that whoever takes decisions about the curriculum or contributes to the taking of such decisions must be encouraged to appreciate the slender nature of the foundations on which any system of values or set of criteria he is using will be based. His choices should, therefore, be tentative and of such a kind as to avoid dogmatism. Furthermore, they should be open to continuous evaluation and modification since that is the essence of curriculum development. If knowledge were God-given and if values enjoyed a similar status, then curriculum development could have only one meaning as the slow progression towards perfection that Plato had in mind. Such a notion is no longer tenable.

It is for this reason that some educationists have encouraged us to look to another source of criteria of choice in making decisions about the curriculum, a source that derives from a consideration not of the nature of society nor of the nature of knowledge but of the nature of the educand, the child our activities are directed towards. For that empiricist approach to epistemology, which we saw began with Locke and Hume, has in turn spawned a new view of education (Blenkin and Kelly 1981) which, in accepting both that the status of knowledge is and must be problematic and that all that is to count as knowledge must be ultimately derived from experience, has come to regard the experience of the child as central to the educational process. This 'child-centred' view of education and approach to educational planning has gained some credence not only from its adoption by a number of well-known 'progressive' private schools, such as Summerhill and Bedales, but also because it has been recommended for adoption in the primary sector of state-provided education in the United Kingdom by the two major government reports on education in that sector, those of the Hadow (Board of Education 1931) and the Plowden (Central Advisory Council for Education 1967) committees. It is perhaps particularly worthy of consideration at the present time too in the light of that growing awareness of the problems created by other approaches which has just been outlined (Blenkin and Kelly 1981). It is, then, to a brief examination of this proposed basis for decisions about the curriculum that we must now turn.

'Child-centred' approaches

The idea that in seeking answers to our questions about what should be taught we look to an examination of the nature of the child is not new; it is certainly not a product of the twentieth century. The revolt against the traditional view of education as concerned with the purveying of certain kinds of abstract knowledge and the development of rationality was begun by Rousseau in the eighteenth century and carried forward by other, perhaps more influential, educators, such as Froebel and Montessori in the last century. The main thrust of that revolt was against the idea that we plan our educational practices by a consideration of knowledge or of society, and that we begin to look instead to the children who are the objects of those practices and plan according to what we can discover about them. It is for this reason that this general movement has been termed 'child-centred'.

What is recent is the rigorous examination of what this entails, since for many years, while admittedly encouraging a more humane approach to education and requiring a more careful consideration of the child's feelings and his reactions to educational practices, it was highly suspect theoretically, leading more to the generation of a romantic reverence for childhood than to any rigorous analysis of what education fundamentally is or should be. It is one thing to claim that education should be planned according to what we know about the nature of children; it is quite another to spell out precisely how our knowledge of children should be reflected in our educational planning. Thus some of the early theories seemed to suggest that no planning should be done at all, since they advised us to leave the child alone to develop naturally, to grow like a plant in a garden, free from the corrupting or confining influences of adults.

With theories such as these it is very difficult to decide what practical provisions they should lead to. They may be helpful in our attempts to decide on appropriate methods but they offer no criteria by which we can make choices of suitable content. It is largely because of this ambivalence that attempts have been made in more recent times to produce more coherent accounts of the practical implications of this fundamental view of the central role of child nature in curriculum planning.

Three related kinds of answer have been offered to this question – claims that our main concern should be the needs of the child, assertions that the content of the curriculum should be decided by reference to his interests and attempts to give a coherent account of the nature of growth. We must look at each of these briefly in an attempt to assess whether they will offer us the yardstick we are looking for.

Needs

The idea that we should begin our curriculum planning by attempting to discover what children need is an attractive one. It appears at first sight to dovetail naturally into a theory of education that takes as its main focus the nature of children and suggests that that should be our first concern in planning educational provision. The whole thrust of the naturalist 'child-centred' movement, as we have seen, is away from the view that education should be planned by reference to the nature of knowledge or the needs of society towards claiming that the main, perhaps the sole, concern should be with the nature of the child and, therefore, with his needs. This whole movement gave great impetus to the development of the study of child psychology, and, indeed, in return has received much support from the work of developmental psychology in particular (Blenkin and Kelly 1981). For clearly, if we are to pay heed to the nature of children we need to discover as much as we can about that nature, and the translation of this into the idea of needs was one attempt by educational psychologists to spell out what kind of educational provision this concern with child nature should lead to. In fact, the concept of need has been an important one in psychology generally and was therefore a popular and attractive notion to educationists at the time when education theory was mainly influenced by the results of psychological researches.

The use of the notion of children's needs, however, as a criterion of choice for the planning of their education is one that is fraught with difficulties (Dearden 1968; Wilson 1971). In the first place, the argument that we can resolve questions of what anyone ought to have by reference to what they are seen to need involves an illicit process from 'is' to 'ought' which can never constitute sound reasoning and which, amongst other things, begs a good many questions of a moral and social kind. For it may be claimed that the whole fabric of society is held together by the ability of most people to go without some of the things they might feel they need in the interests of social cohesion.

Furthermore, even if this were not so, the problem of identifying needs still remains. It may well be that much human behaviour, and especially the motivation for that behaviour, is explicable in terms of the reduction of needs through their satisfaction or part satisfaction (Maslow 1954), since clearly if a felt need is reduced in some way the pattern of behaviour associated with that reduction will be reinforced. But to characterize all learning as being of this type is to go too far and in any case, even if this were the model for all learning, we would still be left with the problem of evaluating between needs, of deciding which patterns of behaviour should be reinforced by these processes of need reduction, since the notion of need in itself, as we have just seen, does not provide us with the criteria of evaluation, with a framework of values, with grounds for asserting what ought to be done.

This becomes apparent when we consider the detailed accounts of human needs that the psychologists offer us. Maslow, for example, identified three kinds of need – primary needs for food, air, sleep and so on, emotional needs for such things as love and security and social needs for acceptance by one's peers and such like (Maslow 1954). However, the further we move up this hierarchy of needs, the more problematic our acceptance of them becomes and even greater difficulties arise over questions of whether, and in particular how, these needs are to be satisfied. A moment's consideration will reveal this.

In fact, as many writers have pointed out, 'needs' is a value term and thus cannot of itself offer us a firm criterion of choice. There can be and are many differing views and opinions concerning what children need or what any particular child needs, ranging from those of the child himself to those of the politicians responsible for the public funding of the educational system. Each individual or group will assess such needs in terms of further criteria that will constitute a particular ideology, a particular view of the goals or principles of education.

In short, the term 'need' does not offer us a straight objective description of certain features of human nature that we can use as a basis for planning any kind of social or educational provision. At all but the very basic levels it is impossible to distinguish what we need from what we want or, worse, what someone else thinks we ought to want or ought to have. We still have to choose between the things that people need or think they need and again the notion of need in itself will not provide us with the criterion by reference to which we can make such choices.

The notion of 'needs' in itself, then, cannot resolve our problem, since some further basis is required from which we can evaluate both the competing needs and the different interpretations that will be offered.

Interests

It is partly for this reason that we have been offered a second device by which it is suggested we can implement at a practical level the idea that education should be based on the nature of the child – a recommendation that we should base our decisions concerning the content of the curriculum on a consideration of the interests of the child. This was a feature of John Dewey's philosophy of education and this theory has recently been developed more fully in an attempt to resolve some of the difficulties that a 'child-centred' approach to education presents (Wilson 1971). Briefly, it is suggested that we plan our curriculum not in the light of what we think to be the nature of knowledge nor by reference to what appear to be the requirements of the society or culture in which we live, but in response to what we can find that is actually of interest to the children themselves.

At one level such an approach has obvious advantages. For there is no doubt that children do work better and learn more effectively when they are interested in what they are being required to do. Conversely, it is a lack of interest in the work that teachers require of them that is responsible for the failure to learn and the ultimate alienation and disaffection of many pupils. Every good teacher appreciates this elementary fact of child psychology and all teachers endeavour to make their lessons, and the work in which they are engaging their pupils, interesting in as many ways as possible – by using all kinds of visual aids, for example, or by incorporating practical work and sometimes even organizing outside visits. We all know that children will learn more in one visit to a museum, provided that visit is properly organized, than in ten lessons offering them descriptions of what could be seen there. Again we note, therefore, that this kind of approach will lead to an improvement in our methodology; we will be better teachers for taking account of children's interests in planning how we will present our material to them.

Interpreted in this way, this approach to educational planning through a consideration of children's interests, therefore, is no more than a methodological device for improving our teaching of what we want them to learn, by making them interested in what we feel they should be interested in or by starting from their interests and leading them on to what we want them to do.

However, it has been argued (Wilson 1971) that this use of children's interests trivializes them by using them as means to the achievement of our ends rather than recognizing them as having for the child an intrinsic value. It is certainly the case that such an approach will not solve the problem we are concerned with here; it provides us with no criteria to decide what we should encourage children to be interested in or how we should develop the interests they already have. We have to look elsewhere for a basis upon which we can build our curriculum content, if we interpret the idea of using children's interests in this way.

However, there is a further and deeper level at which we have been offered this idea of children's interests as a basis for our curriculum planning. It has been suggested (Wilson 1971) that we should actually decide on the content of our curriculum by reference to the interests of children and that we should plan our work, not in order to use these interests to achieve our own purposes, but to help the children to pursue their interests more effectively and with more discrimination and to organize their experiences in such a way as to extend and deepen those interests and gain a clearer view of their intrinsic value.

If education is concerned with activities that have an intrinsic value rather than with those that are instrumental to the achievement of ends beyond themselves and if, as we have argued, it is not possible to identify certain activities as being characterized in some way as having this intrinsic merit, then we must accept that intrinsic value, like beauty, is to be found not inhering in objects or activities but in the eye of the valuer, that those activities that are intrinsically valuable are those that the children do actually value in themselves and that, as a result, a curriculum can only be truly described as educational if its content consists of those things that children value.

In brief, then, it is argued that a consideration of the interests of children is central not only to an effective methodology but also to the educational content of our curriculum. It is further argued that only an approach such as this will enable us to avoid the problems that arise when a curriculum is planned by reference to other considerations and, as a result, lacks relevance, becomes reified and leads to the total alienation of pupils from their education.

What is being recommended here is very clear. If we are to avoid all the ills that are said to follow for many pupils when teachers or others decide for them what they shall learn and thus impose their values on them, we can only do this by letting them decide what the content of their education will be by revealing to us what they are interested in. Such an approach creates many practical problems for teachers and others in matters such as the organization of work in the classroom, the planning and setting of public examinations and so on. None of these, however, would be insuperable if we were convinced on theoretical grounds that this was the only proper approach to the planning of curriculum content. There are, however, several difficulties of a more theoretical kind with this view and we must consider some of these now.

In the first place, the identification of children's interests is not the straightforward matter it may appear to be at first glance (White 1964, 1967; Wilson 1971). Distinguishing an abiding interest from an inclination, a passing whim or a temporary fad, even at the conceptual level, is not easy and clearly we must first know what sorts of thing interests are if we are to use them as the basis of our curriculum planning.

But even if we sort that question out there still remain many difficulties in actually recognizing what we are looking for and identifying children's interests. It is clearly not enough to think only in terms of what children enjoy doing since pursuing an interest is not necessarily always a pleasurable activity, as I have often found as I have worked on this book. Some interests which people pursue with enormous devotion and enthusiasm are of a kind that appear to be characterized mainly by being 'nice when you stop'. Nor is it merely a matter of asking children what their interests are, since they cannot always tell us, and their behaviour can often be misleading, an appearance or show of interest not always being a reliable indication of the existence of a real interest in the full sense.

Secondly, we need to know more than we do about the origins of children's interests and we need to give some thought to this before too readily accepting them as the basis of their education. A child whose home background is a very limited one is unlikely to have a very wide range of interests and we may not be doing him the greatest of favours by underwriting those limitations. For all children there are likely to be areas of understanding they will miss if we only attend to what they are already interested in and, even though the dangers of reification and alienation will immediately again rear their heads, there will be occasions when teachers will need to stimulate interests in children where they do not already exist. If this is not so, then we run the risk of depriving some children of large areas of experience that they might otherwise have profited from – a problem we shall need to consider again when we look at the issues of the common curriculum. If, on the other hand, this is so, then again the presence or absence of an interest will not in itself constitute the central criterion for deciding whether a particular activity or body of knowledge should be included in our curriculum or not.

The same difficulty also arises when we consider the question of selection of interests. It is likely to be the case that some of children's interests will appear to be of a trivial kind, unless we define interest in such a way as to exclude all such. Certainly not all interests will appear to be equally valuable or important and some may even seem to require discouragement on moral or social grounds. In this context we are always given the example of the child whose interest lies in pulling wings off insects – I have never met this child myself, although I have often wanted to – and clearly in such cases the interest is not to be encouraged on the mere grounds that it is an interest. Furthermore, every child will have many interests and it will not be possible, even if it were desirable, for him to pursue them all, so that again choices need to be made among these interests and decisions taken as to which of them should be developed. Again, therefore, we need some criterion of choice other than the fact that certain interests are believed to exist. As we have seen already, to say that education should be child-centred, in whatever sense we use the term, cannot be to be advocating complete freedom of activity for the children and, if the teacher is to play any part at all in the child's education, he must select the activities that he will encourage and promote. He must also decide on the directions in which he will promote them since there are countless ways in which an interest can be developed and not all of them will appear equally valuable or desirable.

It is at this point that some of the theorists who have taken this kind of view introduce into the debate the notion of 'growth', suggesting that the ultimate criterion we should appeal to in making a selection among both the interests and the needs of pupils is to be found in the idea that the main function of education is to promote their continuous growth.

Growth

Much the same problem arises, however, when we attempt to explicate the demand that we base our curriculum planning on a consideration of the nature of the child by reference to the idea of natural growth. For the idea of natural growth in itself is of little real help to educationists since what they really want to know is how, when and where they might be justified in interfering with that growth. Similarly, analogies drawn from gardening are not very helpful since the main need of the gardener is to know when to interfere with the natural development of his flowers, tomatoes or hops. The notion of growth in itself cannot enable us to distinguish education from maturation and, therefore, cannot provide us with any of the criteria we are looking for (Dearden 1968).

To speak of guided growth, as, for example, John Dewey does, would appear *prima facie* to beg the question or at least to do no more than push the question one stage backwards. For we now have to ask what criteria we should appeal to in deciding how to guide children's growth. Again we see that the idea of growth is helpful to us in reaching decisions about appropriate methods in education, since it suggests that these should be such as to ensure that the development of children involves fundamental and permanent changes and that their learning should not be superficial, that it should not consist of 'inert ideas' (Whitehead 1932) that remain as outward manifestations rather than becoming inner transformations, but should involve understanding and knowledge in the full sense. Thus it has led to claims such as that of the Hadow Report of 1931 that the curriculum should be thought of in terms of activity and experience rather than knowledge to be acquired and facts to be stored. We have noted already the central role played by the notion of experience in Dewey's educational philosophy. There is also support for this view of education in the work of people such as Piaget and Bruner who view education as a process of cognitive growth and see the main concerns of the teacher as being to assist pupils to acquire those concepts which will enable them to interact successfully with their environment.

Some choice must be made, however, of the particular concepts we are to help children to acquire, so that again we see it is not sufficient even to define growth in terms of conceptual development. Nor does the notion of guided growth help us in decisions of content. The idea of guidance in itself implies direction; a guided activity is an activity with an end or aim in view. To stop a man in the street and ask him to guide you without knowing where you want to go is to invite psychiatric help or perhaps something more violent. However, neither the notion of growth nor that of guidance can in themselves offer answers to this question of direction.

Dewey's own answer to this problem is an interesting one. He is aware that growth must be directed and he is also aware that this implies the existence of some kind of goal. On the other hand, his view of knowledge, as we have seen, will not allow him to produce any theory that implies that teachers, parents, adults generally or even society as a whole have the answers to this question of goals, since, as we have seen, for him knowledge must be allowed to develop and evolve and this cannot happen if the knowledge of one generation is imposed on the next, no matter how gently this is done. His answer is to assert that the only criterion we can use in attempting to evaluate one kind of activity, one body of content, one set of experiences in relation to others is an assessment of the extent to which each is likely to be productive of continued experience and development. Thus he speaks of an 'experiential continuum' (Dewey 1938, ch. 3) which is for him the essence of education as a continuous lifelong process and which offers us the principle by which we can reach decisions concerning the content of each child's curriculum, that principle being always to choose that activity or those experiences likely to be most productive of further experience. Thus he offers us the notion of experience, rather than that of needs, interests or growth, as the ultimate criterion of educational choice.

There is a good deal that is of value in this concept of the teacher as one who keeps constantly open the options available to each pupil and tries to ensure continuous development and progress, for ever widening horizons and steering pupils away from any experience that will have the effect of closing them down. The idea is an attractive one and as a principle to underlie all of our educational practice it would appear to be of great importance.

As a practical criterion by which we can pronounce upon the competing claims of different activities or bodies of knowledge for inclusion in a curriculum, however, it does not take us very far, as any teacher will know. Furthermore, it does not help us to decide where or how this continuous process is to start, what experiences we are to offer pupils initially to get them started or, perhaps more importantly, which experiences we should steer them away from. Nor is it enough to suggest that this kind of decision can be left to the evidence the psychologists offer us concerning ages and stages of development. Again this is not enough, because again it is merely the argument from needs in a slightly more sophisticated guise. We still require a framework of values to enable us to make choices among the many possibilities that exist for pupil activity both at the beginning of and throughout this process of education by means of continuous and productive experiences. There are many directions in which growth can be guided and many of these will be as productive and as praiseworthy as each other, just as there are many different ways in which I can train up the roses in my garden. We still need to be able to assess which of these directions is the most appropriate or likely to be the most prolific, and the idea of continuous experience offers little if anything more than the idea of continuous growth itself. It will not provide us with the practical answers we need.

However, this approach to the debate does have the merit of directing our attention towards the object of the educational process, the child himself. It also leads us again to ask whether we might not find more satisfactory answers to some of the fundamental questions of education by looking at it as a process or a series of processes rather than by concentrating our attention on its intended outcomes, its end-products or its content. This is an issue we shall examine in greater detail in Chapter 4.

In particular, it suggests that we might do better to base our educational planning on the premise that the central concern of education should be the development of understanding rather than the acquisition of knowledge. A major mistake of many of those who have contributed to this debate, especially those who have wished to argue a case for the objective status of certain kinds of knowledge, has been to confuse these two. They all, of course, stress the importance of understanding but they have often failed to appreciate the relationship of understanding to knowledge or have misplaced the emphasis, being more concerned that children should understand what they learn than that they should develop certain intellectual capacities through their learning. Paul Hirst's work does draw our attention to the important distinction between regarding education as initiation into several 'forms of knowledge' and seeing it as initiation into several 'forms of understanding' or 'forms of thought' (Hirst 1965). That is a distinction that must be made. Unfortunately, very few people have appreciated the subtleties of this distinction and even Hirst himself does not always escape from the clutches of the former view.

Similarly, Mary Warnock (1977), while agreeing with John Dewey that all knowledge must be recognized as provisional and hypothetical, appears to view education as a matter of transmitting the currently received corpus of such knowledge rather than of fostering in each individual child the capacity to contribute to the continuing development of that corpus.

The essence of the distinction is the relative weighting that is given to each of these considerations. While it is true that understanding cannot be developed in isolation from bodies of knowledge, it does not follow that decisions about the knowledge content of the curriculum should or must be made first. On the contrary, it suggests rather that they are secondary considerations. We need first to be aware of the kinds of intellectual capacity we are concerned to promote in pupils and, only then, to make decisions about the kinds of content they must be initiated into in order to develop these capacities. This, in my view, is what Dewey meant by 'education as growth' and by 'education as experience', and this too may enable us to reconcile those conflicting views both of knowledge and of culture which we discussed earlier. For, on this view, differences in curriculum content need not lead to differences in the kind or the quality of educational experience (Kelly 1980).

Curriculum content cannot be ignored in curriculum planning; it is an essential factor. We must recognize, however, that it is only one such factor and that there is a strong case for claiming that it should not be treated as the prime consideration of the curriculum planner. Most of the problems we have discussed in this chapter are a result of giving it that kind of pole position. Most of them, therefore, may be expected to disappear when its prominence is reduced.

Summary and conclusions

We have considered in this chapter some of the arguments put forward for the inclusion of particular subjects or particular kinds of content in the curriculum from three perspectives – epistemological theories of the nature of knowledge, views of the nature of society and of culture, and ideas that have been expressed about the nature of children and ways in which a consideration of this can be the central concern of curriculum planning. We have also considered some of the problems of establishing a framework of values within which choices of curriculum content could be made, concluding that such a framework must be recognized as subjective and, as a result, highly tentative.

We must end this discussion of curriculum content by recognizing that in practice we shall, as teachers, make decisions about the content of the work of each of our pupils by reference to all of the criteria that the theorists offer us. We will be concerned with theories of knowledge, although, as we have seen, this may be the least useful source of advice to teachers or curriculum planners; we will be unable to ignore the demands of society; and we will pay due regard to the individual needs, interests and experience of each child in so far as we feel we can identify them. In fact, as is so often the case, the oppositions and polarities exist more in the minds of curriculum theorists than in the realities of curriculum practice.

Furthermore, in reaching these decisions we shall all display a degree of subjectivity that is only to be expected in any human activity. This subjectivity must be recognized and accepted if we are to achieve a proper perspective for our curriculum planning. The main fault with all or most of the theories we have looked at is that they represent attempts to achieve some kind of objective basis for decisions about curriculum content and this, as I have tried to show, is an impossibility. The very idea itself of curriculum *development* implies that we are not dealing with an issue which will be productive of hard and fast answers, unless we see it as a progression towards some ideal state. The notion of development implies continuous reappraisal and change and, therefore, suggests that we should not be searching for some once-for-all, God-given criteria but rather accepting the idea that any criteria we find will themselves be continuously evolving, so that decisions we make about the content of our pupils' work will inevitably be based on our own subjective judgements of those criteria and their impact and import.

This is not to say that we should not endeavour to ensure that all activities are, as far as is possible, educational in the broad sense. It is rather to accept that many kinds of justification are possible, so that the whole process of planning the content of any curriculum is a good deal more complex than some of the arguments we have been considering would suggest. Again, in the last analysis it all rests with the professional judgement of the individual teacher. The most that we can hope, therefore, is that that judgement is truly professional; in other words, that while being subjective it is also informed and firmly based on a full knowledge and understanding of the issues involved. It is to help teachers to develop that knowledge and understanding as a basis for the crucial decisions they must make that this chapter, and indeed this book, has been written.

CHAPTER 3

CURRICULUM INTEGRATION

Demands that the curriculum be made relevant, meaningful and so on have been the most potent factor in the development of the idea of curriculum integration, one of the most significant features of curriculum development and change in the United Kingdom over the last ten years or so. This is the direction in which many teachers have felt it appropriate to develop the curriculum, in spite of the fact that the most influential educational philosophers have been first of all asserting it to be logically impossible and later searching without real success for the logical and epistemological basis upon which it has been accomplished. It is a development which more clearly than any other illustrates the problems of curriculum content which we discussed in the last chapter.

The most interesting feature of this phenomenon is the fact that it has ever been seen as a serious problem. That it has been so viewed has been in the main a result of looking at the questions it raises from the point of view of one particular theory of knowledge. Curriculum integration, even in the terms of that particular theory of knowledge, has been with us for years. For man has always integrated his knowledge as he has focused it on certain concerns that have been important to him. It is only because people have felt it necessary to refocus knowledge in order to deal with new concerns that the problem of integrating hitherto separate areas of knowledge has been raised. Clearly it is a problem, since it raises certain practical difficulties for school organization; but, as this chapter will attempt to show, it is not a logical problem since, if it were, either we would have been aware of it long ago or we should by now have encountered real difficulties in dealing with long-existing kinds of integrated knowledge, such as the study of geography. 'How can the curriculum be integrated?' is thus to some a question rather like 'Have you stopped beating your wife?' since it is only meaningful if one accepts as true the assumptions that lie behind it.

Forms of knowledge and understanding

The source of the logical difficulties that it is claimed the integration of the curriculum raises is to be found in that view of knowledge which regards knowledge as organized into several logically discrete forms of knowledge, forms of understanding (Hirst 1965) or realms of meaning (Phenix 1964). It is this initial assumption about knowledge that creates the difficulty, since clearly, if these bodies of knowledge are different from each other in their logical structure, it will be not merely difficult but downright impossible to integrate them in any real sense.

In an issue as central to recent curriculum planning as this, it is important to be absolutely clear about the point that is being made here. It is not a matter of knowledge being divided up into *subjects* that we are concerned with; it is the supposed existence of logical differences between kinds of knowledge, which leads us to recognize their existence as separate *disciplines*. Thus it is not, or it should not be, the integration of *subjects* that creates difficulties; it is the integration of *disciplines*. How crucial this distinction is will become apparent later.

There are four main aspects to the logical differences that it is being claimed distinguish each of these forms of knowledge from the others. Firstly, each form has 'certain central concepts that are peculiar in character to the form. For example, those of gravity, acceleration, hydrogen and photosynthesis characteristic of the sciences; number, integral and matrix in mathematics; God, sin and predestination in religion; ought, good and wrong in moral knowledge' (Hirst 1965, p. 129). These concepts are of course sometimes used in the context of other forms of knowledge, but it is claimed that in a rational structure of knowledge these concepts fall naturally into one particular form.

Secondly, each form has its own distinctive logical structure. A systematic body of knowledge consists of networks of relationships through which experience is understood and these networks fall into several categories, such as mathematics, the physical sciences, the human sciences, literature and fine arts, morals, religion and philosophy. Each of these networks of relationships, it is claimed, is of a kind logically distinct from the others. There is of course overlap, as between, for example, mathematics and the physical sciences, but the fact that there is overlap does not imply that important logical differences do not exist.

Thirdly, each form is said to have its own distinctive truth criteria, its own method of validating the assertions it consists of. Mathematical assertions, for example, are to be verified by procedures that are quite different from those that are used to verify scientific assertions and there are further different verification procedures, each appropriate and peculiar to a particular form of knowledge.

Lastly, each form has its own distinctive methodology. Each has its own 'particular techniques and skills for exploring experience' (Hirst 1965, p. 129). Each form therefore represents a different set of procedures for extending human knowledge and experience in the area with which it is concerned.

Such an analysis of human knowledge, as we noted in Chapter 2, provides a clear-cut basis for curriculum planning in that it indicates seven or eight distinct forms of rationality into which, it is claimed, the developing rational mind must be initiated. It also, however, creates problems whenever we feel for any reason that some form of integration of knowledge is necessary or desirable. We must be quite clear, however, about exactly what these problems are and how far-reaching they are, since a good deal of confusion is apparent both in what is said about the integration of knowledge and what in practice is done about it.

The integration of knowledge

Although this theory has been seen as providing a basis for curriculum planning, it does not of itself, even when it is accepted as such, dictate the subjects that are to be included in the curriculum. For it will be clear that there can be many different routes to the development of, for example, literary or aesthetic understanding and even of scientific understanding. In practice, however, it has often been interpreted as providing a justification for the retention of certain traditional school subjects and of the barriers which have separated them from each other. This kind of misunderstanding has often created unnecessary problems for those who have attempted some form of curriculum integration.

We must begin, therefore, by reminding ourselves again that no logical problems are created when we wish to integrate subjects but only when the integration of separate disciplines is involved. The development of what is being called 'integrated science' does not raise logical problems since all the subjects to be integrated fall within the same form of knowledge. Often the problems that face those wishing to develop some kind of integrated studies programme are administrative rather than logical, the term 'integration' being used in this case not to indicate the need to put two or more logically different forms of knowledge together but merely (although often this proves to be a greater problem) to get two or more departments or university boards of studies to work together. Thus, in a particular context a subject such as nutritional studies might not be seen in itself as a form of integrated study, which on this kind of analysis of knowledge it clearly is, but the integration of this with, say, home economics would be regarded as present-ing problems of integration. We must be clear that the problems such developments create are entirely administrative; logical difficulties either do not exist since all are branches of the same discipline, as in the case of integrated science, or they have already gone unnoticed, as in the develop-ment of an integrated field such as nutritional studies.

Secondly, we must also not lose sight of the fact that not all attempts to put subjects, or even disciplines, together will raise problems of integration. Certainly not all will raise epistemological problems. It is possible to devise integrated studies programmes – and there are many such about – in which no attempt is made to do any more than to develop related kinds of content in each subject area, to try to achieve, for example, more point to a geological study of the British Isles by linking it to an historical study of the development of forms of physical communication. The intention here is not that the content of each element should be interwoven into one complete 'whole', but merely that each should be related to the other.

Similarly, some programmes offer a choice of activities to pupils which include several subjects and span several disciplines, but the actual work each pupil does is within rather than across disciplines. Such programmes are multidisciplinary rather than interdisciplinary and do not therefore generate the logical difficulties that have caused some people such concern. Only when it is intended that the different packages of knowledge should be welded into one do we have an apparent logical problem and only here, if anywhere, is there a need to develop an interdisciplinary logic.

Thirdly, before we become too dismayed at the prospect of having to develop such an interdisciplinary logic, let us remember that it has already been done with apparent success. Many of the subjects that stand unques-tioned on the curricula of schools, colleges and universities are forms of integrated study; they are *fields* of knowledge rather than *forms* of knowledge, *subjects* rather than *disciplines*. Geography, drawing on mathematics, the physical sciences and the human sciences, is perhaps the most immediately obvious example of this, as we have already noted, but there are many others – domestic science, physical education, design and technology studies, comparative education and, indeed, the study of education itself. Nothing reveals the confusion of thinking that has been characteristic of this area more clearly than the problems some people are prepared to find in integrating, say, health education with education studies generally, while being unaware of and unable to give any account of the problems that on their own analysis must already have been overcome in integrating mathematics, the physical sciences, the human sciences and moral knowledge to form the area of study known as health education itself, in the first instance.

If the integration of disciplines creates logical problems then it must also create them for those attempts at integration that took place before the notion of logically discrete forms of knowledge was first mooted, just as much as for those attempts that have been made since. Alternatively, if such subjects have solved the logical difficulties, then it should not be difficult for us to find similar solutions for new forms of integration. In fact, the whole issue continues to appear to be a non-problem or at least a problem created, as we commented at the outset, by too close an adherence to a particular theory of knowledge.

Other theories of knowledge

These natural changes in the organization of human knowledge, then, and the corresponding developments in the curriculum have not always raised serious logical problems and often the problems they do raise are not epistemological but merely administrative, as we noted above in the case of such developments as integrated science courses.

For some, however, they do not raise such problems even when integration of disciplines seems to be involved, since, as we have seen, many do not accept the existence of these logical distinctions in the first place but regard all knowledge as one and indivisible. We have already examined in some detail John Dewey's view that all knowledge is ultimately reducible to the form of scientific knowledge, the results of that experimentation we constantly engage in to resolve the problems presented by all aspects of our human environment, not only the physical aspects but also the social, cultural, aesthetic and moral.

If one accepts that kind of view of knowledge, then integration of subjects will present us with no logical problems at all. In fact, on this sort of view we will start by seeing knowledge as undifferentiated, in the way that on the whole most primary schools do, and accept that subject divisions will only emerge in the later stages of formal education and then only when they have point for the learner in the organization of his own knowledge. Furthermore, the divisions that appear even then will not be of a logical kind; they will represent the organization of knowledge into convenient fields on the basis of social and personal relevance and will acknowledge the need for constant change, reorganization and reappraisal of these fields. In short, we will accept that the way in which the adult generation has structured its knowledge will not necessarily continue for ever to be the most satisfactory structure for subsequent generations and the need to plan for constant integration and reintegration of knowledge will be acknowledged. Such a notion has been criticized as representing an instrumental view of knowledge, but it is difficult to understand what knowledge is if it is not to be instrumental to man's purposes either individually or collectively.

In brief, the epistemological basis for all such views is one that denies the 'out-there', God-given, objective nature of human knowledge and regards all knowledge as subjective, as socially constructed, as 'a product of the informal understandings negotiated among members of an organized intellectual collectivity' (Blum 1971, p. 117), or which even takes the phenomenologist's completely personalized view. The debate is, therefore, again between those rationalist and empiricist theories of knowledge that we examined in Chapter 2, and it is the influence of the latter kind of theory which explains why curriculum integration has presented comparatively few problems in the primary sector of education (Blenkin and Kelly 1981).

A second, and perhaps largely negative, reason for rejecting this theory of knowledge as divided into logically discrete forms, and therefore not recognizing any fundamental difficulties in the notion of curriculum integration, is the fact that no really clear account has yet been given of what constitutes the differences between the forms of knowledge, other than that between the logical/mathematical and the empirical/scientific forms, a distinction which is itself open to debate. It is one thing to assert that seven or eight different species of knowledge exist; it is quite another to give an account of the logical form of each. Until such an account can be given it is perhaps unwise to take on trust the existence of such divisions and particularly to base far-reaching curricular decisions on them. There is also the related fact that we can observe that much of human knowledge, as we keep on asserting, has been organized quite effectively and without difficulty in an interdisciplinary way. This must lend support to the argument that knowledge is socially constructed or at least organized to achieve certain social purposes and therefore to the view that the curriculum planner must also look to sociological considerations.

If, nevertheless, we wish to cling to the view that there are logically discrete forms of knowledge while at the same time recognizing, as we must, the need for the organization of knowledge also into fields, then we have indeed got a logical difficulty to resolve. Furthermore, the same kinds of logical consideration would seem to suggest that to find a solution to this difficulty must be a logical impossibility, if the logical differences are as marked as is being claimed. For to argue that we must seek for an interdisciplinary logic that will enable us to operate between or across forms of knowledge (Hirst and Peters 1970) is to suggest that it is possible to find a form of logic that will enable us to achieve some kind of unity of knowledge. This in turn would seem to imply, firstly, that the logical differences between the forms are not as hard and fast as we have been encouraged to believe and, secondly, that we might be more profitably engaged in seeking for this form of logic that will weld knowledge together rather than in continuing the search for those forms which create problems for us when we want to organize our knowledge to some useful but novel end.

The alternative solution that has been offered to this problem of integrating discrete disciplines is no more satisfactory since it seems to beg the whole question. It has been suggested that we can plan the curriculum in terms of certain groupings of subjects, broad fields of experience, such as the practical subjects, the humanities, mathematics and the sciences (Newsom Report) or 'cores', such as mathematics, the sciences, the humanities, the expressive arts and moral education (Lawton 1969, 1973, 1975).

While this kind of approach may well make practical sense and may result in resolving some of the problems of alienation, relevance and so on that we have been considering, it certainly begs the epistemological question. For in telling us, probably quite rightly, that we should concentrate on fields of knowledge, it is not providing us with any kind of logical argument for integration but rather again asserting the sociological case. To claim that in the case of the humanities, for example, there is a conceptual unity which transcends the boundaries of the disciplines is not to solve the logical problem – rather it is to compound and confuse it; it is also to fail to recognize that what holds them together is that they constitute a field of knowledge focused on a central concern – man.

Furthermore, to describe these areas as 'disciplines' and then to add, as Denis Lawton does (1969, 1973, 1975), a sixth unit of interdisciplinary work is merely to introduce further confusion into the debate. For it represents a failure to recognize that incompatibility between rationalist epistemological views and sociological perspectives, which we noted in both Chapters 1 and 2 when we were discussing his claim that curriculum planning should be based on considerations of both the nature of knowledge and the culture of society.

Such views, in other words, tell us yet again that there are strong sociological arguments for integration but they do not begin to deal with any of the logical problems that such arguments may raise. The theories are not necessarily themselves in error, but they are incompatible with theories about the existence of logically discrete bodies of knowledge.

Social and political implications

The fact that we constantly return to the social and sociological sources of justification for the organization of knowledge within the curriculum should alert us to the need to examine some of the social and political implications that it has been claimed curriculum integration has. It is to this aspect of curriculum integration that we must now turn.

'How a society selects, classifies, distributes, transmits and evaluates the educational knowledge it considers to be public, reflects both the distribution of power and the principles of social control' (Bernstein 1971, p. 47). If this is so, then a major change such as the move towards different forms of integration that we are discussing must itself reflect changes in the distribution of power and principles of social control in contemporary society. What sorts of change are being reflected?

It has been posited (Bernstein 1967, 1971) that this move from a curriculum in which the subject boundaries are relatively fixed and strong, a 'collection code', to one in which the boundaries are wide and there is a trend towards increased integration, an 'integrated code', is one aspect of a more general trend in education towards 'open' rather than 'closed' schools towards a mixing of categories, towards diversity rather than purity; and that this is symptomatic of basic changes in the culture of our society, particularly changes in the principles of social control (Bernstein 1967); in short, a corresponding move from a 'closed' to an 'open' society, from what Durkheim has called 'mechanical solidarity' to what he called 'organic solidarity'. Hitherto knowledge has been seen as dangerous and needing to be confined to certain people; the different categories of knowledge must be well insulated from each other, since the results of admixtures are difficult to predict; specialization, it is claimed, makes knowledge safe and therefore helps to maintain the social order; the transmission of knowledge is best left in the control of the teacher. Integration, involving education in breadth, threatens the principles of social order; it weakens the authority systems of society; it represents a move away from a society in which the form of social integration is mechanical, based on a shared system of values and assigned social roles, a 'closed' society, to one in which the form of social integration is organic, that is, a society which is pluralist, tolerating many different value systems, in which social roles are achieved and in which, therefore, social integration arises out of differences between individuals, an 'open' society.

These are some of the social implications that have been found in a move within the school and especially within the curriculum from a collection to an integrated code, from purity of categories to diversity, from a concern with pure knowledge to a concern with its application, from education in depth to education in breadth, from specialization which stresses difference to generalization which stresses commonality.

This same trend therefore results in similarly far-reaching changes in the social order of the school. In the first place, it has immediate implications for the hierarchy of order and control within the school, for teachers' relationships with each other and for their roles. When subject boundaries are strongly maintained, the organization of the institution remains firmly in the hands of the head and the heads of the subject departments; individual staff members are for the most part only involved professionally within their departments. Thus strong subject loyalties are maintained. A move towards an integrated code will challenge this loyalty, threaten the departmental base and, therefore, materially alter the relationships between teachers, since they must now learn to work together, to cooperate with each other across subject departments. This in turn is likely to lead to changes in the hierarchy of the institution and a major shift in its power base; decisions will be reached by different procedures and individual teachers will be more closely involved in them; indeed, it is likely also to lead to situations in which the need for the participation of the pupils or students themselves in decision making will be recognized.

Important changes are likely to take place too in what will count as knowledge in such an institution. We have already referred to the distinction to which sociologists are currently drawing our attention between educational knowledge and common-sense knowledge. A collection code will tend to be largely concerned with educational knowledge since, as we have seen, it has been suggested that such a code will be concerned more with pure than with applied knowledge. It will tend also to see knowledge as some 'out-there', God-given entity rather than as the product of human endeavour. A move towards an integrated code will represent a move towards recognizing the man-made nature of knowledge and towards including common-sense knowledge in the curriculum. Indeed, this is borne out by the fact that many teachers justify the adoption of an integrated curriculum in terms of its increased relevance and its relation to the pupil's own experience. For the same reason, there has been a tendency to introduce such curricula initially for the benefit of the less able pupils and we may note here this added indication of its connection with social control.

Thirdly, a point which follows closely on what we have just said, such a development has important implications for attitudes towards knowledge and especially the attitudes of pupils towards it. 'Knowledge under collection is private property . . . Children and pupils are early socialized into this concept of knowledge as private property. They are encouraged to work as isolated individuals with their arms around their work' (Bernstein 1971, p. 56). Again an integrated code brings with it a more open attitude to knowledge and to its acquisition. The emphasis is much more on collaboration and sharing of knowledge, cooperation ceases to be 'cheating' and becomes acceptable and, as a result, the whole substance of inter-pupil relationships is changed.

This in turn will have its impact on the authority structure of the institution and in particular on the relationships between teacher and taught. In a school in which a relatively fixed view of knowledge holds sway, in which it is seen as something external to be acquired and in which the boundaries between subjects are strongly maintained, the relationships between teachers and pupils will tend to be distant, largely formal and impersonal and the authority structure hierarchical, clear-cut and for the most part positional, the teacher deriving his authority more from the fact that he has been set *in* authority than that he is *an* authority. Where his expertise is relevant it will be that expertise that he has as an authority in a particular subject area. Tradition will also play its part in helping the teacher to establish his authority in this kind of school (Hargreaves 1972).

In a school which takes the view of knowledge and of education that we have seen to be implicit in an integrated code, teacher–pupil relationships will have to be more personalized, since the teacher will be less distant from the pupil. Position and tradition will not offer much support to the development of authority. A much greater premium will be placed on being *an* authority, on possessing expertise, and that expertise will need to embrace a wider range of pedagogic skills than mere knowledge of a subject area.

This kind of analysis of what is involved in a move towards curriculum integration has been offered as an objective, descriptive outline of some of its implications. In view of what it reveals, however, it is not surprising that this kind of development has been deplored by some people both within the teaching profession and outside it, nor that it has met with a good deal of opposition at all levels. Some of these objections have come from those who, like the contributors to Black Papers (Cox and Dyson 1969a,b), appear to be opposed to any change in education, except perhaps a return to the practices of former times, and who must therefore be assumed to be of the opinion that current educational practices or traditional methods are wholly right. The opposition of some teachers can be put down to the fact that change of this kind or, indeed, of any kind in schools brings with it many practical difficulties of a kind that some teachers are unwilling to invite too readily. It can also lead to a loss of status and even of career prospects for those whose expertise and qualifications it may render less significant. Some theoretical objections have been raised, however, to curriculum integration and its social implications and we must consider these briefly.

It has been claimed that subject specialization is one instance of the division of labour and that this is our only defence against centralized autocracy (Musgrove 1973). In other words, integration is seen as introducing sameness into the curriculum and therefore as likely to lead to centralized control and a loss of that very pluralism which is seen as essential to the integration of society. The concept of organic solidarity, as defined by Durkheim, is again used here but this represents a totally different application of that concept to the school situation from that of Basil Bernstein, by whom the move towards integration was seen as one aspect of the move towards organic solidarity rather than away from it.

Similarly, it has been argued that within the school or any educational institution this development is likely to lead to a loss of power by individuals and that it should be seen therefore as an attack on departments and the power of their heads and as a step towards increased autocracy for head-teachers, principals and vice-chancellors (Musgrove 1973). This again represents a totally different analysis of the situation rather than opposition to what others have seen as the main thrust of integration, that is, towards increased individuality and diversity and therefore away from centralization of control and homogeneity of values. It is difficult therefore to understand how it can be claimed at the same time that the integrated curriculum is in the last resort a prescription for social anarchy. Either it leads to tighter centralized control or to anarchy but it surely cannot lead to both. This amounts therefore not so much to a criticism of integration as perhaps to a misinterpretation of its implications.

It has also been argued that integration with its eroding of boundaries between specialist subjects will lead to a loss of structure to pupils' learning and a loss of quality in learning, that subject categories are necessary to bring order into children's learning and that quality of educational experience can only be maintained if teachers can develop expertise in a narrow area of knowledge (Musgrove 1973). There are several points that need to be made in reply to this.

In the first place it fails to recognize that the whole thrust of the movement towards integration has been prompted by a desire to introduce more order and structure, more meaning and relevance into children's learning, but that it has at the same time recognized the importance of endeavouring to ensure that that order and structure should be the child's order and structure and that it should therefore have meaning and relevance for him.

Secondly, there would seem to be no basis for the assumption that an integrated curriculum necessarily leads to the erosion of specialisms or to any loss of rigour or quality of learning. Indeed, one of the main points of the particular brand of integration that Goldsmiths' College pioneered under the name of IDE, Interdisciplinary Enquiry (Goldsmiths' College 1965), has been that a return to a generalist approach in teaching must be avoided and that a prime need of any integration of disciplines is that it should be done by teachers who have, if anything, a greater expertise in their subject areas rather than a lesser, since greater understanding of what one's subject has to offer in the total education of the child becomes necessary as soon as one sets about attempting to integrate it with other subjects. Furthermore, as we have seen, certain versions of curriculum integration are the result of a need that has been felt to reorganize and restructure knowledge to meet new and changed purposes. There is no reason to believe that such new subjects as emerge need reveal any less rigour than those they replace and there is certainly no basis for the assumption that existing subject groupings have status that they must maintain for all time, regardless of diminishing relevance, of social change or of change of any other kind. We are here back to views of knowledge as a God-given entity.

Lastly, we must note the danger of the polarization that is implied by this kind of contrasting of subject-based and integrated curricula. Few secondary schools have adopted a totally integrated curriculum. Most include some form of integrated studies as only one aspect of a two- or three- or four-fold curriculum (James 1968). Nor is there anywhere where one can see an integrated code of a kind that can be contrasted so directly with a collection code. Basil Bernstein was speaking of ideal types not of realities. There are real dangers in using these ideal types as a basis for criticism of the practical realities of curriculum innovations which in themselves only loosely conform to them. There is very little in educational theory that can profit from the adoption of polarized stances of this kind. In most cases we should not be being invited to choose one extreme or another but rather to find a balance between them.

However, this claim that curriculum integration leads to a loss of rigour and of structure for pupils' learning is prompted by, and must be accepted as a fair comment on, some of the schemes that have been implemented. On the other hand, it is not reasonable to assume that, because some schemes have lacked rigour and structure, the loss of these is inevitable. For what these schemes have lacked is a clear view of their purposes and thus of their theoretical bases. Such a clear view is necessary if rigour and structure are to be maintained. It is to a consideration of this aspect of curriculum integration that we must now turn.

Purposes and principles

We must now ask why it is that, in spite of the administrative difficulties and the stated logical problems, so many teachers in schools, colleges and universities have wanted to undertake the chore of developing new forms of integrated studies.

There are at least two different, although both practically and theoretically interrelated, reasons for this, two kinds of purpose that teachers have had in embarking on such a course. What they have in common is that they both represent an attempt to develop a curriculum from a consideration of factors other than those deriving from beliefs about the nature of knowledge. In other words, they lend support to the claim that has already been made that the main thrust of recent curriculum development has rightly been towards seeking justification for curricular decisions from sources other than those of philosophy in general or epistemology in particular, and they add strength to the assertion we made in Chapter 2 that epistemological considerations in themselves have little if anything that is positive to contribute to curriculum planning.

In the first place, we have what we might call a psychological reason for curriculum integration. As we suggested at the beginning of this chapter, many people have looked towards some form of integration as a possible solution to some of the problems raised by the apparent rejection by many pupils of the content of their education. We have already referred to notions such as that of the alienation of pupils from the curriculum, the absence of any kind of interest or source of motivation, the feeling that there is little relevance in what schools are offering. For these reasons, as we saw in Chapter 2, many have recommended that we should start curriculum planning from a consideration, not of the nature of knowledge, but of the needs and interests of the pupils.

Others have looked to a complete change of methods, to the idea of promoting pupil enquiry rather than proceeding entirely through a teacher-dominated didacticism. Either or both of these devices have been seen as likely to enhance motivation and to ensure therefore a higher level of work and achievement. One slightly worrying feature of this kind of development has been that it has often been confined to the curriculum planned for the less able pupil where the problems of motivation and, indeed, of control of behaviour have been most apparent. However, this factor provides further evidence that this has been a major purpose of many schools and teachers in introducing these new approaches to the planning of their curriculum.

It is of course possible to pursue both interest-based and enquiry-based methods within existing subjects and many examples can be found of this being done, not least in those schools where such schemes as the Nuffield science projects are being operated. It will be apparent, however, that it is not easy to confine children's interests or their enquiries within particular subject boundaries, so that if we wish to pursue seriously these particular methods some form of integrated studies programme will often follow. This has been the experience of many schools where the improvement of the children's response to the school has been the main purpose behind the introduction of integrated studies programmes of various kinds. This is also why the notion of curriculum integration has never been regarded as a serious problem or as anything other than a necessity in those primary schools that have adopted an enquiry-based approach to teaching (Blenkin and Kelly 1981).

The second reason for the introduction of some form of curriculum integration, although closely related to the first, is sociological rather than psychological. Some curriculum content can appear and can actually be irrelevant to pupils, not only because they do not see the point of it but because it has no point. Conversely, some areas of knowledge which do have point and relevance do not appear on the curriculum because they do not fit the discipline or subject categories traditionally reflected there.

This is one aspect of a wider feature of human knowledge which we must recognize. We have already noted that some areas of knowledge are not characterized by being logically discrete forms but by being fields of knowledge, issues of importance around which different bodies of knowledge tend to cohere or become organized. Thus, as we have noted several times, geography is a field of knowledge which focuses several different kinds of knowledge on the issue of man and his environment. Traditional groupings of subjects will therefore represent those areas of knowledge that had value and importance when these groupings were made. A changing society will inevitably create new bases for the organization of knowledge and these will require that the traditional forms of organization, whether of subjects or disciplines, be changed constantly and continuously to meet the changing needs.

An interesting example of this kind of reorganization and regrouping of subjects is that which is taking place in that area of the curriculum that was once called 'handicraft' through the linking of design studies with science and technology to form 'Craft, Design and Technology', a new and very different curriculum subject (Hicks 1976). Clearly, this development is to a large extent a response to the kinds of pressure we are discussing to restructure knowledge to meet changing social needs.

Teachers have been aware also that many of the issues that appear to be important and relevant to children growing up in present-day society fall neither into the disciplines nor into the subject categories of the traditional school curriculum. In fact they often fall right through the gaps. Live issues in most spheres straddle the boundaries between the disciplines and, while they continue to be live, they require a constant reorganization of knowledge. One of the best examples of this has been the Schools Council's Humanities Curriculum Project (Schools Council 1970) which, in endeavouring to encourage senior pupils in secondary schools to explore topics of crucial interest and concern to them as members of contemporary society – topics such as relations between the sexes, law and order, living in cities, war and so on – immediately realized that such topics could not be dealt with adequately within any traditional subject area but would necessarily involve some kind of interdisciplinary development. Similarly, recent years have also seen the emergence of other kinds of humanities course, as we have come to recognize that many or all of the subjects normally subsumed under that heading can profitably be pursued together as all contributing to our understanding of man. This has, therefore, been a prime reason for the introduction of new forms of integrated studies in our schools.

This is of course one particular aspect of that view that sees education as being essentially a matter of the developing experience of the individual. If relevance is to mean anything in relation to the content of the curriculum, or conversely, if alienation is to be avoided, then as A.N. Whitehead told us a long time ago we must avoid 'inert knowledge' (Whitehead 1932). In other words, we must put the pupil in a situation in which he can organize his knowledge in ways that are meaningful to him as well as to society. This is the point of those claims that are made that education be seen as a dialectical relationship between the pupil and his environment (James 1968) or that it should be concerned with the intentions that lie behind the conscious activity of the pupil (Freire 1972) or that it should be seen as an extension of the 'common-sense knowledge' that the pupil brings to the teaching situation (Keddie 1971).

One direct implication that should be noted here is that this view requires that any attempt at curriculum integration should be centred on an organizing theme or concept that is properly meaningful. The idea of using a theme to unite the various contributions to an integrated programme or enquiry has been a popular one, not least because it provides a manageable framework within which both teachers and pupils can work. Sometimes, however, the themes are tenuous in the extreme as in the, probably apocryphal, example of the theme 'Hands' being used to focus the integration of biology (the physical structure of hands), industrial sociology (working with one's hands) and religious studies (the 'laying-on of hands') or in the example Lawrence Stenhouse gives to the theme 'Water' being used to link irrigation, boiling kettles, swimming and water on the knee (Stenhouse 1969). If we are to justify the introduction of new combinations of subjects and areas of knowledge on the grounds that such reorganization is necessary to meet changing social needs or to ensure that learning has meaning and relevance for the pupil, then those new combinations cannot be arbitrary collections of subject matter but must have some central focus such as is provided by the controversial issues of the Humanities Curriculum Project. In short, they must represent changes in the organization of knowledge that are meaningful both in social terms and to the individual pupil.

It is important, then, for teachers to be clear about the purposes or principles underlying their proposed schemes of integration. For, unless they are, the theoretical basis of their work will lack coherence and their practice is likely to lack rigour and structure and to become muddled and ineffective, as has been the experience of many such schemes. Once one is clear about the purposes or the principles behind one's practice, one can begin to establish that practice on a firm base. For different intentions or different reasons for integrating will require different forms of integration. We now turn to a brief consideration of some of these and, in so considering them, we shall see that what is crucial in all cases is the need for clarity of purpose.

Forms or models of curriculum integration

The criticism that curriculum integration must lead to a lack of rigour and a loss of structure is based also on the assumption that curriculum integration is a single phenomenon and a failure to recognize that there are almost as many kinds of integrated curricula as there are schools practising integration. Like all other forms of curriculum innovation, curriculum integration takes its character in each case from the particular requirements and features of the context in which it is to be found (Warwick 1973). As we have seen, there are a number of different purposes that teachers might have in introducing programmes of this kind so that the particular form in which they emerge in each situation will vary according to those purposes. Thus there are schemes in which the academic content of each contributory discipline is very carefully fixed and structured by the specialist department or teacher responsible for it, while there are others in which the individual child has almost unlimited freedom of choice. Sometimes the methods are largely heuristic; sometimes a good deal of direct instruction is employed of a completely didactic kind. There are some schemes in which teachers are encouraged to adopt a 'generalist' approach; there are many others, again like Goldsmiths' IDE, which hinge on a pattern of team-teaching in which each teacher contributes as a specialist. One can also find almost every possible permutation of subject involvement according to such basic local factors as the consideration of which departments have heads who believe in integration or are prepared to accept the extra work that will be involved in getting it off the ground. Thus we hear of integrated science schemes, integration of various combinations of humanities subjects with the addition sometimes of one or more of the expressive arts, and occasionally schemes which attempt to combine all kinds of subject. Each form of integration will present its own problems; not all will present epistemological problems, as we have seen, but each will have to be looked at on its own merits. There is so much variety that it is not possible to generalize.

For this reason, the Keele Integrated Studies Project set out not to promote one distinctive form of integrated curriculum but rather to explore the range of possibilities this approach offered, to provide guidelines for teachers and to supply them with materials and ideas that they could adapt to their own purposes and to suit their own particular needs (Schools Council 1972b). In other words, unlike many of the projects contemporary with it, it 'did not aim to provide a teacher-proof blueprint' (Shipman 1972, p. 147).

However, commendable as was the intention of projects such as this to support teachers in developing their own schemes, the result of this policy was in many cases the emergence of a large credibility gap between the thinking of those at the centre of these innovations and the practice of the teachers at their periphery. And it was this gap which was responsible for the appearance of many of those botched-up schemes of integration which it was suggested earlier would justify the charges of loss of rigour and of structure. For examination of many of these schemes reveals a lack of clarity over their purposes and principles and thus the absence of any kind of fundamental rationale.

It was to meet this difficulty that several analyses were undertaken of the different forms of integration that were possible, the different theoretical models that might be adopted; and it was suggested that, even though there might be many different versions of curriculum integration, as we have just noted, they could all be reduced to a few basic forms. The only route to a proper clarity of purpose and thus to satisfactory practice on the part of teachers, it was argued, was via a prior clarification of which of these forms or models was to be adopted.

Those concerned with the Keele Integrated Studies Project suggested that teachers' interest in curriculum integration may have arisen primarily out of one of three concerns:

(a)   to increase individual pupils' power to decide and pursue their own learning paths
(b)   to use subjects to full advantage by exploring cross-links between them
(c)   to make possible the study of large and complex human issues.

(Schools Council 1972b, p. 7)

They go on to suggest that the adoption of any one of these aims does not necessitate the dismissal of the others, but they stress that it will lead to a different form of integration.

An extension of this view was offered by David Bolam (1971) as a result of his experience with this same project. He suggested that there are several theoretical models which might form the conceptual bases of different kinds of integration. Thus he suggests that a programme of integration might be organized around a single area of study, in the way that a subject like classics has often been approached; or it might be organized around 'an overarching concept distinctive of the humanities' (Adams 1976, p. 119), exploring a theme like 'expressionism' or 'communication'; or it might be focused on a human issue, of which he proposes there might be three kinds: a 'perspective' unit concerned with very broad issues in the way that the project 'Man: A Course of Study' (MACOS) is concerned with the question of what is man; a social problem unit like those of the Humanities Curriculum Project; or 'cognitive and evaluative maps which tackle theoretical and practical issues with an emphasis upon building up conceptual nets' (ibid.).

Similarly, Richard Pring (1971b) lists five different meanings or principles of curriculum integration. Firstly, he speaks of 'expediency integration', the purpose of which is merely to ensure effective learning; secondly, he suggests there is 'social integration', whose purpose is to promote social adjustment; thirdly, he offers us 'meaning-based integration', the intention of which obviously is to assist pupils to achieve a meaningful organization of their experience; fourthly, we have 'motivation-based integration', whose concern is to arouse the interest of pupils and to get them launched on a worthwhile enquiry; and, lastly, there is 'concern- or needs-based integration', which is the form of integration we have when we set about the identification and exploration of those important social issues which have so often been the focus of schemes of integrated studies.

It will be clear that, as we suggested, the important question to be faced is that of the purpose or purposes of each particular scheme, so that these analyses should be considered alongside our earlier discussion of the different reasons or purposes which teachers might have in attempting curriculum integration. These, it will be remembered, included a desire to arouse the interest of pupils and thus to avoid the problems of alienation, the related desire to encourage enquiry-based methods of learning, an attempt to assist in the process of the reorganization of knowledge to focus on new and important areas of concern, especially in the social field, and even the adoption of a particular epistemological stance, one that acknowledges the evolving nature of knowledge and regards it as important that we make due allowance for its evolution by making possible, and indeed encouraging, the regrouping of subjects.

We can now see that what is being suggested and proposed throughout this debate is that, if schemes of curriculum integration are to be successful and, in particular, if that loss of rigour and structure we have noted on several occasions is to be avoided, then the planning of any scheme must begin with a careful analysis of the particular purposes we have in mind, the resultant principles that the scheme must be based on and the form or theoretical model of integration that must be adopted. This kind of approach will offer the only proper basis for the development of a programme that can be seen to have some educational point and impact.

To do this, however, is merely to provide ourselves with a firm theoretical base for our work. There are many practical issues which will also claim our attention and it is with an examination of some of these that we will close our discussion of curriculum integration.

Practical issues

Some of the practical aspects of curriculum integration have already emerged in our earlier discussion, particularly in relation to Bernstein's analysis of its implications for the social order of the school. We must not lose sight of the risks to teachers from the possible loss of the identity and security that association with a particular subject gives them, if indeed this is going to be lost. On the other hand, it is perhaps salutary to note that this is a characteristic only of some teachers in secondary schools; teachers of younger children have for a long time had to find their professional identity and security in their pedagogic expertise and their understanding of aspects of child development and of the processes of education. Who is to say that it would be a bad thing if all teachers had to look towards such quarters for their professional status and security? Finally, we must not forget all of the effects of the changed relationships between teacher and teacher and especially between teacher and pupil that most forms of curriculum integration will bring about.

Integrated studies schemes often also raise problems for the organization of the school. Again, not all will do so, but those that involve increased freedom for pupils both in choice of work and of movement about the building, and those that involve a wider use of discovery techniques will raise particular problems of accommodation and timetabling.

Accommodation will need to be of a kind that will lend itself to these new purposes, workshops rather than traditional classrooms, and facilities will need to be provided for all of the activities it is envisaged pupils may be engaged in. Alternatively, it may be necessary for pupils to move to different kinds of room for different purposes and it will clearly be desirable in such cases for these rooms to be as close to each other as possible.

Most schemes of this kind will also necessitate major adjustments to the timetable. Subjects that are to be integrated will need to be timetabled together and a freer style of working will call for greater flexibility of organization and larger blocks of time than the normal 40–45-minute period. In practice, many schools have found that both flexibility and greater scope for sustained work can be provided by blocking time, that is, by allocating double periods or even full half-days to integrated studies programmes (Warwick 1973; Kelly 1974, 1978), as is the normal practice in the primary school. Furthermore, such a solution makes the actual task of timetabling easier on the whole rather than more difficult once agreement of departments has been reached as to how much of their 'private' allocation of time is to be put into the pool for reallocation in this way.

Again, most integrated studies programmes make demands on material resources of a kind that cannot easily be met from within the normal stock of books and equipment of the contributing departments. Much additional material and quite new kinds of resource have to be provided. Many teachers have found it helpful to produce work cards or work sheets of various kinds to guide pupils' work, but these need to be backed by sources to which pupils can refer in carrying out the tasks assigned to them or chosen by them. Furthermore, once this kind of material has been produced, it needs to be kept for future use, unless we are to find ourselves having to produce totally new material each time we deal with a certain topic or area of work. The production of new resources and the organization of an effective system of storage and quick retrieval become key tasks for teachers in this kind of situation (Kelly 1974, 1978) and it is not advisable to enter any scheme of curriculum integration without giving some prior thought to questions of this kind.

The keeping of records also becomes of more importance if pupils are to be allowed greater freedom of choice in their work. It is no longer enough to remember what each class has covered; we need to know what each pupil has been engaged on. In part this has to be done to ensure that we can attend satisfactorily to the continuing educational development of each individual; it is also necessary, however, to allow for the fact that in any kind of school situation there will be some pupils who will attempt to find loop-holes in the system and will work on the same project and offer up more or less the same collection of work every time if we do not take steps to ensure that they cannot.

All of these organizational problems become more important if a system of team-teaching is also adopted (Lovell 1967; Freeman 1969; Warwick 1971; Kelly 1974, 1978). Provision of suitable accommodation, proper timetabling, production of resources and the keeping of adequate records are even more necessary if the collaboration of several teachers is planned. In addition, it is vital that the team of teachers is able to meet regularly to plan and to exchange notes. Such regular meetings should be a formal feature of the timetable and should not be left to chance encounters over coffee, tea or lunch. Team-teaching has a great deal to offer in any educational situation but it is also fraught with many dangers and needs the most careful and elaborate planning and organization.

Team-teaching also highlights another aspect of the practical issues of curriculum integration which we have touched on before. If an integrated studies programme is to involve a totally new approach to teaching (and, unless it is, it may well not be worth venturing on it), it is going to create new roles for teachers and make new demands on their skills. Unless they are prepared to accept these new roles and develop these new skills, little good will come of it. A good deal of preliminary work is necessary, therefore, as with all curriculum innovations, both to persuade those teachers who are unconvinced of the advantages of the changes that are proposed, since to a large extent the success of any such venture will hinge on the attitudes of the teachers who are attending to it (Barker-Lunn 1970), and to help them to prepare adequately for the new work by producing the schemes of work, resources and so on they feel will be needed, by developing the new skills that will be required of them and by adopting the new attitudes required towards their professional tasks, their colleagues and their pupils. Much can be done and has been done by teachers' centres and other special in-service provision to meet these needs (Kelly 1975). In planning such preparation we must again never lose sight of the additional demands, especially on the relationships of teachers with each other, that team-teaching will make and of the new professional attitudes that teachers need to learn if they are to operate successfully within such schemes. Over a long period of time every teacher has become used to working in the isolation of his own carefully guarded territory; it is not easy, especially for the old dogs, to learn new tricks of cooperation, collaboration and sharing.

A final practical issue that we must refer to before closing this discussion of curriculum integration is the implication that it has for assessment generally and for public examinations in particular (Kelly 1974, 1975, 1978). The whole question of the implications of assessment and examinations for curriculum development will be considered in detail in Chapter 7. It is enough here to note that curriculum integration poses special problems in this area. Several solutions have been found by teachers to meet these problems, but again this is an aspect of this kind of development that needs to be well thought-out in advance. New attitudes are needed to internal assessment and examination procedures but, more importantly, the external procedures must be available to match any such development. There are now public examinations at all levels in integrated studies of one form or another. For the most part these have been produced to answer the demands of teachers who were generating such programmes within their schools. This, of course, is the right order of procedures – curriculum innovation first and then the development of examination procedures to fit the new curriculum practices. But it is important when introducing any scheme to ensure either that the public examination system is already in a position to deal with it or to take the necessary steps to ensure that it will be in such a position by the time that one's first pupils are ready for it.

Summary and conclusions

We have examined some of the epistemological problems that it has been claimed are raised by attempts at curriculum integration and have suggested that epistemology, like all branches of philosophy, can do little more than attempt to clarify the questions for us and that there may be dangers in expecting it or allowing it to dictate answers, not least because different theories of knowledge quite clearly offer different answers. We then went on to suggest that it might be more profitable to examine the question of curriculum integration from a sociological point of view. In endeavouring to do this we discovered both certain kinds of rationale for curriculum integration and also some far-reaching political and social implications both for the internal societies of educational institutions themselves and for society at large. Finally, we considered some of the practical issues that are raised for schools and for teachers by such a development and suggested that these should be carefully thought-out against the background of a thorough theoretical understanding and in relation to the particular purposes of the individual institution if such a step is to be taken successfully and chaos and confusion avoided.

Curriculum integration does in fact create many administrative, practical and theoretical problems, but it only presents a logical problem if we take too rigid a view of knowledge and allow that view to dominate our approach to curriculum planning. If we do not, then we suddenly find that a good deal of curriculum integration has been with us for a long time. To extend this is to do no more than to accept that in any developing society the organization of knowledge must change and schools must produce pupils who can adapt and contribute to such changes. If schools are to do this, they must themselves be flexible, open to change and development, prepared to cope with the necessary organizational change and not tied too firmly to the past or to a fixed view of knowledge. As Dewey said, 'We live forward.'

This, in fact, is the general conclusion of the whole of our rather lengthy discussion of the nature of knowledge and its implications for the content of the curriculum. Questions about the nature of knowledge do raise a number of important issues for curriculum planners, some of which we have considered in some detail. But our discussions have led us always nearer to the conclusion that we must ultimately accept the 'man-made' and hypothetical nature of knowledge rather than try to maintain a mystical 'out-there' view.

If this is so, then, as was suggested earlier, it has important implications not only for the selection of curriculum content but also for curriculum planning and development generally. For we have seen that the issue of content, especially when taken together with the related question of values, is an inextricable part of whatever model we adopt for planning the curriculum. It is against the uncertain and shifting backcloth which this view of knowledge offers, then, that we must now turn to an examination of planning models and especially of that planning model which appears to be currently in fashion, that which begins from the prespecification of curriculum objectives.

CHAPTER 4

CURRICULUM PLANNING MODELS

We saw in Chapter 2 some of the difficulties which follow in the wake of attempts to begin curriculum planning from a consideration of the nature of knowledge or of the culture of society and thus to make questions about the content of the curriculum the first and most important problem to be faced. The suggestion was made there that, while issues of curriculum content cannot be ignored, they should not be regarded as having a prior claim to our attention. Thus it may be said that we have already noted the inadequacies of a planning model which requires us to begin from a consideration of the content of our curriculum.

We noted too, in Chapter 1, that there have been many attempts in recent years to encourage a recognition that there are several aspects of the curriculum other than its content and to suggest, in particular, that a consideration of its purposes, its aims and objectives might be a more appropriate starting point, that this might be a more suitable planning model. We have noted too that others have suggested that the consideration of the principles underlying the processes of education might be a better basis for planning, and thus yet another model has emerged.

In fact, once we acknowledge that curriculum content cannot of itself be the first consideration, that some justification of the choice of such content is required, we have to recognize that the emphasis in curriculum planning must be placed elsewhere and that questions of content become secondary to questions about purposes or principles. Furthermore, such differences of emphasis will lead to the generation of different planning models.

It is to an exploration of these alternative approaches to planning that we turn in this chapter, and in particular to an examination of that planning model which begins from the prespecification of curriculum objectives. For this appears currently to be the model which is in fashion, and yet it is clear that not everyone who wishes to advocate its use is fully aware of its implications.

One other preliminary point must be made before we begin this exploration. It must be stressed that the question of the suitability and the characteristics of planning models is as relevant to the individual teacher in the planning of his own work as to a development team concerned to plan a national curriculum project. The question of whether educational planning should begin from a consideration of its content, its objectives or its underlying principles is an important issue for every teacher, not least because of the pressures he may face to adopt that model which is favoured by someone else. The truth of this will not need to be emphasized to those teachers and student teachers who have wrestled to meet demands for the prestatement of lesson objectives from tutors, headteachers, advisers or inspectors.

Curriculum objectives

A concern with objectives has been one of the most striking features of the recent move towards deliberate curriculum planning which we also referred to in Chapter 1. It is not the case, of course, that educators were not concerned with objectives before this. It is probable that people have had aims and goals for any instruction or teaching they have engaged in almost from the beginning of time. From the beginning of the present century too, one can see, especially in the work of American educationists, a desire to examine questions of how educational objectives can best be specified (Popham 1969). It is also the case that for many years teachers and student teachers have been expected by those responsible for supervising their work to begin the preparation of their lessons with statements of their objectives.

For a long time, however, little real attention was given to this issue of specifying objectives in curriculum planning, nor was it taken as a serious exercise by most teachers in planning their work.

Recently, however, this situation has changed and there has been revived a genuine interest in the problems involved in specifying educational objectives and a concern to pay due regard to them in curriculum planning, so that this has been the starting point, for example, for many curriculum projects developed under the aegis of the Schools Council.

It is also the case that many of those external pressures on teachers, which, as we noted in Chapter 1, have grown in strength in recent years, have taken the form of requiring them to state the objectives of their teaching and/or to keep records of what they have done in similar form. The current requests for information from those who are framing the guidelines and criteria for the new single 16+ examination are also often expressed in this form. In short, people outside the schools, including many of those in the advisory service, appear to be making the tacit assumption that this is the only model one can adopt for effective curriculum planning.

At the same time, there are still those who positively eschew such an approach. The Humanities Curriculum Project, for example, has taken this line and, indeed, its Director, Lawrence Stenhouse, has suggested that prespecification of objectives is not appropriate within the humanities generally (Stenhouse 1970). Interdisciplinary Enquiry (IDE), as propounded by Goldsmiths' College Curriculum Laboratory, has also deliberately and consciously rejected an objective approach (James 1968), regarding it as unsuitable to attempt to state in advance what the result of pupil enquiry should be.

Furthermore, it has been argued (Blenkin and Kelly 1981; Kelly 1981) that planning through the prespecification of curriculum objectives is inappropriate, not to say inimical, to that educational tradition that has emerged through the 'progressive' movement and has developed in some British primary schools, especially those concerned with the very young child. External pressures for this kind of planning, however, are to be felt as much in that sector of schooling as elsewhere. It thus becomes particularly important for teachers to sort out the issues that are involved if they are to be able to respond to such pressures appropriately and not merely by yielding to them. It was for this reason that a detailed discussion of this problem was undertaken in *The Primary Curriculum* (Blenkin and Kelly 1981), and readers of that book will recognize in what follows much that was included there.

The growth of the objectives movement

It has been argued with some justification that this movement is as old as teaching itself, that, for example, primeval man had clear objectives in mind when he set about teaching his offspring the arts of axe-making (Popham 1969). It is certainly the case that this approach to educational planning of a more sophisticated kind can be discerned from quite early times, as, for example, in the taxonomy offered by Cicero for the planning of a curriculum in rhetoric (Davies 1976). The influence of that approach can also be seen in the work of men like Herbart and Spencer in the nineteenth century (Davies 1976).

It is only in the present century, however, that this style of educational planning has been spelled out in detail and serious attempts made to persuade teachers to adopt it. The impetus for this came initially from those who were impressed by the progress of science and technology and believed that the same kind of progress might become possible in the field of education if a properly scientific approach were to be adopted there also. As is so often the case, the origins of this movement can be traced to the United States; in the United Kingdom it is a much more recent phenomenon.

The tone of this movement was set by one of its earliest proponents, Franklin Bobbitt (1918), who expressed great concern at the vague, imprecise purposes that he felt characterized the work of most teachers, announced that 'an age of science is demanding exactness and particularity' (1918, ch. 6; Davies 1976, p. 47) and suggested that teachers be required to write out their objectives in clear, non-technical language that both pupils and their parents might understand. He also distinguished between what he called 'ultimate' objectives, those for the curriculum as a whole, and 'progress' objectives, those for each class or age-group.

The cry was taken up by others. In 1924, for example, Werrett Charters attempted a 'job analysis' of teaching and offered a method of course construction based on this kind of approach. His suggestion was that we first determine what he called the 'ideals' of education, then identify the 'activities' that these involve and finally analyse both of these to the level of 'working units of the size of human ability' (Charters 1924; Davies 1976, p. 50), these small steps that need to be mastered one by one. In this way the curriculum could be reduced to a series of working units and its whole structure set out on a chart or graph.

Thus, early pioneers of the movement, like Bobbitt and Charters, gave it from the beginning a scientific, behavioural, job-analysis flavour, their general purpose being to introduce into educational practice the kind of precise, scientific methods that had begun to yield dividends in other spheres of human activity and especially in industry.

The spread of interest in testing that was a feature of educational development in the 1930s can be seen as another aspect of this same movement. For the link between the prespecification of objectives and the testing of performance has long been a close one and that it continues to be so is apparent from the effects on curriculum planning of current demands for a closer monitoring of standards in schools. This link was made quite explicit in the work of the next major exponent of the objectives approach, Ralph Tyler. For Tyler's original aim was to design scientific tests of educational attainment and his solution to this problem was to suggest that this could be done most readily and easily if a clear statement had been made of the kind of attainment that was being aimed at. If course objectives had been formulated and those objectives defined in terms of intended student behaviour, that behaviour could then be evaluated in the light of those intentions (Tyler 1932; Davies 1976).

This provided the foundation upon which Tyler was later to base what has come to be regarded as the classic statement of the objectives approach to curriculum design. In a book which he tells us is intended as 'one way of viewing an instructional programme as a functional instrument of education' (1949, p. 1) and in which he expresses alarm at the level of generality he claims to have detected in teachers' responses to questions about their work, he sets out the four questions which he says must be faced and answered by curriculum planners. Those four questions, as we saw in Chapter 1, are concerned with the purpose, the content, the organization and the evaluation of the curriculum.

The next milestone was reached in 1956 with the publication by Benjamin Bloom and his associates of their *Taxonomy of Educational Objectives Handbook I: Cognitive Domain*. For this introduced a new dimension into this form of curriculum planning with its division of objectives into three categories or 'domains' – the cognitive, the affective and the psychomotor – and at the same time if offered the most detailed and ambitious classification of objectives in the cognitive domain that had yet been attempted. This was matched by the publication in 1964, under the editorship of D. R. Kratwohl, of a second handbook that offered a similar classification within the affective domain.

It was some time before the work of either Tyler or Bloom began to have any real impact but by the mid-1960s their influence was beginning to be felt not only in the United States but in the United Kingdom too, and, in an article published in 1969, Paul Hirst made the same kind of claim that we should begin our curriculum planning with a statement of our objectives, arguing that not to do so is to transgress a basic principle or rationality, since, in his view, an essential feature of any rational activity is that it be goal-directed.

At the level of educational practice, initially little interest was shown in this style of planning. Some response to the early promptings of Bobbitt, Charters and others can be seen in the planning of vocational courses but that was as far as things went. One reason for this may well have been the wordy and jargon-ridden nature of most of what was written about it. But at least two other reasons have been posited (Hirst 1969). One of these is the fact that at secondary level the obsession with subject content, reinforced by the demands of largely monolithic examination syllabuses, rendered it unnecessary for teachers ever to think about what their purposes or objectives might be. The second of these is the suggestion that at primary level the 'romantic' or 'progressive' movement, in particular because of its emphasis on 'child-centredness', also had the effect of deflecting attention from a clear formulation of objectives. Paul Hirst explains this as an obsession with methods or procedures but it has also been interpreted (Blenkin and Kelly 1981) as the result of a concern with education as a process and this, as we shall see, has very different implications. At all events, although teacher trainers demanded from their students and inspectors from their probationer teachers, and even some headteachers from all of their staff, lesson notes that began with a clear statement of the aims and objectives of their lessons, few responded to such requests with any degree of clarity or effectiveness and the practice was not taken seriously by any who were engaged in the realities of teaching.

The statement of clear course objectives, however, was a major feature of most of the curriculum projects that emerged during that period of widespread innovation that followed the establishment of the Schools Council in the United Kingdom in 1964, and this was a key factor in the growth of interest in this approach to curriculum planning that came in the 1960s. The allocation of public money to curriculum development on this scale brought with it the requirement that a proper account be given of how that money was being spent. For this reason, as well as because of considerations of a purely educational kind, evaluation was a central concern of most new projects from the outset and a proper evaluation was interpreted as requiring a clear statement of goals, aims, purposes, objectives.

It was through the work of the Schools Council, therefore, after a long and interesting history, that the concept of curriculum objectives finally entered the consciousness of the practising teacher. Its apparent significance was reinforced by some of the criticisms offered of the Plowden Report which was accused of being weak on aims, although strong on method, and of reflecting a general looseness and lack of clarity that was said to be characteristic of the planning of work in the primary sector (Peters 1969). And so, when in the late 1970s, as a result of several factors of a largely political kind which we will explore more fully in Chapter 8, pressures began to be felt by teachers to plan their work more carefully and precisely, it was to this model that they were inclined and, indeed, encouraged to turn (Blenkin 1980).

This approach to curriculum planning, however, requires more careful analysis than most teachers were able to give it, and it is to that kind of examination that we must proceed. Before we can do so, however, it will be helpful to try to pick out the major characteristics of this approach.

The main characteristics of the objectives approach to curriculum planning

We might begin this exploration by noting a generally accepted distinction between objectives and aims (Taba 1962). Aims are usually seen as very general statements of goals and purposes. Such aims by themselves, however, have often been regarded as too general and lacking in specificity to provide clear guidelines for planners or teachers, so that curriculum planning has been seen as a process of developing more precise statements of goals from these general aims. It is these more precise statements of goals that are normally termed objectives. Indeed, some writers have even suggested that we should recognize three or more levels of specificity (Kratwohl 1965): general statements of goals that will guide the planning of the curriculum as a whole, behavioural objectives derived from these which will guide the planning of individual units or courses, and a third level of objectives appropriate in some cases to guide the planning of specific lessons; to use Wheeler's terms, 'ultimate', 'mediate' and 'proximate' goals, the latter providing specific classroom objectives (Wheeler 1967). This, as we saw earlier, is the kind of structure that was envisaged by the early pioneers of the movement, and the important point to note is that this approach to curriculum planning assumes that education must be planned in a step-by-step, linear manner.

The classic statement of this kind of hierarchy of goals is to be found in Bloom's taxonomy of educational objectives (Bloom et al. 1956; Kratwohl et al. 1964). The notion of the hierarchical nature of the interrelationship of these objectives is fundamental and is apparent from the gradation of objectives in the cognitive domain from the acquisition of the knowledge of specifics, through such higher level cognitive abilities as classification, comprehension, application, analysis, synthesis and so on to the making of evaluative judgements. Similar gradations are offered within each of the categories, comprehension, for example, being broken down into translation, interpretation and extrapolation.

However, Bloom also offers us another distinction within this range of objectives since, as we have seen, he divides them into three clear domains: the cognitive, the affective and the psychomotor – the head, the heart and the hand. Thus he is suggesting that in framing our objectives we need to be clear not only about the sequential nature of the activity but also about the different categories of behaviour we might be concerned with. For the cognitive domain is defined as comprising 'objectives which emphasize remembering or reproducing something which has presumably been learnt, as well as objectives which involve the solving of some intellective task for which the individual has to determine the essential problem and then reorder given material or combine it with ideas, methods or procedures previously learned' (Kratwohl et al. 1964, p. 6). The affective domain, we are told, comprises 'objectives which emphasize a feeling tone, an emotion, or a degree of acceptance or rejection' (Kratwohl et al. 1964, p. 7). Finally, the psychomotor domain consists of 'objectives which emphasize some muscular or motor skill, some manipulation of material and objects, or some act which requires a neuromuscular coordination' (Kratwohl et al. 1964, p. 7).

Thus these two dimensions which Bloom and his associates offer us enable us to prespecify our objectives at varying levels of specificity in order to outline in great detail the kinds of behaviour which are the objectives of our curriculum. We are offered a hierarchy of goals, of 'intended learning outcomes' defined in terms of the kind of behaviour the pupil is intended or expected to display through his thoughts, actions or feelings if we are to be able to claim that our objective has been achieved. It is easy to see why this approach has proved so attractive to some curriculum planners.

Conversely, however, it is when we are offered this kind of highly detailed statement of how a curriculum is to be planned in terms of objectives that we begin to see what it is that other people have found unacceptable in this approach, or at least we begin to become aware that it is not such a straightforward matter as it may at first have appeared to be.

The results of Bloom's work, therefore, have been twofold. On the one hand, recent years have seen a proliferation of curriculum projects which have begun diligently with detailed statements of their objectives; on the other hand, we have also witnessed a developing movement away from the idea of prespecified curriculum objectives, a reaction against what has begun to appear to some as an undue limitation on the scope of the teacher and, indeed, of education.

A good example of the former would be the elaborate table of objectives given by the Schools Council's Science 5–13 Project team (Schools Council 1972a) which begins by listing nine broad aims focused on the central goal of developing an enquiring mind and a scientific approach to problems and then proceeds to break these broad aims down into a detailed list of shorter-term behavioural objectives, grouped in such a way as to be closely linked to the children's stages of conceptual development. Thus at the second part of Stage 1, the early stage of concrete operations, the broad aim of developing interests, attitudes and aesthetic awareness is broken down into four objectives:

Desire to find out things for oneself
Willing participation in group work
Willing compliance with safety regulations in handling tools and equipment
Appreciation of the need to learn the meaning of new words and to use them correctly.

(Schools Council 1972a, p. 60.)

Another example is the statement of the objectives of the teaching of home economics as outlined in Schools Council Curriculum Bulletin No. 4. These are given under the general headings, 'Development of personal qualities', 'Intellectual development', 'Discrimination and aesthetic appreciation', 'The needs of the adolescent', 'Future needs', 'Skills and knowledge'; they include such things as 'to develop a sense of responsibility and service towards other pupils and towards the home and school communities', 'to cultivate an intelligent attitude towards home-making, including the social, financial, nutritional and practical aspects', 'to develop recognition and appreciation of craftsmanship, quality and good design', 'to encourage the constructive use of leisure time', 'to give the girls an awareness of their potential as women, wives and mothers of the future', 'to teach pupils to understand the topics which we consider most important, e.g. basic nutrition, budgeting, hygiene, home safety', 'to encourage enjoyment of the subject and the development of particular interests and talents', 'to train girls to act sensibly in an emergency' (Schools Council 1971b, pp. 9–10).

A further example, taken from the field of primary education, is even more directly derivative of Bloom's taxonomy. For the Schools Council's Aims of Primary Education Project divides its aims into those related to intellectual, physical, spiritual/religious, emotional/personal and social/ moral development and then divides these different kinds of aim on a second axis into those 'to do with knowledge, skills and qualities' (Ashton et al. 1975, p. 13). Thus again the interrelationships of objectives are seen as essentially hierarchical and all learning is viewed as a linear activity. There are many examples of this kind of approach to be found among the schemes for the teaching of reading that teachers have been offered in recent times and, in particular, among the more sophisticated 'reading workshops' or 'reading laboratories' designed for use with pupils in junior schools and middle schools, or in the lower classes of secondary schools. The Kent Mathematics Project is also an example of the use of this model in the teaching of mathematics.

An attempt to impose a hierarchical structure on educational planning, then, is one major feature of this model. Even the most cursory reading of these examples will make immediately apparent some of the difficulties that have been identified in this kind of approach to curriculum planning and will explain why other projects, notably the Humanities Curriculum Project and the more recent Bruner-sponsored project, 'Man: A Course of Study' (MACOS), have deliberately eschewed the idea of prespecifying their objectives.

A further important characteristic of this view of curriculum planning is that the objectives it requires us to prespecify are clearly and unequivocally behavioural. Tyler, for example, tells us that 'the most useful form for stating objectives is to express them in terms which identify both the kind of behaviour to be developed in the students and the context or area of life in which this behaviour is to operate' (1949, pp. 46–47). Bloom calls them 'intended learning outcomes' and says that they are to be defined in terms of the behaviour the pupil is intended to display through his thoughts, actions or feelings. Mager (1962, p. 13) says, 'A statement of an objective is useful to the extent that it specifies what the learner must be able to *do* or *perform* when he is demonstrating his mastery of the objective.' And Popham (1969, p. 35) tells us that 'A satisfactory instructional objective must describe an observable *behaviour* of the learner or a *product* which is a consequence of learner behaviour'. The observable behaviour might take the form of something like 'skill in making impromptu speeches or performing gymnastic feats' (ibid.). Products might be an essay or 'an omelet from the home economics class' (ibid.).

This being so, 'a properly stated behavioural objective must describe *without ambiguity* the nature of learner behaviour or product to be measured' (op. cit., p. 37). For example:

> When given a description of a research design problem, the student can select correctly from the twenty statistical procedures treated in class that one which is most appropriate for analyzing the data to be produced by the research.

> Having been given a previously unencountered literary selection from nineteenth-century English literature, the student will be able to write the name of the author and at least three valid reasons for making that selection (ibid.).

The Schools Council's Aims of Primary Education Project offers the same kind of definition, declaring that 'if the teacher's aims are to help guide his practice, then they should be expressed in behavioural terms. That is to say that they should state what the child will actually be able to do when the aim is achieved' (Ashton et al. 1975, p. 15). This concern with observable changes of behaviour is also apparent in some of the forms of record-keeping that have recently been urged upon primary teachers to which we referred earlier.

The focus of this approach to educational planning, then, is on the modification of pupil behaviour and the success of such a curriculum is to be evaluated by an appropriate assessment of the behaviour changes that the curriculum appears to have brought about in comparison with those that it was its stated intention to bring about.

A final feature of the behavioural approach to curriculum planning that we must note is that, like all scientific approaches to the study and planning of human activity, it endeavours to be value-neutral. This is not entirely true of the work of the early exponents of this view. In fact, it does seem that one of the sources of the confusion surrounding the interpretation of what Werrett Charters meant by 'ideals' and 'activities' is that he was attempting to make some due allowance for the value dimension of educational activities. Subsequent writers within the behavioural tradition, however, have avoided such confusion by refusing to acknowledge this dimension and denying that questions of value are their concern. Bloom's taxonomy, for example, has been criticized on these grounds, since it is not based on any clearly worked out concept of education (Gribble 1970), but this is not a criticism that he or any of the others would accept as valid, since they are concerned only to present teachers and curriculum planners with a scheme or a blueprint for them to use as they think fit; it is not their concern to tell them how to use it. They regard education as a matter of changing behaviour but they do not accept responsibility for questions about what kinds of behaviour education should be concerned to promote or what kinds of behavioural change it should be attempting to bring about. They maintain their scientific stance, therefore, and leave it to the persons using their scheme to make the decisions about how it should be used. Thus this approach deliberately sidesteps the most difficult and intractable problem that faces curriculum planners – that of deciding what kinds of activity shall be deemed to be educational.

Arguments for the use of objectives

These, then, are the major features of this approach to curriculum planning. We must now consider briefly the main reasons why some people have been and still are concerned to urge it upon curriculum planners. There would seem to be four of these which we might call the logical, the scientific, the politico-economic and the educational arguments for the use of objectives.

The logical argument we have already referred to in considering the case put by Paul Hirst. Briefly, it claims that part of what it means for an activity to be rational is that it should be directed towards some clear goal or purpose. If education is to be regarded as a rational activity, therefore, it must state its goals or purposes. If it does not, then, as both Tyler and Hirst have argued, it becomes literally aimless. Another way of putting this is to accept the analysis made by Israel Scheffler (1960), Richard Peters (1967b) and others of teaching as an intentional activity and to claim that we should, therefore, acknowledge and state the intentions of our teaching. How can one teach, it is asked, if one doesn't know what one is doing it for. The power of this argument is difficult to deny, although, as we have just seen, it is not regarded even by its proponents as leading necessarily to the use of objectives of a strictly behavioural kind. On the other hand, as we have also just suggested, it leads to some comparable difficulties.

The scientific argument we have also touched upon briefly. This represents an attempt to bring into the practice of education some of the precision, accuracy and technological efficiency that is admired as the key to advances elsewhere and thus to render it more 'respectable'. This was clearly the major motivation of the early exponents of this view and the application of scientific method to the study of human performance and achievement in industry by men such as Frederick Taylor obviously aroused the interest and enthusiasm of certain educationists of his day (Davies 1976). This argument also gained force from the predominance of psychology within educational theory in the 1920s and 1930s. For the main impact of psychology on education theory, if its effects are not modified and tempered by the application or acceptance of other disciplines, is to reduce it to scientific analysis of an essentially means–end kind and to advocate this sort of approach to educational planning.

The politico-economic case is made at a rather more mundane level but it is one that is becoming increasingly influential, so that both its existence and its effects must be clearly recognized. Fundamentally, what it claims is that most educational provision is made at the expense of the taxpayer and that most curriculum development is financed in the same way, so that the taxpayer is entitled to a clear statement of what his money is being spent on and thus of what it is intended should be achieved by it. More significantly, perhaps, it is argued that there must be a careful evaluation of the effectiveness of measures that are taken in schools or at other levels of curriculum planning in order to ensure that public money is not being wasted and that the country is not being deprived of the talents and skills its economic welfare requires of its citizens. Such evaluation, it is felt, can only be made properly if it is based on a clear statement of intentions. Thus, as was suggested earlier, the effect of current attempts to monitor standards, particularly in primary schools, in the United Kingdom and to raise the level of teacher accountability is to push teachers towards the prespecification of their objectives, just as the need for evaluation to demonstrate that the taxpayer was receiving value for money pushed most of the early Schools Council projects towards the same curriculum model.

Lastly, some reasons that might be described as educational have been advanced in support of the prespecification of curriculum objectives. Again, however, they make the assumption that evaluation requires such prespecification. Thus it has been argued by Hilda Taba (1962) that objectives must be prespecified because this is crucial for evaluation and that evaluation in turn is crucial for effective teaching, the continued presence of certain subjects on the curriculum and for curriculum development itself. 'It is well known', she tells us (op. cit., p. 199), 'that those things that are most clearly evaluated are also most effectively taught.' She also advises us that 'it is difficult to defend the "frills" from current attacks because attainments other than those in "essentials" are not readily demonstrable ... With a clearer platform of objectives and more adequate evaluation data, both the necessity and the efficacy of many aspects of the school program would be vastly more defensible' (ibid.). Lastly, she claims that this is essential for the continued development of the curriculum since we can only change it effectively if we obtain appropriate data concerning its effects. 'Evaluation thus serves not only to check the hypothesis on which curriculum is based but also to uncover the broader effects of a program which may serve its central purpose well, but may, at the same time, produce undesirable by-products' (op. cit., p. 315).

This emphasis on evaluation and the assumption that it can only take place if objectives are clearly prestated is typical, of course, of an approach to education whose base is essentially psychological. It is important to note, however, that recent studies of curriculum evaluation (MacDonald 1973; Hamilton 1976), as we shall see in Chapter 6, have demonstrated that it is possible to evaluate a curriculum whose objectives have not been clearly stated in advance. Indeed, it might be argued that those very educational advances that Taba is concerned with are better promoted by the use of more sophisticated forms both of evaluation and of planning.

The case for the prespecification of curriculum objectives, then, is a powerful one. Many of the objections to it, however, are equally cogent. It is to a consideration of these that we now turn.

Some problems presented by the objectives model

We must begin by noting that this approach raises some fundamental theoretical issues concerning the nature of education and also concerning the nature of man. For the most fundamental criticism that has been levelled at this approach to curriculum planning is that its attempt to reduce education to a scientific activity, analogous to the processes of industry, commits it to a view of man and of human nature that many people find unacceptable and even unpalatable. For to adopt this kind of industrial model for education is to assume that it is legitimate to mould human beings, to modify their behaviour, according to certain clear-cut intentions without making any allowance for their own individual wishes, desires or interests. Like the materials upon which the industrial worker operates, children's minds are to be fashioned by teachers according to some preconceived blueprint.

This kind of view also requires us to accept that human behaviour can be explored, analysed and explained in the same way as the behaviour of inanimate objects, that it can be studied scientifically by methods similar to those used by the physical scientist or even the biologist and that it can be explained in terms of causes rather than purposes, by reference to external forces acting on the individual rather than internal drives and choices of a personal kind. Fundamental to the view, therefore, is a psychological theory of a behaviourist kind and it is with behaviourist psychology that the movement has been associated from the start. In fact, most of its theoretical proponents have been psychologists rather than educationists or teachers.

This passive model of man is endemic to the theory and it is thus not acceptable to those who take the view that man is to be regarded as a free and active agent, responsible for his own destiny and who, as a direct consequence of this, believe it to be morally wrong to deny him that responsibility and freedom by attempting to mould his behaviour to suit the ends of someone else. Such a process, they argue, is indoctrination rather than education and thus to be deplored.

It is for this reason that it has also been attacked as being based not only on an inadequate and unacceptable model of man but also on an equally unsatisfactory concept of education, or perhaps on no concept of education at all. For those who have attempted to disentangle the concept of education from other related concepts such as training, instruction or indoctrination have done so by drawing attention to certain features of education that are not necessary parts of these other processes and, indeed, are sometimes explicitly excluded from them (Peters 1965, 1966). Pre-eminent among these features is that of individual autonomy without a concern for which, it is argued, no process of teaching can be called education. Such a view of education clearly entails the kind of active model of man we have just been discussing and precludes an approach to educational planning that begins from a clear idea of the kinds of behaviour modification that teachers are to try to bring about in their pupils.

A second feature that it has been claimed must be present if an act of teaching is to be properly described as educational is that pupils must be engaged in it for its own sake. This is sometimes expressed by saying that it must be a process of initiation into activities that are intrinsically worthwhile (Peters 1965, 1966). Whether such activities can be accurately defined or identified is, as we saw in Chapter 2, a difficult question. What is apparent, however, is that in a properly educational process the teacher must view the content of his teaching as being of value in itself and his intention must be to persuade his pupils so to view it. For if its justification lies in what it leads to, if, in short, the process is an instrumental one with ends or purposes outside itself, then we would more naturally refer to it as 'training' or 'instruction'.

In this context, it is interesting to note how many of the books and articles that have been written to promote an approach to educational planning through the prespecification of objectives contain the word 'instruction' in their titles or use that word to describe the kinds of teaching they have in mind. It is also interesting to consider the examples that they give, since most of them are of a relatively simple, instructional kind.

This in itself illustrates either that their concept of education lacks this dimensions that Richard Peters and others wish to give it or that their theories lack any concept of education at all. For if one of the things that characterizes education as opposed to other activities that involve teaching and learning, such as training or instruction, is that education is essentially concerned with activities whose value is intrinsic to them, such a notion of education is clearly at odds with the idea of activities planned according to extrinsic behavioural objectives, goals extrinsic to the activity itself. It was John Dewey who first drew our attention to this feature of education when he asserted that education can have no ends beyond itself, since it is its own end. This view has subsequently been developed more fully by Richard Peters (1965, 1966, 1973a) who claims, for example, that 'to be educated is not to have arrived at a destination; it is to travel with a different view. What is required is not feverish preparation for something that lies ahead, but to work with precision, passion and taste at worthwhile things that lie at hand' (Peters 1965, p. 110). On this kind of analysis not only does the notion of pre-specified behavioural objectives run counter to the very concept of education but the broad aims of education must also be seen from a different perspective, not as what education is *for* but as what it *is*, so that to assert that education is concerned with the development of personal autonomy, understanding, a cognitive perspective, a recognition of the value of certain kinds of activity and so on is not to state extrinsic goals for education so much as to identify features that should characterize any process that is to be described as educational.

Another way of expressing this is to say that education on this kind of analysis contains a value element, a commitment to the intrinsic worthwhileness of certain kinds of activity, and that this element is essential to it. Any approach to educational planning that ignores this element, that sets out deliberately to be value-neutral, as we have seen the behavioural objectives approach does, must be inadequate as a basis for the planning of activities which are educational in the full sense. Such an approach might be quite satisfactory for the planning of schemes of training or instruction and this would explain why, as we suggested earlier, its main impact at the practical level has been on the planning of vocational courses. But for those activities that most teachers would wish to argue constitute the education they offer their pupils, the things that they would claim were for their 'personal development' rather than for their vocational advancement, those things whose presence on the curriculum would be justified in educational or intrinsic terms, the model is quite inadequate. In fine, while the concept of an *instructional* objective is not difficult to grasp, that of an *educational* objective would appear to have no substance at all and to be, in fact, a contradiction in terms.

To take this kind of instrumental view of education further involves adopting a similarly instrumental view of knowledge. For the content of the curriculum on this theory becomes the means by which we achieve our objectives; decisions about content are answers to the question 'What educational experiences can be provided that are likely to attain these purposes?' (Tyler 1949, p. 1). At no stage, therefore, do we select knowledge because we believe it to be valuable in itself but always because it is seen as the means to something else. Thus all knowledge comes to be regarded as of utilitarian value only and this is a view which has wide-sweeping implications not only for education but for attitudes to human existence in general (MacIntyre 1964). It is also a view that few teachers would consciously subscribe to.

The third major difficulty of the objectives approach to curriculum planning follows naturally from this. Once we adopt a model that allows us to see content as instrumental, we immediately risk slipping into some kind of indoctrinatory process, as an examination of Plato's theory of education will again quickly reveal. For there are many areas of the curriculum which involve content of a kind which is highly controversial and to approach these areas with a clear prespecification of intended learning outcomes in behavioural terms is to abandon education altogether for what must be seen as a much more sinister process. In the teaching and learning of music and the fine arts the prime concern is to elicit an individual response from the pupil; it is clearly not appropriate to decide in advance what that response should be (Eisner 1969). 'How can you put on the blackboard the mysterious internal goal of each creative person?' (Pirsig 1974). In literature too the whole purpose of introducing pupils to great literary works is lost if it is done from the perspective of intended learning outcomes (Stenhouse 1970). Again that purpose is to invite the pupil to respond in his own way to what he is introduced to. To approach a reading of *Hamlet*, for example, in any other way is either to reduce it to an instrumental role, as we have just seen, designed to promote an understanding of words, poetic forms, even philosophy, or to attempt to impose one's own moral and aesthetic values, one's own subjective interpretation of the play and response to it on one's pupils. If appreciation of literature or any of the arts means anything at all and has any place in education, it cannot be approached by way of clearly prespecified objectives.

This is one of the major reasons why the Schools Council's Humanities Curriculum Project has deliberately eschewed any kind of statement of objectives and, indeed, has gone so far as to make teacher neutrality its central principle. Being concerned to introduce older pupils in secondary schools to some of the controversial issues that face modern society, issues like those of relations between the sexes, living in cities, war and so on, and being of the opinion that these are issues upon which a number of different value stances can be taken with equal validity, it has recognized that the involvement of pupils in these issues cannot be undertaken justifiably with clear objectives as to what the outcome of their learning and discussions should be, but only according to certain procedural principles that will allow them to reach their own informed opinions on them. To do anything else would be to indoctrinate rather than to educate.

We must also note the criticism that this approach is based on an inadequate view of knowledge (Pring 1971). There are several aspects of this. In the first place, the hierarchical form of the relationships between objectives that is characteristic of taxonomies such as that of Bloom (1956) does not reflect the realities of the learning process. The linear model that it assumes, which attempts to break down all learning into a step-by-step procedure, is not suitable for most of the learning that goes on in schools. We do not acquire knowledge and then, at some later stage, attain understanding; the two must go hand in hand. Any view of knowledge that does not recognize this must be regarded as too simplistic to serve as a basis for any but the most unsophisticated of teaching activities.

To look at this from a different point of view and in more detail, the real thrust of this criticism is that the relationship that exists between educational objectives is too complex to be reduced to an unsophisticated model of this kind which sees that relationship as a hierarchy of simple to ever more complex objectives (Hirst 1975). The relationships existing between the many things that teachers are endeavouring to achieve with their pupils are far more complicated than such a model supposes.

Secondly, the division of objectives into domains that is a major feature of Bloom's taxonomy or into the categories or spheres offered by the Aims in Primary Education Project (Ashton et al. 1975) is an attempt to create distinctions that are unrealistic in practice and untenable in theory. For it is not possible to envisage an activity that concerns itself only with certain cognitive or intellectual goals without simultaneously involving affective or emotional considerations and probably the development of psychomotor skills too. Indeed, we have been arguing that it is of the essence of an educational activity that it should be concerned not only to develop cognitive abilities but at the same time to promote a recognition of the intrinsic value of the activity and a feeling for those standards of truth and beauty which are an essential component of what it means to have knowledge and to be educated (Pring 1971). For how could one attempt to ensure that 'the child should be able to read with understanding material appropriate to his age group and interests' (Ashton et al. 1975, p. 17) without, at the same time, endeavouring to see to it that 'the child should be developing a personal appreciation of beauty in some of its forms, both natural and artistic' (op. cit., p. 19) and that 'the child should find enjoyment in a variety of aspects of school work and gain satisfaction from his achievements' (op. cit., p. 21), not to mention that 'the child should be happy, cheerful and well balanced' (ibid.)? Conversely, how can one hope ever to achieve these affective goals if one has largely to ignore them when setting out to attain the former 'aims related to intellectual development' (op. cit., p. 17)?

Every activity in which a pupil engages will have a range of objectives both within and between the three 'domains'. This is brought out very well in the general statement of the traditional objectives of craft teaching offered by the architects of the Schools Council's project, 'Education through the Use of Materials', as 'developing motor skills, such as sawing, planing and filing, and appreciation of design and craftsmanship in furniture and engineering, with all the satisfaction that attainment in these activities can bring to some pupils and which for so long have been the "bread and butter" activity of the workshop' (Schools Council 1969a,

p. 10). It is also well illustrated by the assertion already referred to that one objective of the teaching of home economics should be 'to encourage enjoyment of the subject and the development of particular interests and talents'. The Science 5–13 Project too has stated quite clearly that 'a teacher will have many objectives for her children in mind at any one time, and in general there is potential for working towards several objectives through any one activity, (Schools Council 1972a, p. 32). Thus, in practice, every activity will embody a range of objectives, involving 'some intellective task', 'a degree of acceptance or rejection' and probably 'some manipulation of materials and objects' too.

This brings us to the third point that needs to be made in criticism of the view of knowledge upon which this curriculum model is based. The teaching of basic skills, even those of a psychomotor kind, cannot be separated out from other kinds of goals without risking the loss of that essential ingredient of education that we must also be concerned with. It is possible to teach basic skills in an instructional manner – the basic skills of reading, for example, of using a saw or a wood-chisel, of drawing straight lines or circles and many others – and it is in this area that the use of the behavioural model has appeared to be successful. The wide adoption and evident commercial success of those 'reading workshops' and 'reading laboratories' we mentioned earlier provide ample evidence of this. However, if we do not at the same time have clearly in mind the educational dimensions of the activities we are engaged in, then, while our efforts might well result in highly skilled performance at the behavioural level, they are likely to result in our achieving little beyond that and may even be counterproductive to any further attainment and, indeed, to education itself. For, as the Bullock Report (DES 1975) pointed out, it is possible to help pupils to a high level of reading performance and at the same time to kill or to inhibit any love or appreciation they may have developed for the written word. Indeed, as the Report also pointed out, even that high level of skilled performance itself will be short-lived. There are more 'non-readers' about than those who merely cannot decipher the symbols of the written word. This is a major danger of attempts to measure standards of attainment in schools in terms simply of performance or behaviour. It is thus a danger not only of the objectives model of curriculum planning but also of those popular, public and political demands for improved standards in the 'basic skills' which have this kind of simplistic model of education at their tap-root.

It is much the same point that Charity James (1968) makes, although from a slightly different perspective, when she argues that this approach restricts the freedom of both teacher and pupil. For both will be inclined to see the objectives as fixed or given, just as secondary teachers tend to see examination syllabuses as immutable, so that not only will they concentrate on what must be rather simple instructional goals, they will also lose the opportunity to play an active role in the educational process, a process which, it is claimed, is only fully educational if both teachers and pupils are active within it. Thus it is argued that the prespecification of intended learning outcomes to an educational process denies autonomy not only to the teacher but also to the pupil and anything that does not take account of the incipient and developing autonomy of the pupil cannot be accurately described as educative (Pring 1973). The curriculum on this view has to be seen as the dynamic interaction of teacher and pupil and this cannot be promoted by a scientific, 'industrial' model requiring careful preplanning of outcomes. If education is seen as a continous, ongoing, open-ended activity, then the idea of constant modification and reassessment must be endemic to it, so that any approach to the planning of an educational activity that starts with a clear specification of objectives will be based on a misunderstanding of what an educational activity really is. Every act of education takes place in its own individual context (Sockett 1976a) and thus cannot be predetermined. Education is an art as well as a science and far too complex and sophisticated an activity to be elucidated in terms of this kind of simple model.

This view of education as an ongoing, open-ended process, subject to constant reassessment and modification as a result of pupil–teacher interaction is supported by the practical experiences of many teachers. We noted earlier that teachers and student teachers, even in the face of concerted pressures upon them to prespecify the objectives of their lessons, have in practice rejected this approach and we suggested that this might be seen as evidence of its impracticability. We can perhaps see now that it is precisely those teachers who are concerned to offer something that goes beyond mere training or instruction who have found this model impossible to use. The realities of the teacher's task are too complex to be met by an approach like that of the industrial planner. This has been reinforced by the experience of many of those curriculum projects that have attempted to use this kind of model, such as the Schools Council's project, 'History, Geography, and Social Science 8–13' (Blyth 1974) and the Nuffield 'A' level Biology Project (Kelly P.J. 1973). For even when sets of objectives are presented to them in clear terms, teachers do find it impossible not to modify them continually in the light of the experiences that they and their pupils have from the moment the work begins. As John Dewey once pointed out, objectives have a tendency to change as you approach them. It is thus not bloody-mindedness on the part of teachers that causes them to cannibalize what they are offered; it is a realization that, if they do not make this kind of constant adjustment, then the goals of their teaching will remain at a simple level and that which is truly educational will be at risk. It is here that the practitioners may fairly claim to have been ahead of the theoreticians. It is here too that the most serious threats are posed by the growing pressures on teachers from outside the school.

Furthermore, it is clear that the attempts of some projects, such as the Schools Council's Integrated Science Project (SCISP), to require teachers to work from prestated objectives have had the effect of complicating their work unnecessarily – if only through the vast number of such objectives they have been expected to bear in mind. Thus teachers have been rendered less effective rather than more so by the requirement to adopt a form of teaching that was ill-suited to their customary approach.

One major reason, then, why some people have recently wished to argue against the prespecification of objectives is the conviction that education is a more sophisticated activity and curriculum planning as a result a more complex process than this simple theoretical model suggests. This is a point we have noted several times already. In Chapter 1, for example, we suggested that the model of curriculum planning as a straight linear progression from prespecification of objectives via decisions about suitable content and procedures to evaluation of intended learning outcomes is far too unsophisticated and inadequate for the planning of any educational activity. We suggested then that the continuous interaction of all the elements involved in curriculum planning was important and had to be allowed for by the adoption of a model that was at the very least cyclical, resulting in modifications of our objectives in the light of the evaluations made, or, preferably, one that allowed for constant modification of objectives in the light of continuous evaluation.

We must note now that this latter kind of model accords more closely with the practice of teachers in most kinds of educational situation. Sensitive teachers do make constant adjustments to their procedures and to their objectives in the light of the continuous feedback they get from their pupils as any piece of work progresses. This is true even of those teachers who do begin by setting out their terminal objectives very precisely. We must note too that factors other than prestated objectives will influence their decisions about content and procedures and these factors in turn will also result in modifications to these objectives (Taylor 1970).

Furthermore, we must recognize that, as we have just suggested, all such modifications will be made according to the individual teacher's interpretation of the values implicit in the originally prespecified objectives (Stenhouse 1970), his own reaction to the response of the pupils to the work and any other factors which he regards as relevant. In short, they will be made in relation to the individual context of each teacher's work. It is for this reason that the results of any educational programme will always differ from the expectations of its planners (Stenhouse 1970); this is one factor in the recent move towards seeing curriculum development as essentially a matter of local development within a particular school rather than in terms of the generation of projects to be disseminated nationally.

Any model we adopt for curriculum planning must allow for the personal and professional autonomy of the teacher, especially in relation to the framing and modification of objectives. If we do not allow for this, then we create constraints on the activity of teachers and their scope for exercising their professional judgement on the spot. This is clearly a very real danger with too simple an objectives model.

The criticisms of the objectives model, then, are as strong as, if not stronger than, the case for its use. That strength derives largely from the claims that for proper educational planning a concept of education is necessary and that the only satisfactory concept we can attain is one that refuses to see man as a passive creature and to regard the process of education and the acquisition of knowledge as purely instrumental processes. On the other hand, it is desirable that the process of education should be a rational process, even if it is not to be scientific in a narrow sense, that it should not appear to be aimless and that teachers and others should have a reasonably clear idea of what they are about. We must finally turn, therefore, to a consideration of some of the attempts that have been and are being made to find a solution to this dilemma.

Alternative approaches to curriculum planning

There ought not to be any fundamental contradiction between the idea of rational curriculum planning and that of promoting the process of education. In other words, the fact that we are faced with this dilemma is more likely to suggest that our thinking has gone wrong somewhere than that a real impasse exists.

For this reason it has been suggested that it is not the specification of objectives in itself which causes the troubles we have listed but rather a misunderstanding as to the kind of thing an educational objective is (Hirst 1975). In short, it is said that we must look for another model for curriculum objectives, since the behavioural model of curriculum objectives is unsatisfactory. Firstly, it is unsatisfactory precisely because it is behavioural and, therefore, loses sight of the fact that educational objectives must of their very nature be concerned with much more complex forms of 'personal and mental development' (Hirst 1975, p. 15). Secondly, it is based on a misunderstanding of the relationship between objectives. Thirdly, it leads to a view of curriculum planning as a kind of engineering or computer programming which fails to understand how curriculum objectives come to be framed. Lastly, it operates at too general a level, assuming that curricula can be planned in a Utopian, *carte blanche* manner rather than recognizing that curriculum development must be seen as a piecemeal activity taking place in specific contexts (Hirst 1975).

Thus, it is not the idea of having a purpose to our planning that is at fault. It is the way in which we view that purpose and its relations to the activities that will embody it. Given that the engineering or computer-programming model is inadequate and accepting that a horticultural model of largely undirected growth is equally unsatisfactory, it is argued that we must set about the search for a more suitable model rather than reject the idea of specifying objectives altogether.

On the other hand, it is difficult to know what an educational objective would be if it were not to be seen as a statement of the intention to change or modify behaviour, unless it were a general statement of principle, a long-term aim. Any short-term goal must be expressed in terms of the behaviour changes we hope to bring about. Certainly the only way in which we could measure the achievement of a short-term goal would be by examining the behaviour of our pupils. Thus, even if we attempted to express the goals of a lesson in terms of *educational* objectives, such as 'to develop habits of enquiry', rather than tight *behavioural* objectives or 'intended learning outcomes', our intention would still be to change behaviour and our success or failure must still be evaluated by observation of pupil behaviour. Any short-term goal, therefore, must be behavioural in nature, although this does not need to be interpreted from the perspective of the behavioural psychologist.

A second attempt to resolve this problem has taken the form of suggesting that we should examine each area of the curriculum separately on the assumption that different subject areas or curriculum activities will require different approaches to their planning.

This argument has taken two main forms. The first of these has distinguished the teaching of science and mathematics from teaching in other areas of the curriculum and has proposed that, while the prespecification of objectives would appear to be inappropriate in the latter context, the teaching of 'factual' material in 'linear' subjects like mathematics, where a clear progression of step-by-step learning may be discerned, does lend itself to clear initial statements of intended outcomes. Certainly, it is the case that most of the examples used by those who have wished to argue the unsuitability of the objectives model have been derived from humanities subjects. The most cogent and often quoted example is that used by Lawrence Stenhouse (1970) in the attack he mounts on the objectives model, the example, which we noted earlier, of the teaching of *Hamlet*.

This case against the prespecification of objectives in such contexts would appear to be irrefutable and it is not difficult to appreciate its force in relation to all those subjects that comprise the humanities. However, is it possible to approach the teaching of mathematics and the sciences differently? Some have certainly felt that it is and in practice a good deal of the teaching of these subjects can be seen to reflect an acceptance of the validity of this model. This is particularly true of some of the schemes for the teaching of mathematics in the primary school, such as Fletcher Mathematics and the Kent Mathematics Project, to which we referred earlier. We have also noted already the degree of preoccupation with curriculum objectives shown by the team associated with the Science 5–13 Project.

It has been argued, however, that this distinction between the humanities and the sciences is difficult to maintain. For it is difficult to sustain the view that science is value-free and that it is not, therefore, subject to the same problems as the humanities subjects. In particular, it has been suggested that nothing could be more unlike true scientific method or inquiry than to begin an experiment with a clear statement of what one intends to prove by it (Sockett 1976a), that the old-style 'required-to-prove' approach to the teaching of science indicates a misunderstanding of the nature of scientific exploration and is unlikely to promote an appreciation of what science truly is. For this reason, although, as we have said, the prespecification of objectives played a major part in the evolution of the Science 5–13 Project, those objectives on examination prove to be rather more loosely framed than at first sight they appear to be and in practice they have been used to support an approach to the teaching of science in the primary school that is enquiry-based. This is even more apparent in the work of the follow-up project, 'Learning through Science' (Richards 1979). Similarly, there is no evidence to support the assumption that an understanding of the logic of mathematics will best be achieved if mathematics is experienced in a logical sequence.

It becomes increasingly clear, then, that in all areas of the curriculum, if our concern is with education and we wish to distinguish this from instruction, training and other teaching activities, one of the things we must do is to eschew the prespecification of objectives.

It is this that has led some to propose a different kind of division of curriculum activities, a separation of those whose justification is clearly educational from those which are equally clearly instrumental, forms of training for which statements of intent are not only acceptable but even necessary. Some support for this view comes from the fact we have already noted that the most widespread practical use of systems of objectives has occurred in the area of vocational preparation and training. Certainly, in such contexts the content of what is taught is clearly chosen on instrumental grounds, so that most or all of the objections that have been raised would seem not to be applicable. In teaching someone to drive a car, for example, it would be foolish not to have a clear idea of one's goals, expressed in quite explicit behavioural terms – 'he shall be able to bring the car to an immediate halt when confronted by an obstruction, human or material' and so on.

However, while this is undoubtedly a proper and acceptable approach to the teaching of basic skills, it is not as easy to identify and single out these skills in the context of schooling as many theorists appear to believe and, as we have just seen, serious dangers lurk in those attempts to make this kind of distinction within the school curriculum. Not much of what goes on in schools has this kind of single-minded vocational goal.

Elliot Eisner's suggestion that we distinguish between 'instructional' and 'expressive' objectives can be seen as an attempt to combine both of the solutions we have considered. For it attempts both to offer an alternative model of an educational objective, in the way that Paul Hirst suggested, and to recommend that we approach the planning of different parts of the curriculum in different ways. The distinction he is attempting to make also suggests a resurrection of that made by Charters between 'ideal' and 'activity' objectives that we referred to earlier. For Eisner, an 'instructional' objective is a behavioural objective of the kind we have been discussing. An 'expressive' objective, however, does not specify an outcome of instruction in behavioural terms. 'An expressive objective describes an educational encounter. It identifies a situation in which children are to work, a problem with which they are to cope, a task in which they are to engage; but it does not specify what from that encounter, situation, problem, or task they are to learn. . . . An expressive objective is evocative rather than prescriptive' (Eisner 1969, pp. 15–16).

Eisner gives as examples of expressive objectives:

1) To interpret the meaning of *Paradise Lost*,
2) To examine and appraise the significance of *The Old Man and the Sea*,
3) To develop a three-dimensional form through the use of wire and wood,
4) To visit the zoo and discuss what was of interest there.

(op. cit., p. 16.)

He goes on to suggest further that it is this kind of objective that teachers have more often than they have instructional objectives of a behavioural kind and that this is particularly so in 'the most sophisticated modes of intellectual work' (op. cit., p. 17).

It is this kind of thinking that lies behind those statements of objectives offered by several Schools Council projects which we noted earlier were not strictly behavioural in form but appeared to be seeking a more satisfactory educational basis. It is also another way of attempting to express as objectives those complex forms of development of which Paul Hirst speaks. This in turn reflects the thinking of many teachers who, while acknowledging the difficulties created by attempts to specify the goals of their teaching in narrow behavioural terms, feel it quite appropriate to speak of the 'broad aims' of education.

It is clear that both Eisner and Hirst are endeavouring to avoid defining an educational objective in instrumental terms because they are aware of the fundamental contradiction that that entails. However, if that contradiction is fundamental, then it cannot be resolved by seeking a different kind of goal for educational activities; it can only be resolved by replacing the notion of an educational goal with something entirely different. This, in effect, is what Eisner's notion of an expressive objective actually does. For, as the examples given clearly show, it does not provide us with a goal so much as offer us a statement of procedures or principles. It is, however, misleading to use the term 'objective' with its connotations of extrinsic purposes to denote a notion whose central concern seems to be with processes. This is a point we shall return to.

A third kind of solution has emerged from the practical experience of a number of curriculum projects that we have already briefly referred to. A number of project teams have discovered that no matter how carefully their objectives have been framed they quickly come to be modified by teachers in the light of the experience and feedback they begin to receive as soon as they begin to implement the project. They have thus come to realize that the objectives they framed would have to be regarded as tentative and open to constant modification and adjustment. Those, for example, who were associated with the Schools Council's project, 'History, Geography and Social Science 8–13', came to recognize that they must regard their objectives only as 'provisional' (Blyth 1974) and those concerned with the Nuffield 'A' level Biology Project came to describe their objectives as 'mutable' (Kelly P.J. 1973). This view not only reflects more nearly the practical realities of the classroom and of teacher behaviour and experience, it is also closer to what we really mean by scientific exploration which, as we pointed out earlier, is characterized not by possessing a clear idea of where it is going but rather by being hypothetical, open-ended and subject to constant modification. This development is reflected in the growing practice of some local authorities of offering curriculum 'guidelines' to their primary teachers rather than statements of objectives, although it is sometimes the case that these guidelines are so tightly framed that their point is lost and their impact on the curriculum continues to be restrictive.

Such an approach is also supportive of the development of the curriculum, since it allows for the kind of continuous change and adjustment that the notion of development entails. It thus recognizes that in education 'objectives are developmental, representing roads to travel rather than terminal points' (Taba 1962, p. 203). It also acknowledges the force of one of those criticisms levelled by Paul Hirst at the behavioural objectives model of educational planning, namely that it assumes that curricula can be planned in a Utopian, *carte blanche* manner rather than recognizing that curriculum development must take place in a specific context and must be seen as essentially a piecemeal activity (Hirst 1975).

It is for this reason that we are now being encouraged from a number of sources to adopt a much more flexible approach to the framing of objectives so as to avoid a tight computer-programming approach to pupil activities. It has been suggested, for example, that we do begin by stating course objectives but that we avoid the temptation to frame them in highly specific behavioural terms and that we should not be afraid to state long-term objectives, since many important educational outcomes may not be achieved except after many months or years of effort (Hogben 1972).

A recognition of the developmental nature of educational goals leads also to a willingness to accept unintended learning outcomes (Hogben 1972) and it is further suggested that we be on the alert for these and that we do not reject or discourage them merely because they do not conform to our prestated short-term goals.

In short, we should regard our objectives, certainly those of a short-term variety, as provisional, mutable and subject to modification in the light of the continuous experience both of ourselves as teachers and of our pupils once a course or piece of work has got under way.

This solution, however, although commending itself in many ways, not least in its obvious reflection of the actual practice of teachers and other curriculum planners, suffers from one major theoretical weakness which must render it, in the long term, an inadequate basis for satisfactory curriculum planning. For, apart from the fact that it embraces an instrumental model of education, the problems of which we have already discussed, its fundamental weakness is that it advises and encourages us to change and modify our objectives and to accept learning outcomes from our teaching which we did not intend to bring about, without offering us any criteria by which we can make judgements about the desirability of such changes and modifications or of these unintended outcomes. If we change our objectives or accept the validity of experiences or learning we did not intend or foresee, and if at the same time we do not accept the validity of all such changes or outcomes, we do so only because we have some criteria of judgement against which we can assess these unexpected and unplanned events. If this is so, and logically it must be, then it is these criteria which are the real bases of our curriculum planning, and not our initial, mutable, provisional objectives, which must be seen as essentially second-order considerations. Until we get to grips with those basic principles, both our theorizing and our practice will continue to be muddled.

In fact, a common difficulty evinced by all of the proposed solutions we have so far examined is that, while ostensibly seeking new models of educational objectives or attempting to identify areas of the curriculum where existent models might apply, they have all failed to realize that all educational planning must begin from a consideration of its basic principles or of the processes it is concerned to promote.

Indeed, this is a basic weakness of the objectives model itself. For, in rejecting, as we have seen it does, all responsibility for those value choices which are essential to education, it refuses to offer us any basis upon which we can even make a selection of the objectives we are to aim for. Nevertheless, as we shall see when we come to discuss the problems of curriculum evaluation in Chapter 6, even those who advocate this approach recognize that it is necessary for evaluative procedures to ask questions not only about the effectiveness of a programme in attaining its objectives but also about the desirability of the objectives themselves, to provide data for their subsequent modification. The model itself, then, draws our attention to the fact that educational planning must begin from considerations which are logically prior to statements of its objectives.

It is for this reason that others have recently stressed the need to begin educational planning from statements of principles rather than goals, assertions of the value positions that are to act as a base for all subsequent decisions.

A process model

Paul Hirst's claim (1969) that all rational activities are characterized by having clear goals or objectives has perhaps been accepted by many educationists too uncritically. For, while this may be a major characteristic of rational activity, it is certainly not peculiar to human activity, since it is quite apparent that much of the behaviour of animals is goal-directed. It is also true that much animal behaviour is characterized by the ability to generalize, since, as Mark Twain wrote, a cat who sits on a hot stove-lid will not sit on a hot stove-lid again. It is a reflection on the quality of, rather than the existence of, the ability to generalize that he is able to go on to claim that such a cat will not sit on a cold stove-lid either.

What is uniquely characteristic of human behaviour and does offer a valid and important contrast with animal behaviour is that it is in many cases based on adherence to principles. Thus it might be argued that it is this feature of human behaviour which offers the appropriate kind of basis for the planning of education, so that some educationists have advised that we turn from this search for objectives of any kind and devote our attention instead to achieving agreement on the broad principles that are to inform the activity or course we are planning and in the light of which all on-the-spot decisions and modifications will be made.

Lawrence Stenhouse, for example, has suggested that 'in mounting curriculum research and development, we shall in general . . . do better to deal in hypotheses concerning effects than in objectives. To attach the value-laden tag, *objectives*, to some of our hypotheses is an odd and usually unproductive scientific procedure' (Stenhouse 1970, p. 80). Such an approach, he is claiming, will encourage us to be much more tentative, less dogmatic and more aware of the possibility of failure and the need for corrective adjustments than statements of objectives which may lead us to feel we know where we are going without fear of contradiction. He has also suggested that we should begin by defining the 'value positions embodied in the curriculum specification or specifications' (op. cit., p. 82). Again, to do this will provide us with a clear view of the principles upon which the original planning was founded which can act as a basis either for later changes in our procedures or for modification of these value positions themselves in the light of subsequent experience.

This is a point that Richard Pring has taken up in urging teachers and curriculum planners to seek for agreement on the principles of procedure that will guide the conduct of any particular curriculum project and to concern themselves not with prespecifying goals but with statements of the norms and principles that will inform the activity of both teachers and pupils (Pring 1973). Only thus, it is argued, will it be possible for us to reconcile the idea of rational curriculum planning with that of education as a continuous lifelong process to which terminal goals cannot be attributed.

It was on this kind of base that the Schools Council's Humanities Curriculum Project was established, making no attempt to specify learning outcomes but stating quite clearly the principles to be adhered to in the classroom. In fact this has been the practice of most curriculum projects. For where objectives are stated, these are seldom really short-term, but usually have a kind of 'middle-ground' appearance and are stated in general procedural terms. In other words, they are often neither very broad educational aims nor immediate intended outcomes but rather statements of the general principles that the project team felt should underlie the work of a particular subject area. If they are to be called objectives at all, they resemble Eisner's expressive objectives rather than instructional objectives framed in behavioural terms.

This is the only interpretation that can be put on a statement of objectives such as that of the Schools Council Working Paper No. 24 – *Rural Studies in Secondary Schools*, which set out the following five objectives:

a)   To promote an understanding of the countryside and man's relation to his natural environment and to develop a respect for living things
b)   To develop an understanding of science and scientific method through observation, first-hand investigation, and experiment
c)   To give enjoyment and satisfaction, and to encourage a profitable use of leisure
d)   To develop aesthetic appreciation and an outlet for creative thinking
e)   To arouse the interest of all pupils through acceptable and enjoyable practical work, and in this manner to provide valuable starting points for further studies.
(Schools Council 1969b, pp. 9–10.)

Such a statement clearly does not offer a programme of behavioural objectives but it does provide a set of guidelines for teachers to refer to in the planning of their own particular programmes or the work of individual pupils.

What has happened seems to be that people are very confused in their thinking about objectives, so that they call what they are doing framing objectives but then proceed to make these of such a general kind that they are not objectives in the instructional and behavioural sense of the term at all, but rather expressive objectives or principles of the kind we have been discussing. Thus even the Schools Council's Science 5–13 Project, which sets out a programme of objectives with a very taxonomous look to it, is at pains at the same time to stress that all of these objectives are at a level of generality such as to give both teachers and children a good deal of freedom over choices of activity, materials, experiments and so on (Schools Council 1972a). Indeed, the experience of that project points up precisely the problem we have been endeavouring to air, since its objectives could not be tightly framed without being in conflict with the enquiry approach to science that it was also at pains to promote.

Most people do seem in fact to accept that an educational curriculum must be viewed in terms of processes rather than content or behavioural outcomes. One might express this by saying with Richard Peters that it is the manner rather than the matter of learning that we must look to in defining an educational activity (Peters 1965). Or one might agree with Paul Hirst's claim that to be initiated into the several forms of thought is more important than to acquire the ability merely to perform certain intellectual feats (Hirst

1965), the ability to think scientifically, for example, being what the notion of education requires rather than the mere display of certain behaviours recognizable as regurgitating statements of scientific fact. Or one might argue with Alfred North Whitehead that education is 'the art of the utilization of knowledge' and not the acquisition of 'inert ideas' (Whitehead 1932). Again one might accept John Dewey's claim that all knowledge is to be seen as the developing experience of the individual. One might even take the line of those sociologists who argue that education, to be meaningful to the pupil, must be a development of the knowledge he brings to the school with him (Keddie 1971).

It all comes down to the same thing fundamentally, namely that education and, therefore, the curriculum have to be planned in the light of those processes they are seen to comprise rather than in terms either of the subject content it is claimed they should contain or include or a set of behavioural outcomes they are designed to promote or achieve. Aims and processes cannot be separated; the aims are reflected in the processes and the processes are embodied in the aims.

The difficulty arises when the framing of short-term goals is seen as a tight deductive process from these broader statements of aims, processes or principles. It is the relation of our short-term objectives to these longer-term aims that is the crucial issue. The model that is unacceptable for all the reasons we have listed at length is that which offers us a hierarchy of goals, beginning, for example, with the *ultimate* goals of all education, deriving from these *mediate* goals for different stages of learning, deducing from these *proximate* goals for shorter-term activities and finally drawing from these specific classroom *objectives* (Wheeler 1967). This kind of deductive process becomes almost inevitable when one calls these broad statements of intent 'aims', and it is important to recognize why they are to be seen clearly as principles rather than as aims, as well as why this approach to curriculum planning is to be regarded as different from, and even incompatible with, an approach through the prespecification of aims and objectives.

The answer to these questions is to be found in the difference, which is more than a semantic one, between a principle and an aim. For an aim is extrinsic to the activities which constitute the attempt to attain it, while a principle is integral to those activities. An aim can be viewed as something which will be attained at a later stage in the process, while a principle must be seen to be present at every stage. Thus a teacher of young children who regards literary appreciation as an aim of education may be encouraged to approach the teaching of reading as if it were merely a step on the road to that extrinsic goal, and thus may adopt methods of teaching, perhaps unduly emphasizing the 'basic skills', which may even turn out to be counterproductive to its attainment, while one who sees it as a principle will be concerned to ensure that it should inform even the earliest steps of linguistic development. For the same reason, ideas such as those of autonomy, freedom of thought, critical awareness and all of those other qualities we listed earlier in our attempt to define what it means to be educated, are of as much concern to teachers in nursery schools as to those in universities. In short, the adoption of a principle ensures that the end only justifies those means which are compatible with it.

It is quite understandable that teachers should want to be given some idea of what should be the end-products of several years of continuous effort on their part. However, what is wrong with this approach is that it assumes that these qualities can be regarded as end-states and thus as extrinsic to the processes and activities of education, when in fact, as we have suggested several times, the two cannot be separated in this way, since they are integrally linked and interwoven. Such qualities of mind are not the objectives, goals, purposes, intentions of educational activity but rather the principles which must inform all such activity and the processes of teaching from the outset. A concern with the principle of autonomy, for example, must be there from the beginning – even in the work that is done with the three-year-old – if autonomy is to be developed. To suggest that we might engage pupils in certain activities now in order that they may achieve autonomy later is to misunderstand totally the educational process or at least to offer a gross caricature of it. For, if we take this view, what we do now will often be counterproductive to our intentions, since the temptation will always be present to permit the end to justify, rather than to permeate, the means. It is this that is at fault with all forms of educational planning that are instrumental and thus with all forms of educational objectives.

It is because the term 'aim' has been used by most of those concerned with major attempts at changing the curriculum in recent years that they have been tempted into proceeding to deduce from these aims more specific teaching objectives. It is because they have done this that teachers have felt the need to modify and change those objectives, as well as to accept the educational validity of some of the learning outcomes which were unintended. Where teachers have done this, however, they have usually done it in response to and in accordance with principles which they have felt to be embodied in the broader aims. It would avoid much confusion at all levels of both theory and practice if this were acknowledged, the status of such principles as the essential starting points of educational planning recognized and the principles themselves clearly articulated. Another way of putting this was suggested recently by a friend and colleague, HMI Roger Shirt-cliffe, who suggested the acceptance of the maxim of the artilleryman, that if the aim is good enough the objectives are destroyed.

It is not being suggested that in educational planning we should take no account of outcomes or products or that these are to be ignored. It is being proposed, however, that in both the planning and the execution of an educational curriculum the major emphasis should be on the processes of development it sets out to promote, so that, if it can be said to be concerned with products or outcomes, these will be defined in terms of intellectual development and cognitive functioning rather than in terms of quantities of knowledge absorbed or changes of behavioural performance.

The recognition that planning must begin from statements of broad principles to be interpreted by the teacher, rather than from statements of aims which can be reduced to a tight programme of objectives, also permits that kind of freedom for the teacher in planning his own work and that of his pupils which we are arguing throughout this book is in the best interests of education. It is infinitely preferable that after agreement has been reached at the level of general principles, teachers and pupils should be given the autonomy to interpret these principles in their own way in the planning of their varied and continuing activities. In practice, this seems to be what most projects in the last analysis do anyway, so that once again it seems that we have a problem created for us by the theorists. There are, of course, dangers here that teachers and pupils will either fail to use or will misuse their autonomy (Blyth 1974) but unless this risk is taken and they are given this freedom, nothing that can be characterized as education is likely to take place and no curriculum *development* will be possible. This looser model is the only acceptable model for both the rational planning and the continuous development of an educational curriculum.

Summary and conclusions

We have in this chapter examined in some detail the objectives model of curriculum. We began by tracing its history and suggesting that it can be seen as the result of a desire to make the practice of education more 'scientific' and thus as an effect of the influence of psychology, especially that of the behaviourist school, on education theory.

We then tried to pick out the essential characteristics of this view and, in doing so, we laid particular stress on the fact that those systems of objectives that have been proposed are behavioural, hierarchically structured and value-neutral. We next suggested that support for this approach to curriculum planning came not only from those who wished to make education more scientific but also from those who felt that in order for it to qualify as a rational activity it needs to have clear goals of some kind, from others who have felt that they could see advantages of an educational kind in it and, most recently, from politicians and others who have seen this as the only way of evaluating what schools and teachers are doing and testing their effectiveness and efficiency.

Having thus outlined the case for this model of curriculum planning, we then considered some of the criticisms that have been levelled at it. Most of these seemed to focus on the claim that both in theory and in practice to approach education in a manner that regards it as an instrumental activity is to lose one essential ingredient that makes education what it is, namely a process whose justification must lie within itself. Thus we saw that the critics of the objectives model base their attack mainly on the fact that it treats education and knowledge as instrumental and, as a corollary of doing so, often adopts a passive model of man, that model of man that is at the root of behavioural psychology. We saw too that in practice this leads to teaching that is better described as instruction or training or even indoctrination than education and that it places constraints on both teachers and pupils that inhibit that freedom of interaction that some have claimed to be central to the educative process.

Inevitably, therefore, when we came to consider some of the solutions that have been proposed to this problem, some alternative approaches to curriculum planning, we found faults in those that fall into this same trap of regarding education as an instrumental process that is to be planned as a means to ends beyond itself. The solutions that appeared to offer something of value were those that in one form or another rejected that means-end stance and attempted to allow for unintended learning outcomes and for constant modification in the light of the continuing experience of teacher and taught.

This led us finally to the view that the notion of an educational objective might be a contradiction in terms and that an educational curriculum might have to be planned by the use of or on the basis of a totally different model. Such a model would have to recognize that if education is not to be viewed in instrumental terms its planning must begin not with a statement of goals but with the specification of procedures, principles or processes, as a basis for the continuous exercise of the professional judgement of the teacher.

We shall find ourselves returning frequently to this issue of curriculum planning models in subsequent chapters. For in considering, as we now must, how curriculum change can be effected, we must examine not only the responsibility of teachers for this but also the role of external agencies. Our discussion must, therefore, embrace questions not only of the influence of external bodies but also those concerning the direct control of the curriculum. We will find throughout this discussion that its implications for the planning strategies available to schools and teachers are wide-ranging and important. In particular, we shall see that the greater the degree of external control, whether it be expressed through the forms of evaluation adopted or those for teacher accountability or, indeed, in attempts to centralize the decision-making process, the greater the tendency will be towards simplistic and instrumental planning models.

CHAPTER 5

STRATEGIES FOR CURRICULUM CHANGE

We have noted in the earlier chapters of this book that if curriculum development is to be promoted and if curriculum change is to be effected, then a good deal of attention must be given to the choice of a suitable theoretical model for curriculum planning and, in particular, to some important questions about the kind of emphasis which can or should be placed on the selection of curriculum content and the use of curriculum objectives. In later chapters we will also note the account which must be taken of a vast range of constraints and influences which together provide the context within which curriculum change and development must occur. This chapter will address itself to questions concerning the possible strategies which might be employed for changing the curriculum, the techniques which have been or may be used in attempts to bring about curriculum change or to accelerate and smooth the path of curriculum development.

First of all, we will look briefly at the work of the Schools Council which is and has been for almost twenty years the major national agency for curriculum change in the United Kingdom. Secondly, we will explore some of the problems of disseminating curriculum innovations, by looking at some of the models of dissemination which have been either postulated or employed and by considering their relative effectiveness. And thirdly, since this kind of exploration must lead to a questioning of the role of a centralized agency in curriculum development, since in fact the main lesson to be learnt from a study of dissemination techniques is that local initiatives have always been more effective than national projects in bringing about change, we will examine the theory and the practice of school-based curriculum development.

The Schools Council

It was suggested in Chapter 1 that planned curriculum development, at least at the level of secondary education, is a relatively recent phenomenon, that the 'unplanned drift' (Hoyle 1969a), resulting from the product of external pressures, which characterized such change as the curriculum once sustained, was replaced by attempts at deliberate planning and curriculum construction only in the late 1950s and early 1960s. This was largely as a result of a concern felt throughout the western world that it might be falling behind in the race for technological advancement.

In the United Kingdom that period saw the beginning of a number of attempts to change the curriculum, supported in some cases by the injection of money for research from such bodies as the Nuffield Foundation, until all of these threads were drawn together by the establishment in October 1964 of the Schools Council for the Curriculum and Examinations, whose brief was 'to undertake research and development work on the curriculum, and to advise the Secretary of State on matters of examination policy' (Lawton 1980, p. 68). It was to be funded jointly by the Department of Education & Science and the local education authorities. It is worth noting also, that its constitution implicitly endorsed the idea of teacher control of the curriculum, in that teacher members formed a majority on virtually all of its committees.

Once established, the Council began its task by identifying its major programmes of work, and, in doing so, it directed its attention towards six main areas of interest: the primary school curriculum, the curriculum for the early leaver (the Newsom Report (Central Advisory Council for Education 1963) had just recommended the raising of the school leaving age to 16), the sixth form, the English programme, GCE and CSE examinations and the special needs of Wales.

It is clear that from the very outset the duality of the role given to the Council – its responsibility for both curriculum development and the public examination system – has been a major factor in determining its policies and its actions. For its task has been to maintain a balance between two potentially conflicting elements of the education system (Becher and Maclure 1978). There is no doubt that these two must be planned in phase, not least because, as we shall see when we consider in Chapter 7 some of the external constraints on curriculum planning and development, the public examination system is probably the most influential of these. For the same reason, however, it is apparent that the Council's inability to bring about significant changes in the examining system has severely limited its effectiveness in promoting curriculum change. For its advice on examinations has never been taken seriously by the Department of Education & Science, as is demonstrated by its many unavailing attempts to bring about significant changes in the system of public examinations for sixth forms (Schools Council 1978a, 1979), and its attempts to introduce a common system of examinations at 16+ (Schools Council 1971a, 1975b), a change which has only recently been given official sanction for implementation in 1987.

As a result, this dual role has also determined the major flavour of its work at least during the first ten years of its life. For, like the examinations system, its work has been largely subject-based and this has made it difficult for it to respond to changes of focus within the curriculum. In particular, it has led it to adopt a differentiated approach to curriculum planning which has been rightly criticized as based on a particular and erroneous view of educational knowledge (Young 1973). For, while it could be claimed that it has been at its most influential in recommending changes in the curriculum for the less able pupil in the secondary school – its ROSLA programme – it must also be recognized that its influence here has often taken the form of advising schools to offer such pupils a different curriculum, consisting largely of low-status knowledge and little else (Kelly 1980). In fairness, it must be conceded that, while such criticism is quite justified, its errors in this area were due to ignorance and inexperience rather than to sinister intent; it must also be acknowledged that one or two projects, such as the Humanities Curriculum Project (Schools Council 1970), realized the errors of these ways and attempted to avoid them. It must be stressed, however, that this trend in its work is the very natural result of both the subject-based approach which a monolithic examination system dictated and the greater ease with which the curriculum for the less able, 'non-examinable' pupil could be changed, precisely because it is largely unconstrained by the demands of public examinations.

A second criticism which is prompted by this subject-based approach is directed at the failure of the Council to view the curriculum as a whole and to plan its development as a totality. Again, one must recognize that its attempts to do so, by first changing the examination system to make this possible, have been frustrated by the unwillingness of outside bodies to accept the changes proposed, as, for example, in the case of the attempts to broaden the sixth-form curriculum which were embodied in the proposals for N and F level examinations (Schools Council 1978a). One must concede also, however, that even in the area of the primary school curriculum, where comparable constraints do not exist and where tradition might be said to favour the idea of total curriculum planning, the main influence of the Council has led to a move towards a more subject-based approach and away from rather than towards the planning of the curriculum as a whole (Blenkin and Kelly 1981). The current emphasis on the need for 'balance' in the curriculum can be seen as a direct result of this failure to achieve this kind of total planning and of the completely unbalanced curriculum experienced by many pupils in the upper reaches of the secondary schools which it has resulted in (DES 1979). Again, it would be unfair to lay this charge entirely at the door of the Schools Council or to fail to acknowledge that its procedures must be seen largely as the product of its dual brief. Its contribution to this trend, however, must be recognized.

A third aspect of the work of the Schools Council which has attracted criticism is the encouragement it has offered to most of its projects to adopt an objectives-based planning model. Again it might be claimed that this is an inevitable consequence of its concern for examinations. It must also be conceded that this was understandable in the context of the general climate existing at the time when it was established. Whatever the reasons, however, it is clear that from the beginning the Council was concerned not only that, in order to demonstrate its proper use of public funds, the work of all of its projects should be evaluated, but inclined also to the view that this could best be done, perhaps could only be done, if they began by making clear statements of their objectives. There were, of course, notable exceptions to this general trend, among which again was the Humanities Curriculum Project (Schools Council 1970), but these exceptions merely prove the rule and there is no doubt that as a whole the Schools Council has added its weight to that growing trend towards regarding this as the only proper basis for curriculum planning, a trend which we both noted and vigorously questioned in our last chapter. The link between the prespecification of objectives and the evaluation of the curriculum we will explore more fully in Chapter 6; we must merely note here that the Schools Council can be criticized for lending its general support to the view that this link is non-problematic.

Lastly, we must note that a further major criticism has been directed at the methods of dissemination adopted by many of the Schools Council's projects. Again, we will look at the problems of the dissemination of curriculum innovation later in this chapter. We must comment here, however, that on the evidence of its own Impact and Take-Up Project (Schools Council 1978b, 1980) the work of the Council has been less effective than one would have hoped and that this may be largely attributable to the forms of dissemination it adopted, particularly in its early years, or to its failures to pay adequate attention to the problem of dissemination. This criticism too is easily made from hindsight and its approach here should perhaps be seen as typical of, if not inevitable in, the context of the first ten years of its work. However, it must also be seen as contributing to the growing criticism of that work.

The force of most of these criticisms has been recognized by those responsible for the work of the Council, so that recent years have seen new trends arising from the emerging inadequacies of the old. There has been a broadening of scope, for example, which has seen some projects extending their sphere of interest down the age-range and a general move towards seeing the curriculum as a whole. There has also been a development away from the starkest forms of objectives-based planning, as more sophisticated forms of evaluation have been developed. The emergent problems of dissemination too have led to a greater concentration on the idea of supporting local, school-based initiatives.

However, it is quite clear not only that the early patterns and structure adopted by the Schools Council have influenced curriculum development generally but also that they are now acting as a continuing constraint on its own work and are thus inhibiting these recent developments (Blenkin 1980). It is equally clear that they have provided ammunition for those who have wished to argue that a teacher-controlled Schools Council has failed to make a significant impact on the curriculum of the schools. It might be claimed that the success of the Schools Council is to be judged not by its direct influence on curriculum change but by the contribution its work has made to promoting debate about the curriculum and to creating an interest and concern for curriculum issues among teachers. But the influence of the Council's work on general development in both the theory and the practice of curriculum change, while it may be very extensive, is difficult, if not impossible, to quantify, while its failure to achieve direct changes through its own projects is manifest from the evidence of its own Impact and Take-Up Project (Schools Council 1978b, 1980). Its attempts to learn from the inadequacies of its earlier practices, then, have been thwarted not only by these practices themselves but also by the strength they have added to the case of its opponents.

Criticisms of the achievements of the Schools Council under a system of teacher control, then, have led to its recent reconstitution. For the attempt to reduce the teachers' control of the curriculum which may be seen to have failed when the Council was first established has gained strength from the criticisms by outsiders of its work (Lawton 1980), and also from the economic stringency which in recent years has led to the availability of less money for curriculum development. These are major features of a general change of political climate which we will examine in some detail in Chapter 8. As a result of them, however, the main thrust of the reconstitution of the Council has been towards reducing the influence of teachers in the formation of its policies and increasing that of many other bodies with an interest in education. In short, in unison with the general trends of the time, it has been designed to open educational policy to public debate, or, as the cynic might argue, to bring it under the control of the administrators.

One major reason for this reorganization can be seen to be its political and economic desirability at this point in time. We must acknowledge, however, that there may be good pedagogical reasons for it too. Many of the criticisms we discussed earlier have come from within the profession and their strength has to be recognized. Some kind of reconstitution, therefore, was needed and it is clear that this has already resulted in some important structural and policy changes.

For the new constitution has created what has been described in one of the Council's information pamphlets as 'an entirely new and more efficient committee structure'. This reorganization has significance at two levels. Firstly, the old structure, which consisted of a vertical and hierarchical organization of committees from the Governing Council through a Programme Committee and three Age Group Committees to the six Subject Committees responsible for the areas listed earlier, has given way to a parallel structure consisting of three main committees – Convocation, the Finance and Priorities Committee and the Professional Committee. Secondly, this has resulted in, and/or from, the abandonment of the subject base adopted by the Council in its early years.

Its research is now concentrated, as the same pamphlet tells us, in five main areas:

- purpose and planning in schools, i.e. the effectiveness of a school's staff as a professional team
- helping teachers to develop their skills
- aspects of the curriculum, including content and pupil's skills, ideas and attutudes

- the needs of particular groups of children such as those in ethnic min-
  orities, the disrupted (sic) and the gifted
- fairness, accuracy and uniformity of standards across the examination
  system.

This has led to the establishment of major programmes, one in each of these
areas – Organization in Schools, Helping Teachers' Professional Development, Developing the Curriculum for a Changing World, The Needs of
Individual Pupils, and Improving the Examination System.

Finally, it should also be noted that although this new constitution has
reduced the involvement of teachers at the top level of management of the
Council, they retain a strong membership of the Professional Committee
and 'now greater numbers of practising teachers are participating in the
earlier development stages of curriculum projects'.

It will be clear from this that many of the lessons of the early years of the
Council's work appear to have been learnt and attempts are being made to
respond to the criticisms we listed earlier by putting right some of the
inadequacies of the early policies which they were directed at. In doing this,
however, this new policy itself raises further questions which only time will
answer. For example, while the importance of school-based curriculum
development is now acknowledged, as we shall see later, it is not yet
established that this is best supported by a national development policy
rather than by local agencies. Nor is it clear that this kind of policy is the
best way to raise the quality of teachers. In fact, many doubts continue to
exist about the viability of attempts of this kind to effect changes in the
curriculum by establishing some kind of national policy, especially when
the body created to do this has a role which is merely advisory and lacks the
power to implement its policies in any way.

These doubts lead us to several major questions which subsequent chapters will explore. They arise particularly, however, from the experiences of
recent years in the crucial area of curriculum dissemination. This is a vital
element in any programme of curriculum change and it is with a discussion
of this that our examination of the strategies of curriculum change now
proceeds.

The dissemination of innovation

It was suggested earlier that a major reason for the failure of the Schools
Council to influence curriculum change more directly and more widely was

to be found in the dissemination strategies that were adopted. The dissemination of innovation is another problem that was created by that shift we have noted on several occasions from unplanned drift to deliberate planning, from random evolution to social engineering. The essence of the change is that dissemination replaces diffusion (although the terms are not always used with meanings as clearly distinct as this). 'Once the curriculum reform movement got into "third gear" the term "diffusion", suggesting a natural social process of proliferation, gave way to the term "dissemination", indicating planned pathways to the transmission of new educational ideas and practices from their point of production to all locations of potential implementation' (MacDonald and Walker 1976, p. 26).

The intentions behind this process were several. It was hoped that it would lead to improvements in the channels of curriculum change; there was optimism that it would accelerate the speed of curriculum change; it was expected that the quality of the curriculum would be improved; and greater cost-effectiveness was also envisaged (MacDonald and Walker 1976).

The problems which rapidly became apparent arose from two major and interrelated sources. Firstly, the effectiveness of this process was seen to be determined to a high degree by those many constraints which limit all forms of curriculum development. At an early stage in its existence, the Schools Council identified several of these as being particularly significant in the constraining effects they were clearly having on innovation – 'finances, staff attitude, the mobility of pupils, parental pressures, and examinations' (Schools Council 1971c, p. 15). This whole issue of constraints on curriculum planning will be examined in some detail in Chapter 7.

The second set of problems for programmes of dissemination arose from the models of dissemination which were used and some discussion of the models which have been identified must be undertaken as a prerequisite to examining the problems themselves.

Two major attempts have been made to identify different models of dissemination – those by Schon (1971) and Havelock (1971). These have been taken as offering the bases of an understanding of the problems of disseminating educational innovation, but it must be noted and emphasized straightaway that their analyses are based on evidence culled from spheres other than education, a process whose dangers and inadequacies we have had cause to comment on in several other contexts.

Schon identifies three models of dissemination which he calls the

Centre–Periphery model, the Proliferation of Centres model and the Shifting Centres model. It is not unreasonable to see the second and third of these as elaborations of the first and thus all three of them as different versions or methods of what is fundamentally a centre–periphery approach.

The essence of the centre–periphery approach is that it assumes that the process of dissemination must be centrally controlled and managed, that the innovation is planned and prepared in detail prior to its dissemination and that the process of that dissemination is one-way – from the centre out to the consumers on the periphery. The effectiveness of this approach depends on several factors which include not only the strength of the central resources, but also the number of points on the periphery that are to be reached and the length of the 'spokes', the distance of these points from the centre.

The Proliferation of Centres model attempts to overcome these factors, or at least to reduce their significance, by creating secondary centres to extend the reach and thus the efficiency of the primary centre. The intention is that the work of the central development team is supported and extended by local development groups. In turn, these local groups are supported by the central team through the provision not only of advice but also of courses of training. It can be seen that the adoption of this kind of model represents an acknowledgement that attention has to be given to the process of dissemination itself and not merely to the details of the innovation to be disseminated. It has been claimed (Stenhouse 1975) that this model reflects most clearly the realities of attempts at curriculum development in recent years in England and Wales. It is certainly true that this kind of approach has been used to some effect by a number of projects, notable among which are Stenhouse's own Humanities Curriculum Project, the Geography for the Young School Leaver project and Joan Tough's project, Communication Skills in Early Childhood.

Schon's third model, the Shifting Centres model, was posited to explain the spread, witnessed in recent years, of ideas such as those of civil rights, black power, disarmament and student activism, in other words changes of values and attitudes of a more subtle and less deliberate kind. These developments are characterized by the absence of any clearly established centre and of any stable, centrally established message. Indeed, this is a model which appears to be more successful at explaining how unplanned diffusion occurs than at offering a strategy for planned dissemination. Schon believes it has potential value for curriculum change but this must be questionable, since it is a model which appears to offer no basis for the development of any specific message (Stenhouse 1975).

Havelock's analysis of dissemination strategies can be seen as an attempt to take us beyond the notion that these must always assume a one-way, centre-to-periphery process. His Research, Development and Diffusion (R, D & D) model has many affinities with Schon's basic centre–periphery approach. For it assumes a developer who identifies the problem and a receiver who is essentially a passive recipient of the innovation developed to resolve that problem. It is a 'target system' and is regarded as the model to be adopted when large-scale curriculum change is the aim. As the difficulties of the centre–periphery approach emerged, two further stages were added to this process – those of adoption and implementation. This again reflects the move towards the more deliberate planning of dissemination.

His Social Interaction (SI) model, however, places great stress on the social interaction between members of the adopting group. Again it is a form of the centre–periphery model; again it is a 'target system'; and again the needs of the consumer are determined by the central planner. But it recognizes that the key to the adoption of the innovation and thus to its successful dissemination is the social climate of the receiving body and that the question of success or failure will hinge on the channels of communication there. It thus represents, like Schon's Proliferation of Centres model, the beginnings of a shift of focus from the centre to the periphery.

It is with Havelock's third model, the Problem-Solving (PS) model, that this shift is completed. For the essence of this model is that the problem is identified by the consumer and the process of innovation is thus initiated also by him. The man on the periphery is thus himself active and involved from the beginning and the process is essentially one in which he recruits outside help. The relationship between the consumer and the external support agent is one of mutual collaboration rather than that of the receiver and the sender of a message; and the whole process is personalized to the point where it has to be recognized that this is not a model of mass dissemination, since the solution that is devised for the problem need not be seen as solving the problems of other consumers. In short, it might be fairly claimed that this is not a model of dissemination at all but rather that it is a model for school-based curriculum development which in turn has led to an idea which goes further still, namely for the establishment of 'change-agents' within the school.

It will be appreciated that there is a good deal of overlap between these schemes and models. It is not an oversimplification, however, if we suggest that the major division is between those which adopt a centre–periphery approach of central development and planned dissemination and those which encourage initiatives from the consumer and have led to the development of the notion of school-based curriculum development. The latter is a relatively new concept; the former was the strategy adopted by the early projects of the Schools Council and, as we suggested earlier, this has been a major factor in its failure to influence curriculum development as directly as it was once hoped it might. For there are some problems which it might be argued are endemic to this approach and which make it quite inadequate as a device for bringing about effective curriculum change.

It is worth noting that it was the intention of the Schools Council from its inception to provide support for teachers in the development of the curriculum by extending the range of choices and variety of materials open to them. It chose to do this initially, however, by establishing national projects in certain areas of the curriculum and adopting a centre–periphery model of curriculum development, hoping that the ideas for curriculum innovation that were developed centrally at the national level could be disseminated to the schools at the periphery and that each school could then be supported in its attempts to attend to its own developmental needs.

As we have seen, however, the inadequacies of this model have gradually become apparent. There is a wide gap between the ideas of a project held by its central planners and the realities of its implementation, if that is even the word, in the classroom by the teachers. The existence of this gap between policy and practice is viewed by Lawrence Stenhouse (1975) as the central problem of curriculum development and, indeed, of the advancement of education itself. Even when a project team sets out deliberately to support teachers in their own developments rather than to provide a teacher-proof blueprint (Shipman 1972), as was the case, for example, with the Humanities Curriculum Project, the Keele Integrated Studies Project and the Goldsmiths' College Interdisciplinary Enquiry Project, the same difficulties have been experienced. It has proved impossible to get across to teachers the concept of the project, the theoretical considerations underlying it, in such a way as to ensure that these were reflected in its practice. And so a gap emerges between the ideals and the realities, a gap that in some cases is so wide as to negate the project entirely, at least in terms of the conception of it by its planners.

In some cases, the teachers have taken the project's ideas and materials and 'cannibalized' them, using them for their own purposes rather than for those for which they were intended. In others, they have merely rejected the proposed change as not capable of being adapted to their existing work. In extreme cases, when an unwanted innovation has been foisted on them, they have even been known to sabotage it.

The main danger then becomes a possible loss of credibility for the project, a rejection of the principles behind it, if a malinformed or maladroit or even malignant implementation of it derived from lack of adequate understanding has led to disastrous practical consequences. That something has not worked leads too readily to the assumption that it cannot work, rather than to a consideration of the possibility that one has got it wrong. This has been especially apparent in the reaction of some secondary schools to the results of ill-thought-out attempts to introduce mixed-ability groupings.

Such a situation is clearly unsatisfactory since it means at one level that the sums of money spent on central curriculum development are not producing anything like adequate returns and at a further level that they can be positively counterproductive, in so far as failures of this kind can lead to an entrenching of traditional positions.

This kind of reaction, however, is easy to understand, once one acknowledges that schools are living organisms and must be helped to grow and develop from within rather than having 'foreign bodies' attached to them from without, like barnacles attaching themselves to a ship's bottom. This kind of attempt at transplantation must lead in almost every case to 'tissue rejection' (Hoyle 1969b) and that has been the experience of all such attempts at the dissemination of innovation.

Hence recent years have witnessed a good deal of attention given to the problems of the dissemination of curriculum innovation. In some cases this has led to little more than a determination to explore ways of promoting projects more positively, through improved in-service provision or closer involvement of the project team in the development of the work within the schools (Schools Council 1974b; MacDonald and Walker 1976), in other words, by the adoption of some form of Proliferation of Centres model, as we saw earlier. Others, however, have begun to identify some of the reasons for this failure of dissemination and to suggest that the model itself is wrong and that attention needs to be given to the development of alternative models.

Various hypotheses have been put forward to explain the inadequacies of the centre–periphery model of dissemination. One piece of research has indicated that even where a lot of positive effort has gone into promoting the dissemination of a project to the schools, barriers exist to its implementation in both the failure of teachers to perceive with clarity their new role and also the absence of conditions appropriate to their being able to acquire such a perception (Gross et al. 1971). 'Our analysis of the case study data led us to conclude that this condition could be primarily be attributed to five circumstances: (1) the teacher's lack of clarity about the innovation; (2) their lack of the kinds of skills and knowledge needed to conform to the new role model; (3) the unavailability of required instructional materials; (4) the incompatibility of organizational arrangements with the innovation; and (5) lack of staff motivation' (Gross et al. 1971, p. 122). The first four of these conditions, they claim, existed from the outset; the last emerged later. Nor would this seem surprising.

It has also been suggested that another major factor in the ineffectiveness of this approach to curriculum change is its failure to take proper account of social interaction theory (House 1974). House posits two kinds of social group, each of which has quite different characteristics. 'Rural' society is homogeneous and within it ideas are communicated by a kind of contagious diffusion brought about by personal contact between individuals of comparable social status. Innovations in this form of society are of a kind he calls 'household' innovations and are adopted by individuals. The only serious barrier to such diffusion is the distance between the individuals concerned. He suggests that the social interaction between teachers is of this kind and that innovations which teachers accept are, therefore, of the 'household' kind. 'Urban' society, on the other hand, is heterogeneous and the barriers created by differences of social status are the most significant since they inhibit social interaction. Innovations here are of a kind which he calls 'entrepreneurial' and these he associates with administrators rather than teachers.

Broadly speaking, then, the case he is arguing is that centre–periphery approaches to dissemination in education are using the wrong model of social interaction or 'personal contact'. They are attempts at imposing a highly depersonalized model and thus they reduce the level of personal contact, leaving the teacher as a largely passive recipient of the innovation. This, he claims, not only restricts the flow of the innovation but invites teachers to modify and adapt it to conform to the norms of their own group.

These have been recognized as valid criticisms of those early attempts at curriculum innovations, like some of those of the Schools Council, which did not plan their dissemination but rather hoped that their ideas, once propagated, would spread with the wind. In response to them, therefore, many devices have been introduced to improve the processes of dissemination by the deliberate planning of it. Most of these may be seen as indications of a move towards Schon's proliferation of centres. House himself recommends the creation of more incentives for local entrepreneurs, the leaders of Schon's secondary centres; he also wishes to increase the number of those participating in the exercise; and his major aim is 'to reduce political, social and organisational barriers to contact with the outside world' (MacDonald and Walker 1976, p. 20). In pursuit of much the same goals, the Schools Council has attempted to establish local development groups, to involve teachers' centres, to gain the support of local education authorities, to promote the in-service education of teachers, to mount regional conferences and even, in some cases, to involve members of the project teams in the work of the schools, as change agents working in secondary centres (Schools Council 1967, 1971c).

In spite of all such developments and the use of all these detailed strategies for planned dissemination, major difficulties have continued to exist. Some of these have been identified by those concerned with the dissemination of the Humanities Curriculum Project. For here it was possible for the problems of dissemination to be considered most carefully in advance and detailed strategies for dissemination developed (Rudduck 1976). In particular, failure to achieve adequate dissemination was attributed to difficulties in communication between the project team and the schools (MacDonald and Rudduck 1971). It would be a mistake, however, to interpret that statement at too simple a level. For a number of features of this failure of communication have also been identified. One of these is the tendency of teachers 'to invest the development team with the kind of authority which can atrophy independence of judgement in individual school settings' (MacDonald and Rudduck 1971, p. 149). The converse of this was also observed, namely the anxiety of some teachers not to lose their own style by accepting too readily the specifications of method included in the project. Both of these factors would seem to point to the need for a full and proper involvement of the teachers with the development of the project. Both of them too draw attention to the significance of House's insistence on a proper regard being paid to the different forms of social interaction.

This draws attention to the importance of the manner in which innovations are introduced. It will be clear that if an innovation is the have a chance of 'taking' in a school, it will be necessary for more to be done than the mere provision of resources and in-service support for teachers. Teachers will need to become committed to it, an ideological change will need to be promoted, if they are to be expected willingly to adapt their methods and approaches to meet the demands of the new work. This offers a far more subtle problem. It is here that the manner in which the proposed change is made becomes important. For if it is imposed by the headteacher, for example, or by powerful pressure from outside, the dictation involved will be counterproductive and will promote opposition and hostility in teachers rather than support. As we suggested earlier, not only will teachers in such circumstances not work to promote the change planned; they will quite often deliberately and actively sabotage the efforts of others.

It will be remembered that the attitudes of staff were one of the major constraints on curriculum change that the early work of the Schools Council drew attention to. When this point was made, it was asserted that 'innovation cannot succeed unless the majority of staff are, at worst, neutral; but it was clearly important to have a majority positively inclined to curricular change' (Schools Council 1971c, p. 15). That report went on to say that 'one solution suggested was that innovation should begin by attempting to solve existing dissatisfactions' (ibid.). This suggestion clearly points to the desirability of shifting the focus from the centre to the periphery and of adopting a model more akin to Havelock's Problem-Solving model. In fact, it would appear to suggest that artificial dissemination by donor is not as good as the real thing.

Support for this view is to be found elsewhere too. For it has further been suggested that this problem goes beyond a mere failure of communication or of the strategies employed to introduce the innovation and is in fact the result of the different views and definitions of a curriculum project that we have already suggested are taken by different bodies of people involved in it (Shipman 1972, 1973). The question must then be asked whose definition is to be seen as valid. To speak of dissemination or implementation, of the barriers to implementation created by schools and teachers, or of the need to improve the teachers' understanding of the theoretical considerations underlying a project is to make the assumption that it is the planner's view and definition that is to be accepted as valid. For this reason, it has been suggested that 'the process of curriculum dissemination, in so far as it assumes a stable message, does not occur. The process to which the term "dissemination" is conventionally applied would be more accurately described by the term "curriculum negotiation" ' (MacDonald and Walker 1976, p. 43). In other words, having recognized that a gap exists between the ideals of the planners and the realities of the work of the teacher in the classroom, we should be concerned to close it by attempting not only to bring the latter nearer to the former but also by seeking to bring each closer to the other. To see the need to do this is to recognize that curriculum development is essentially a matter of local development, that it requires a form of 'household' innovation, and thus that it has to be school-based.

.This leads us finally to the question of the conditions which are most favourable to the implementation of change within a school.

We have mentioned several times how crucial it is that a curriculum innovation should ' "take" with the school and become fully institutionalised' (Hoyle 1969b, p. 230). It has further been suggested that whether this is likely to happen or not will depend on the organizational health of the institution, since only a healthy institution can readily absorb a new development. As Eric Hoyle goes on to say, 'the central problem facing the curriculum development movement is the avoidance of tissue rejection whereby an innovation does not "take" with a school because the social system of the school is unable to absorb it into its normal functioning' (Hoyle 1969b, p. 231).

But what criteria are we to use to define a healthy institution? We face immediately the kinds of difficulty that surround concepts of mental health, namely those that arise from the values that must be implicit in any definition we offer. On the other hand, although much more work needs to be done in this area, there are some indications of what factors are relevant to the question of a school's ability to digest satisfactorily a curriculum innovation.

The style of the headteacher is clearly crucial, since the organizational structure he creates within the school will be of great significance to the reaction of teachers to proposed curriculum change (Halpin 1966, 1967; Hoyle 1969b). The degree to which a school is 'open' is also very important (Halpin 1966, 1967; Bernstein 1967; Hoyle 1969b). The more open a school is the more likely it is to be able to absorb innovation. For an 'open' school will offer teachers a greater degree of freedom and autonomy and will encourage a higher level of collaboration between them. They are thus more likely to have the confidence that change requires and to have been involved themselves in the processes of change. As we have mentioned several times, no kind of change will 'take' if it is not accepted by the teacher at the coal-face. In the last resort, therefore, his motivation is paramount and this is most likely to be high if he feels himself to be completely involved and, indeed, in control of events.

In more detail, the investigation into the 38 schools that were involved in the Schools Council's Integrated Studies Project based at Keele led to the following rather tentative suggestions as to the main characteristics of a school that is ready for innovation. 'The salient points are that the school which is likely to introduce and implement successfully a planned innovation would:

- have teachers who would feed back information to the project
- have teachers who would accumulate supplementary material
- have teachers who had volunteered knowing that they would be involved in a lot of work
- reorganise its timetable to provide planning time for teachers involved in innovation
- have a headteacher who supported the innovation but did not insist on being personally involved
- have a low staff turnover among key personnel
- be free of any immediate need to reorganise as part of a changing local school situation.'

(Shipman 1973, p. 53.)

To this list one might add also a further point that emerged from an exploration of the difficulties of dissemination associated with the Humanities Curriculum Project. 'It seems that an experiment settles well in a school where teachers are confronting a problem and contemplating action. The experiment should extend the range of their strategies for dealing with the problem' (MacDonald and Rudduck 1971, pp. 150–151). If the teachers are aware of a need, then, and the climate of the school gives them the confidence and support to experiment with possible solutions to that need, a project has a far better chance of succeeding.

These, then, are some of the characteristics of the school as a social system that will help to decide whether it is ready for curriculum innovation or not. There are besides, of course, a good many considerations of a more practical kind relating to the geography of the school, the availability of appropriate resources and such like. In the last resort, however, it is the social climate that will be crucial and it is on this that we must concentrate if we wish to develop strategies of curriculum change within the school.

This constitutes a further argument in favour of school-based curriculum development. For it is clear that, if the social climate of the school is to be supportive of innovation, if, to change the metaphor, the organizational health of the school is to be such as to ensure that there will not be the kind of tissue rejection we spoke of earlier, it will be necessary for the initiatives to come from within, for the process to be one of growth and development rather than of transplantation. In short, attention is again directed towards the idea of school-based development.

School-based curriculum development

It is the relative failure of external attempts at the dissemination of innovation, then, that has led to the emergence of the idea of school-based curriculum development. There is, therefore, a real sense in which this must be seen not as a form of dissemination so much as an alternative to it, although it need not be regarded as precluding the possibility that other kinds of curriculum change might be attempted at the same time. We have just noted that the failure of descending modes of dissemination is in part due to the need for the social and organizational climate of the school to be such as to create the conditions for any planned innovation to 'take' in the school, and that this realization, by shifting the focus of attention from the innovation to the school, from the seed to the soil in which it is to be planted, suggests that the process must be considered first from the other end and the initiative sought in the school rather than outside it.

There are several major principles which are reflected in this notion of school-based curriculum development. In the first place, it is based on the beliefs that the curriculum consists of experiences and that these should be developed from the learner's needs and characteristics (Skilbeck 1976), so that it represents a commitment to the view that educational provision must be individualized. It thus reflects a major change of focus from that of the move towards planned curriculum development in the early 1960s. For, as we saw, that was prompted by a concern for the needs of society. Secondly, it acknowledges that a large measure of freedom for both teacher and learner is a necessary condition for education of this kind (Skilbeck 1976). Thirdly, it views the school as a human social institution which must be responsive to its own environment (Skilbeck 1976), and which must, therefore, be permitted to develop in its own way to fit that environment. Lastly, then, it regards it as vital to this development that the individual teacher, or at least the staff of any individual school, should accept a research and development role in respect of the curriculum (Stenhouse 1975), modifying, adapting and developing it to suit the needs of individual pupils and a particular environment.

This philosophy, then, has provided the basis for the positive arguments which have been offered in support of this shift of emphasis. Malcolm Skilbeck, for example, argues that school-based curriculum development 'provides more scope for the continuous adaptation of curriculum to individual pupil needs than do other forms of curriculum development' (Skilbeck 1976, pp. 93–94). Other systems are 'by their nature ill-fitted to respond to individual differences in either pupils or teachers. Yet these differences . . . are of crucial importance in learning. . . . At the very least, schools need greatly increased scope and incentive for adapting, modifying, extending and otherwise reordering externally developed curricula than is now commonly the case. Curriculum development related to individual differences must be a continuous process and it is only the school or school networks that can provide scope for this' (Skilbeck 1976, p. 94).

Such an approach will, of course, lead to great diversity and elsewhere Malcolm Skilbeck argues that curriculum diversity is essential if all pupils are to be given a meaningful educative experience (Skilbeck 1973). This is a point we have returned to many times throughout this book, the need for teachers to be able to devise programmes of work tailored to what they can recognize as the requirements of their own individual pupils. If education is to be meaningful to all pupils and if all are to have truly educative experiences, then it is only by allowing for this local development at the level of the school that this is likely to be achieved, so that we must accept the diversity of provision it entails. In any case, it will not be at the level of educational principles that this diversity is likely to occur but at the level of content where, as we argued earlier, at least if we concern ourselves only with educational considerations, it is of less significance.

For these reasons, then, there is a growing conviction that the only satisfactory curriculum development is likely to be school-based curriculum development and we must now consider what this entails.

We must begin by noting that, to meet some of the problems this approach creates, some schools have recently made senior appointments of teachers with special responsibility for coordinating and guiding curriculum – curriculum coordinators or curriculum development officers, change-agents within the school. This is a practice which has much to recommend it. It is a step towards achieving that kind of coordinated development across the curriculum which we said in Chapter 1 was often lacking, especially in secondary schools where the tradition has been for development to go on within individual subjects in isolation from each other. It also ensures that there is one person in the school who can be expected to attempt to organize support from outside agencies for any group of teachers engaged in any particular innovative activity. Such a person can also act as a focus for curriculum study groups in the school, an innovation which is essential if teachers are to be made fully aware of what is entailed in school-based curriculum development.

It is obviously crucial for the success of the school-based approach to curriculum development that this kind of appointment be made and that some teachers be enabled and assisted to acquire the expertise needed to take up these roles. For the difficulties which face the holders of such posts have already begun to emerge (Lee 1977; Purcell 1981). Their task makes it necessary for them to encroach on the preserves of other colleagues' subjects and classrooms, and often this is resented. Furthermore, this encroachment often has to be undertaken with a view to getting these colleagues to change their ways, by adopting new syllabuses or approaches to teaching, by collaborating with others or even by accepting a reduced share of the timetable. They also need to be able to back up their requests for such changes and modifications by promises of adequate financial support, and this cannot always be assured. It is already clear what a difficult and even thankless task this can be, but it is also becoming equally clear that it is a task that has to be done if school-based curriculum development is to be made to work. More teachers must be given proper opportunities to prepare to undertake this kind of task.

However, if we have been right to identify the teacher in the classroom as the hub of all this activity and the person whose role is quite fundamental and crucial, the most important need will be for adequate support for him. It is clear that what we are describing involves a major change in the teacher's role and there must be corresponding changes in the organization and even the staffing of schools if he is to have the time and the ability to respond to this.

It becomes increasingly important too for his initial course of training to have prepared him to take this central role in curriculum development. It becomes even more important, however, that he be given adequate opportunities for continuing in-service education to enable him to obtain any new skills that the innovations require of him and a developing insight into the wider issues of education, a deep understanding of which is vital for any kind of adequate planning, research or development.

This is why major curriculum changes such as the introduction of mixed-ability groupings in secondary schools have worked most smoothly and effectively when, as in the West Riding of Yorkshire under Sir Alec Clegg's guidance, suitable in-service courses have been made available on demand and tailored not to the advisory staff's ideas of what is needed but to what the teachers themselves ask for (Kelly 1975). It is for the same reason that where national projects have developed training courses for teachers wishing to make use of the project materials, teachers who have had this training achieve more success than those who have not (Elliott and Adelman 1973).

In short, there can be no curriculum development without teacher development and the more teachers are to be given responsibility for curriculum development the more important it becomes that they be given all possible support of this kind. The potential of the role of the professional tutor as the focal point of this kind of teacher development, linking initial and in-service teacher education and developing contacts between the school and colleges and other institutions responsible for these courses has so far not been fully appreciated but it offers opportunities that may be crucial to school-based curriculum development (Kelly A.V. 1973; Lee 1977). Staff development and curriculum development must be closely linked, and it is very important that teachers be put in touch with any outside agency that can provide them with the resources, the skills or the understanding they need if they are to take responsibility for developing the curriculum.

Another aspect of this kind of support for teachers is that with which the Ford Teaching Project has concerned itself. As part of the help teachers need with innovation they need assistance with the monitoring of what they are doing in the classroom. We shall examine in the next chapter the attempts of the Ford Teaching Project to support teachers in developing the skills needed to make reasonably objective appraisals of their own work, to engage in 'research-based teaching'. Without some kind of evaluation any curriculum innovation becomes meaningless and probably also impossible. If teachers are to take responsibility for curriculum development they need to be able to monitor their own work in this way in order to provide themselves with appropriate data for continued curriculum development. We shall see, therefore, in Chapter 6, the emerging notion of a process model of evaluation, of evaluation as action research. One of the main purposes of the Ford Teaching Project was 'to help teachers by fostering an action-research orientation towards classroom problems' (Elliott and Adelman 1973, p. 10). This is offered as an alternative to the model of action research in which researchers from outside come into the classroom and work with the teacher. It is felt that this kind of relationship erodes the teacher's autonomy and that if this is to be protected he must be enabled to take responsibility for his own action research as part of his responsibility for his own curriculum development (Elliott and Adelman 1973). This the Ford Teaching Project has attempted to encourage.

What about the curriculum developer, then? Is there a place for a professional curriculum developer if curriculum development is to be school-based? It is still not clear what role there is for the outside expert. This was a second-order action research project for the Ford Teaching Project team. At the same time as helping teachers to develop the ability to engage in their own 'research-based teaching', they wanted also to explore how best this kind of teaching can be assisted from outside.

The logic of the Ford Teaching Project's approach would seem to be that, once teachers have acquired a research-based teaching orientation as part of their basic weaponry, the need for outside support will disappear, so that perhaps the role of the curriculum developer is to be seen as provisional only, his services being needed only until such times as teachers themselves have acquired his skills.

Two questions, however, must be asked before we too readily accept such a view. In the first place, we must ask how far the average teacher is likely to be able to develop the abilities this will require of him. Apart from the problem of adding yet another chore to his already heavy task, we shall see in Chapter 6 that it has not been easy for the Ford Teaching Project team to develop in teachers the detachment and the security of confidence necessary to be able to make reasonably objective appraisals of their work, although the team did express optimism on this point.

Secondly, however, we must also ask whether there will not always be a need for someone to come from the outside to take a detached view of what is being done and to suggest possible alternatives. Few of us cannot profit from this kind of second opinion. Perhaps this is to be seen as a function of teachers from other schools as part of the process of moderation that should be an essential element in all assessment procedures. But there may also continue to be a need for someone acting as a professional consultant, a role that members of the advisory services should perform. It is interesting to note that these were the two main features of the work of the Goldsmiths' College Curriculum Laboratory from its inception. It brought teachers together not for in-service courses but to give them the opportunity to share problems and solutions with each other. At the same time it provided them with opportunities for consultation with experts in whatever fields they decided were relevant and useful to them. Subsequently too it attempted to provide schools with consultancy facilities.

Again, it is already clear that the idea of school-based curriculum development, as well as generating the change agent within the school, has also given birth to various forms of 'curriculum support team' (Ball 1981). In fact, we have already seen the emergence of two quite different models of such curriculum development, the one relying on initiatives and support from within, the other responding to such from outside. We noted earlier that the provision of such support has become a major focus for the work of the newly reconstituted Schools Council and it is also the case that some local authorities have created their own curriculum support groups.

It is also becoming clear that the role of such support groups is not always an easy one (Ball 1981). To some extent they exist to respond to and support changes initiated within a school and this is not in itself necessarily a difficult task. Their main function, however, certainly at local authority level, is to prompt changes in schools which do not initiate these of them-selves and this is obviously a much more difficult and sensitive task, one which can make that of the internal change agent appear by comparison a pleasant sinecure.

We examined earlier in this chapter the conditions which appear to be most conducive to curriculum development within a school, the factors which contribute to its organizational health. It has been argued (Shipman 1973) that if a school possesses all those characteristics there is hardly any point in getting it to change. Certainly, it would seem that change in such a school can be left to internal processes. However, for those schools which do not enjoy these advantages, strategies must be developed for bringing about both the qualities that will make curriculum development possible for them and that curriculum development itself. In short, it is necessary to go beyond Havelock's Problem-Solving model of change by identifying the problem for the consumer when he appears to be unable to recognize it for himself. In cases of this kind the external curriculum developer or support team has a major role to play and it is clear that it is an unenviable one.

There is also some evidence, albeit at present of a somewhat tentative kind, that one of the most effective ways of meeting this problem may be to provide teachers with opportunities for visiting each other's schools, sharing mutual problems and discussing possible solutions. It may, therefore, be the case that here again teachers need to be given opportunities to support and help each other rather than being offered such help from outside. At the present time, however, it is apparent that some of them need outside help too.

Perhaps there is still a role then for the wandering expert in curriculum development. If there is, and only subsequent research and continuing experience will answer that question for us, it is likely that that role will be to provide teachers with expert advice and the detached appraisal they cannot provide themselves and not to arrive hawking his own pet project, cobbled together in a place somewhat removed from the realities of any particular group of classrooms. His job will be to follow and serve the teachers rather than to lead them into his own new pastures. He can only support curriculum development; he will no longer attempt to direct it.

The question of whether there is a proper role for the external curriculum developer, however, is so closely linked to that of the role of the external curriculum evaluator that we must delay any further discussion of it until we have considered more fully in our next chapter the wider questions of curriculum evaluation. It also, of course, raises important political questions about the control of the curriculum which we shall also take up in subsequent chapters.

Summary and conclusions

This chapter has attempted to explore some of the issues that are raised by questions about how the curriculum changes and especially how it can be changed.

We began by looking at the work of the Schools Council as a major national agency within the United Kingdom for curriculum development. An attempt was made to trace the development of its work and some of its major characteristics and the conclusion reached was that, although its indirect influence on curriculum change through its contribution to the continuing curriculum debate has probably been very great, its direct effect on the school curriculum has been disappointing.

A major reason for this would appear to be the problems that have been encountered in the dissemination of curriculum innovation. Discussion of the major models of dissemination which have been identified suggested that there may be certain problems endemic to any centre–periphery approach and that the models that seemed to offer most hope of success are those whose attention is focused on the schools themselves and which, therefore, perhaps are not models of dissemination as such at all.

One reason why this kind of approach appears to be more successful is that it takes full account of the organizational health of the school and recognizes that this is the most crucial consideration in the planning of curriculum change. It thus points again to the idea that effective curriculum development can only be based on initiatives that come from within the school, that if curriculum innovation is to be curriculum development in the full sense it must be school-based.

The chapter turned finally, then, to an examination of some of the advantages, disadvantages and problems of this device for changing the curriculum, concentrating in particular on the demands it makes on the expertise and skill of teachers and the question of the appropriate kind of outside assistance they need to meet these demands.

Towards the end of this discussion it began to emerge that the ability of teachers to promote the development of the curriculum is clearly dependent on their ability to evaluate its effectiveness and that here again the question of what kind of external help they need is crucial. Curriculum development and curriculum evaluation are integrally linked together; the role of the teacher in the one cannot be properly debated except in association with the issue of his role in the other; the possible role of the external agent in the one is also clearly bound up with the role such a person might play in the other.

A discussion of curriculum evaluation, then, cannot be delayed any longer.

CHAPTER 6

CURRICULUM EVALUATION

It was suggested at the conclusion of the last chapter that a major feature of recent attempts at the planned dissemination of curriculum innovations has been the development of a range of techniques for the evaluation of these innovations. These attempts to measure the effectiveness and, in some cases, the desirability of such innovations have led to the emergence of a further, involved and complex area of study within Curriculum Theory. This development also has important implications for the evaluation of the work of individual teachers, since some kind of evaluation should be undertaken not only of major innovations but also of individual projects and even single lessons. Both the micro and the macro aspects of this issue must be borne in mind, then, as we turn in this chapter to an outline of the major features of recent developments in evaluation theory.

It is certainly the case that many major curriculum innovations have not been accompanied by any attempt at evaluation. This was true of the many projects that were introduced both in Britain and in the USA in the late 1950s and early 1960s when public money was made available for curriculum development on a broader scale than had hitherto been possible. It seemed to be felt at that time that any curriculum change must be for the better. However, experience of later developments, particularly that which began to emerge as teachers in diverse school situations began to make many different uses of the projects and materials the developers presented them with, led to a gradual realization that evaluation had to be seen as an integral part of any curriculum *development*, so that in Britain arrangements for proper evaluation were made an essential requirement of all projects by such funding bodies as the Schools Council and every subsequent project had its own full-time evaluator (Hamilton 1976).

This process has more recently received another kind of support. For economic stringency has encouraged people to look even more closely at innovations that might prove expensive in order to ensure that they are fully justified. Furthermore, several events, such as those at the William Tyndale School, have raised a concern over standards of achievement by pupils and have led to public demand that teachers and other educationists should be made more clearly accountable to society for their decisions concerning the content and methods of their work. We shall look more closely at this issue of accountability in Chapter 8. It is enough to note here that it implies a closer monitoring of the work of the schools, particularly in the area of curriculum development, thereby increasing the felt need to evaluate the curriculum.

Whatever the value of a central organization for the monitoring and evaluation of the work of the schools, it is difficult to argue against the notion that particular innovations need to be evaluated and that we need to assess very carefully the results of any change that we introduce. In fact, it is to make a purely logical point to say that the recognition of a need for change implies an awareness of inadequacies in existent practices and thus of the need for some basis upon which both those practices and the innovations which may be introduced to replace them can be evaluated.

However, the sheer rapidity with which we have reached this awareness has created several kinds of difficulty for both the theory and the practice of curriculum evaluation. For the recent rapid increase in the activities of evaluators in many different areas of the curriculum has led to the emergence of many new and different views of the nature and purposes of curriculum evaluation. Recent years have seen the appearance of a great diversity of curriculum projects and, therefore, a corresponding diversity of evaluation procedures (Schools Council 1973; Tawney 1975; Hamilton 1976). The field we are about to enter, then, is a confused and complex one.

A possible source of such confusion may be avoided if we begin by noting that curriculum evaluation must be distinguished from the assessment of individual pupils. For, although both may involve similar procedures, such as the gathering of evidence concerning changes of pupil behaviour or the extent of pupil learning that has resulted from any particular planned programme of experiences, the uses to which such data may be put and the purposes for which they are collected are quite different in the two cases. The crucial element in curriculum evaluation is that the data are gathered in order to provide a basis upon which decisions can be made about the curriculum and/or perhaps certain resultant and concomitant administrative changes, and not as diagnostic evidence for the making of decisions about any aspect of the work of individual pupils. If we make this distinction at the outset we may avoid one major kind of confusion into which several discussions of this issue have fallen.

However, there is no easy way of avoiding the comparable confusions which can arise from the fact that there is a variety of purposes that one can have in making an evaluation of anything and the range of different conceptions one can have of such an activity, each of which may be perfectly suitable for some area of curriculum development. What might we be doing in evaluating a curriculum project? We might be doing no more than attempting to establish that the curriculum innovation is in fact happening, since we have already commented several times on the gap that often exists between the plans of the curriculum developer and the practice of the teachers supposedly implementing that curriculum project. Or we might merely be attempting to ascertain if we have achieved what we set out to achieve. On the other hand, we might be endeavouring to compare a particular project with other alternative methods, procedures or programmes in the same area. Is it really better than what it has replaced or than other new alternatives that are offered? Again, we might be concerned to do no more than to ascertain if it is acceptable to teachers and/or pupils (Schools Council 1974a). Then again, we might be attempting to assess whether we have got our goals or our principles right.

Every one of these has been the main focus of the evaluation of at least one project and quite often several or all of them are built into the procedures adopted for the evaluation of any particular project. It is not possible, therefore, to provide a single useful definition of curriculum evaluation. It must vary according to the area of the curriculum we are dealing with, the curriculum model we have chosen and the purposes we have in mind when we set up our evaluation procedures. Such definitions of evaluation as are offered beg all or most of these questions, in so far as they represent a commitment to one or more particular views of evaluation (Harris 1963; Cronbach 1963; Wiley 1970; Stenhouse 1975). Furthermore, the term 'evaluation' can describe many processes and can have many meanings; we can have many different aims in view when we set out to evaluate a curriculum, as we have just seen, and we can employ many different techniques in doing so; it can also be conducted by many different categories of people, some of whom will be concerned with its administrative function, others with its educational implications (Taba 1962).

We must note too that the questions to be asked in any process of evaluation are of at least two logically discrete kinds (White 1971). Some of them are empirical questions which, like the investigations of a body such as the Consumers' Association, explore the relative merits of a project in terms of its costs, its effectiveness and so on. For questions of this kind we are looking, therefore, for relevant empirical data. Other questions, however, are asked in the process of evaluating a curriculum which are not of this kind but raise those difficult issues of value that we can never get far from in any discussion of education. These are the questions about ends rather than means, which ask whether the purposes of the activity are the right purposes, whether the experience being offered to pupils is of educational value, whether the curriculum is good in itself rather than merely effective in achieving its ends. Here the concern is to evaluate the goals or the underlying principles of the curriculum itself and not merely the effectiveness of its procedures.

In short, the purposes of any scheme of evaluation will vary according to the purposes, views, conceptions of the person or persons making the evaluation. We noted, when discussing the problems of dissemination in the last chapter, that the conception of any curriculum project will vary according to the angle from which one views it, whether as planner, teacher, pupil, parent or whoever. Each will have his own conception or definition of the project (Shipman 1972, 1973). For the same reason, each will have his own view of the purposes of evaluation and his own interpretation of the data which it produces.

Thus the selection of which information to collect, the range of purposes one may have in collecting it, the variety of uses to which it may be put and the range of the decisions it may lead to, make of evaluation 'a multi-faceted phenomenon encompassing a range of diverse properties' (Hamilton 1976, p. 11).

Again, therefore, it will be helpful to avoid a tight definition of a kind that is likely to inhibit the further development of understanding in this area. The most sensible approach to adopt would seem to be to begin by considering several forms of curriculum evaluation or to consider some of the different dimensions of curriculum evaluation that people have identified.

Forms of evaluation

It might be helpful first of all to note some general categories of evaluation. It is useful, for example, to distinguish in-course and post-course evaluation, those procedures that are designed to assess the work of the project as it proceeds and perhaps also to provide immediate feedback and those which are intended to be employed when the project is completed in order to assess its overall effectiveness. Another way of expressing this distinction, where the in-course procedures are intended to be used for continuous ongoing modifications, is to contrast 'formative' and 'summative' evaluation (Scriven 1967).

'Summative' evaluation is concerned with appraisal of the work, it is a form of 'pay-off' evaluation (Scriven 1967) and is concerned primarily to ascertain if the goals of the course have been achieved. 'Formative' evaluation, on the other hand, is concerned to provide feedback (Scriven 1967; Stenhouse 1975) and thus a base for course improvement, modification and future planning. As such, it may occur post-course, but it is more likely to take the form of continuous in-course monitoring of both goals or principles and procedures. It will, therefore, involve a number of dimensions, since it will be attempting both to assess the extent of the achievement of the purposes of the project and to discover and analyse barriers to their achievement (Stenhouse 1975). It may also be concerned to contribute to a modification of those purposes themselves, in short, to ask the 'value' questions we mentioned earlier.

Again we note that the variables are so many that this is a very difficult area to chart effectively. Several attempts have been made, however, to list the different possible types of curriculum evaluation. Thus Wynne Harlen, for example, has listed four types of evaluation 'which seem to have different purposes and functions in the main, though they overlap considerably' (Harlen 1971, pp. 128–129). First, 'evaluating the suitability of the objectives of an educational programme', in other words attempting to assess whether the objectives are worth trying to achieve and preferable to 'other possible and perhaps competing sets of objectives'. Secondly, 'on-going evaluation'; this is the 'formative' evaluation we have already referred to and 'has as its chief function helping the production of the educational programme once its objectives have been accepted'. Thirdly, 'evaluation of individual readiness and progress', which can be used by teachers themselves for such purposes as 'to diagnose their children's ability to benefit from certain experience, to gauge their progress, to locate their difficulties, and so on'. And fourthly, 'terminal or summative evaluation', the most important function of which is 'to find out whether the final product does, as a whole, achieve what it set out to do, whether it does this any better than other possible materials or approaches and how extended is any effect it may have' (ibid.).

It is important to stress again that these divisions are largely conceptual, since several or all of them are likely to be involved in any one set of evaluation procedures in practice. Nor are they, therefore, to be seen as alternatives; each is likely to have its place at some stage in the development of any programme, according to the purposes of the planners (Harlen 1971). It is also worth noting here that the type of evaluation used will be closely tied to the curriculum planning model that has been adopted (Tawney 1973), as has become clear in the methods adopted by a number of varied Schools Council projects.

We must also acknowledge that a great deal of what has been said about evaluation both up to this point in this chapter and in other writings on the subject has tended to take for granted some kind of objectives model for curriculum planning and we must spend some time considering how far the prespecification of objectives is an essential prerequisite for the evaluation of a curriculum.

Evaluation and the prespecification of objectives

Early discussion of curriculum evaluation certainly tended to be fixed well within the context of the simple behavioural objectives model of the curriculum. Ralph Tyler, for example, is quite explicit on this point. 'The process of evaluation is essentially the process of determining to what extent the educational objectives are actually being realized by the program of curriculum and instruction' (Tyler 1949, pp. 105–106). And again, 'it is absolutely essential that they [the behavioural objectives] be defined in order to make an evaluation since unless there is some clear conception of the sort of behaviour implied by the objectives, one has no way of telling what kind of behaviour to look for in the students in order to see to what degree these objectives are being realized. This means that the process of evaluation may force persons who have not previously clarified their objectives to a further process of clarification. Definition of objectives, then, is an important step in evaluation' (op. cit., p. 111).

A good deal of more recent discussion has also followed a similar line. The prespecification of objectives is made an explicit precondition for all the four types of evaluation listed by Wynne Harlen. The first activity that is involved in all of them, we are told, is 'clarifying objectives and analysing them to the point of expressing them in terms of behaviour changes' (Harlen 1971, p. 129). Nor is this surprising since she is writing from her experience of evaluating the Schools Council's Science 5–13 Project which, as we saw in Chapter 4, attempted to remain very firmly rooted in a classical objectives model. The evaluator, as a member of the project team, helped the team to clarify its behavioural objectives (Harlen 1971, 1973) which were published in detail for the use of the teachers who were to use the project materials and implement the programme in their schools. The actual task of evaluation was then restricted to determining how far the teachers' guides that were produced enabled teachers to achieve these objectives and how they might be modified to increase their efficiency.

A good deal of both the theory and the practice of curriculum evaluation, therefore, has been set well within the context of an objectives-based curriculum model, and for this reason evaluation has been seen as centrally concerned to help with the framing and subsequent modification of objectives, the assessment of the suitability of the learning experiences to the achievement of the objectives set and the measurement of the degree to which the prestated objectives are being or have been attained. The need for proper accountability to which we have already referred also tends to encourage the use of this kind of model and it is relatively easy too with such a model to see the point and purpose of evaluation.

On the other hand, it is equally easy to recognize the dangers that lie in this kind of approach. For it is possible, and perhaps likely, that the kinds of evaluative procedure available will tend to govern or determine the choice of objectives, content or methods rather than merely to offer additional information to those selecting them on other grounds. We are all familiar with the teacher's everlasting complaint that the public examination syllabuses are the strongest determinants of the curriculum and the greatest inhibitors of curriculum change. Furthermore, we have already discussed at great length in Chapter 4 the difficulties and dangers that exist for curriculum planners in the view that all curriculum planning must start from a pre-specification of objectives.

Thus, although there may seem to be a *prima facie* case for the prespecification of objectives if adequate procedures of evaluation are to be found, we must pause to ask whether evaluation becomes quite impossible if we are not prepared to start with a statement of objectives and, if it does not, what differences does this necessitate in our methods of evaluation?

It might perhaps be worth beginning by dispelling the illusion that may have been created by what has been said so far that evaluation is an easy and straightforward matter when we work from a clear statement of objectives. For even here we face a number of difficulties, some of which derive from the unsuitability of this approach to certain areas of curriculum planning, which we have already examined extensively in Chapter 4.

We have already referred to the temptation this approach offers to settle for those objectives whose achievement can easily be measured. The converse of this is the inability of current techniques of evaluation and assessment to measure the more sophisticated objectives teachers and educators adopt, especially in the affective domain (Kratwohl et al. 1964). As Schools Council Working Paper 26 tells us in discussing 'Education through the Use of Materials', 'a problem arises in assessing teaching that seeks to attain such objectives as "the development of desirable personality traits and attitudes" ' (Schools Council 1969a, p. 11). In other words, there exists a wide discrepancy between the scope of most sets of objectives and the scope of evaluation (Taba 1962) which will lead to inadequacies either in evaluation or in our specification of the objectives themselves.

Inadequacy of the available techniques of evaluation leads to further difficulties. At one level it can lead to conflict between the objectives made explicit by the project and those implicit in the evaluative techniques used (Taba 1962). Thus, no matter how far, for example, a project stresses its concern to develop pupils' understanding in a certain area of the curriculum, teachers will emphasize memorization and regurgitation of factual material if the main thrust of the evaluation procedures is towards this and better grades are obtained by those pupils who can reproduce learnt, but not necessarily assimilated, material most readily and in largest quantity. What is worse is that these procedures are often taken as indicators of the extent to which the real objectives of the programme have been attained so that a facility at reproducing scientific facts, for example, becomes confused with or is taken as evidence of the ability to think scientifically (Taba 1962).

On the other hand, if we succeed in avoiding this situation and make the somewhat inadequate techniques we have do a reasonable job of helping us to evaluate the more sophisticated objectives we may set ourselves, a good deal of interpretation of the data our evaluation procedures produce is still needed (Taba 1962). We need to measure against each other such things as memorization and understanding, knowledge and interest, achievement and social or educational background, learning and psychological stages of intellectual and physical growth. The data our evaluation techniques produce, therefore, need to be interpreted against a broad backcloth and related to information from other sources and of other kinds, especially that coming from philosophical, psychological and sociological research. This is far from being a straightforward matter, so that even when objectives are clearly prespecified evaluation is not easy.

Furthermore, a proper evaluation requires a proper level of understanding of the process that is being evaluated (Stenhouse 1975). A simple assessment of the attainment of objectives is concerned only with the success or failure of the programme; it is not concerned essentially with an understanding of it. It assesses without explaining (Stenhouse 1975). Thus the value of such evaluation is limited, since it can offer little feedback, if indeed it offers any at all, upon which the objectives or the procedures can be modified, so that it may well fail to do the very job it is designed to do. It is seldom helpful to know in black-and-white terms whether a project has succeeded or not. In fact, it will seldom be possible to make that kind of simple assessment. What is needed is a far greater complexity of data which can provide a basis for present and future curriculum development. This in turn implies the generation of evaluation procedures which do more than attempt to measure success or failure and which, in order to offer more, must be based upon a full understanding of the educational process itself.

Lastly, we must note that if we are dealing with an approach to education or a project for which the prespecification of objectives is deemed inappropriate, any evaluation based on such a model will be equally inappropriate, will add to the confusion and may have quite disastrous consequences (Weiss and Rein 1969). One of those consequences we have already referred to several times, namely the tendency to modify the project to meet the assessment procedures being used. We noted in Chapter 4 that many teachers, especially in primary schools, have felt that an objectives model is unsuited to their work. We saw too that some project teams have begun their planning from the belief that, at least for some areas of the curriculum such as the humanities or social education, an objectives model is not suitable. Any attempt, therefore, to evaluate the work of such teachers or such projects in terms of what are thought to be their objectives must fail either by providing inadequate, unsatisfactory and irrelevant data or by persuading teachers to alter their approach to the work in such a way as to change its whole conception and scope.

On the other hand, to attempt no evaluation can be equally disastrous. This is well illustrated by the experience of those connected with the Goldsmiths' College development of Interdisciplinary Enquiry (IDE). Although a large number of schools were associated with this development and took it up with enthusiasm, no attempt was made to set up any formal scheme of evaluation. This was mainly due to the fact that no financial support was made available for what would have been an extremely expensive undertaking, although it was also in part a result of a conviction shared by most of the architects of the scheme that its value was self-evident. At all events, it was taken up or not taken up by schools and teachers according to their own private enthusiasms and convictions and it always lacked credibility in the eyes of its sternest critics, and especially those curriculum theorists who, quite rightly, felt it appropriate to ask for evidence of its effectiveness.

Hence others, who have been engaged in curriculum development for which they have felt the prespecification of objectives to be unsuited, have nevertheless recognized the necessity to design procedures by which it could be evaluated and have thus faced squarely the problems presented by the evaluation of a programme whose objectives cannot be stated in advance and whose evaluation procedures, therefore, must be based on a different, more sophisticated view of what the whole process of curriculum evaluation is. Certainly it would appear that a more sophisticated, developed view has begun to emerge from the work they have done.

Evaluation without prespecified objectives

The Schools Council's Integrated Studies Project which was set up at Keele University in 1968 had a brief which required it to consider a new way of organizing the curriculum rather than to measure the outcomes of pupils' learning in particular subjects, since its task was 'to examine the problems and possibilities of an integrated approach to humanities teaching in secondary schools' (Jenkins 1973, p. 70). Thus its concern was not to assess the extent to which certain purposes had been achieved but rather to evaluate the aims and purposes themselves of such an approach to the organization of the curriculum. To specify objectives at the beginning and to work on the production of materials designed to achieve those objectives was quite inappropriate.

The team, therefore, adopted a 'horizontal' curriculum model 'in which aims, learning experiences and material were developed concurrently' (Tawney 1973, p. 9). As a consequence of this, evaluation was seen not as a process for measuring the results of an experiment but as a device for continuously monitoring the project as it developed and constantly reviewing its aims, the packs of material that were produced and the practical problems that arose when it was introduced into schools. A major technique that was used was that of participant observation (Tawney 1973) and what emerged was not so much objective scientific data as a growing collection of experience and understanding of the issues and problems involved, which offered teachers, therefore, not a curriculum package as such, but a set of principles and a body of knowledge to which they could refer and from which they might profit in developing their own schemes.

The most interesting project from the point of view of evaluation procedures, however, is the Humanities Curriculum Project, to which we have already referred on several occasions. We saw in Chapter 4 that this project has eschewed the idea of the prespecification of objectives more vigorously and more completely than any other. Being concerned to encourage pupils of secondary age to explore areas within the humanities and through discussion of all kinds to reach their own conclusions, the project team saw from the outset that to prespecify learning outcomes would be to contradict their own first principle and to beg the very questions they wanted to raise.

However, 'in an approach which is not based on objectives, there is no ready-made niche for the evaluator' (MacDonald 1973, p. 82). Furthermore, the team also felt it inappropriate to evaluate a curriculum project during its trial period so that, although Barry MacDonald, the project's evaluator – or Schools' Study Officer as he was significantly called – was appointed during the developmental stage of the project, his job was to prepare evaluation procedures for use after the project was firmly established in schools.

Both of these factors combined to present a particularly difficult set of problems in evaluation (Stenhouse 1975), difficulties which were acknowledged but which nevertheless were regarded as being there to be overcome. 'The evaluation then had to cope with an attempt at creative curriculum development with variable components, obvious disturbance potential and a novel approach' (MacDonald 1973, p. 83).

To meet these difficulties, Barry MacDonald adopted a 'holistic' approach. 'The aim of that stage [i.e. during the trial period] was simply to describe the work of the project in a form that would make it accessible to public and professional judgement' (MacDonald 1973, p. 83). It was not possible to define in advance what data would be significant, so that all data had initially to be accepted. 'In view of the potential significance of so many aspects of the project, a complete description of its experience was needed initially, as was awareness of a full range of relevant phenomena' (ibid.). Selection within and between such data could only be made later when the criteria of such selection began to emerge from the continuing experience. 'Evaluation design, strategies and methods would evolve in response to the project's impact on the educational system and the types of evaluation problems which that impact would throw up' (ibid.).

In this spirit the work of the 36 schools which experimented with the project was monitored, all possible techniques being used to collect a wide variety of data. Then attention was narrowed to eight schools which became the subjects of detailed case studies. The procedure appears to have been entirely justified since this method resulted in the acquisition of data and a recognition of phenomena that would never have been expected or envisaged in advance of the project's arrival in the classroom (MacDonald 1973).

Furthermore, there also emerged from this holistic approach a number of principles of significance for curriculum planning as a whole rather than merely for the evaluation of this particular project, principles which reflect in an interesting way some of the general points that have recently been made about curriculum development.

For example, it emerged very clearly that what actually happens when a project is put into practice varies considerably according to the local conditions prevailing in each school, whereas more simple evaluation procedures have tended to assume that there is or should be very little variation between schools. It also became apparent that curriculum innovations have many unexpected results, many unintended outcomes, and that again these are not allowed for in simple evaluation procedures. Furthermore, the variations in the reaction of different schools led to the conclusion that the judgements of the teachers in them are crucially important, every bit as important as those of the project designers, in the making of decisions concerning the curriculum of any individual school. It also became obvious that a gap often yawned between the conception of a project held by its developers and that held by those implementing it in the school. 'We have seen the Project used as a political resource in an existing power struggle, as a way of increasing the effectiveness of a custodial pattern of pupil control, and as a means of enhancing the image of institutions which covet the wrappings, but not the merchandise of innovation' (MacDonald 1971, p. 166; Stenhouse 1975, p. 111).

What was learnt from these processes of evaluation was seen, then, not as contributing to some statement of the project's effectiveness but as providing information for 'consumers', those who have the responsibility of making the decisions concerning the curriculum. Four main groups of these were identified – sponsors, local authorities, schools and examining boards – and the task of evaluation was seen as to provide them with the kind of understanding of the problems of curriculum development that will help them to make their decisions (MacDonald 1973).

The same general approach has been adopted by those who have proposed the notions of evaluation as 'portrayal' (Stake 1972) and as 'illumination' (Parlett and Hamilton 1975). Portrayal evaluation is seen as an attempt not to analyse the results of a project in terms of its prespecified goals but to offer a comprehensive portrayal of the programme which will view it as a whole and endeavour to reveal its total substance.

Similarly, the primary concern of illuminative evaluation is 'with description and interpretation rather than measurement and prediction' (Parlett and Hamilton 1975, p. 88). Such an approach to evaluation has three stages: 'investigators observe, inquire further and then seek to explain' (op. cit., p. 92). As a result of this threefold procedure an 'information profile' is put together which is then available for those who need to make decisions about the project. 'Illuminative evaluation thus concentrates on the information-gathering rather than the decision-making component of evaluation. The task is to provide a comprehensive understanding of the complex reality (or realities) surrounding the project: in short, to "illuminate". In his report, therefore, the evaluator aims to sharpen discussion, disentangle complexities, isolate the significant from the trivial, and raise the level of sophistication of debate' (op. cit., p. 99).

In similar style, the objectives of the evaluation unit of the Humanities Curriculum Project were defined as:

a)   to ascertain the effects of the project, document the circumstances in which they occurred, and present this information in a form which would help educational decision-makers to evaluate the likely consequences of adopting the programme;

b)   to describe the existing situation and operations of the schools being studied so that decision-makers could understand more fully what it was they were trying to change;

c)   to describe the work of the project team in terms which would help the sponsors and planners of such ventures to weigh the value of this form of investment, and to determine more precisely the framework of support, guidance and control which were appropriate;

d)   to make a contribution to evaluation theory by articulating problems clearly, recording experiences and, perhaps most important, publicising errors;

e)   to contribute to the understanding of the problems of curriculum innovation generally.

(MacDonald 1973, p. 88)

It is perhaps these last two points, and especially the last one of all, that are most interesting and draw our attention to the full significance of the developments in evaluation procedures consequent on the adoption of a non-objectives curriculum model. For what seems to be emerging as a result of the work of projects of this kind is a new and more sophisticated model of curriculum evaluation – a process model – which does not content itself with measuring the results of one project in simple and often consequentially unhelpful terms but sets out to provide continuous feedback to all of those concerned with the planning and implementation of this particular project and of curriculum development generally. Its concern is to disclose the meaning of the curriculum as much as to assess its worth (Stenhouse 1975), and, in order to do this, it attempts to document 'a broad spectrum of phenomena, judgements and responses' (Hamilton 1976, p. 38). In some situations this will be done to help the planners to modify their objectives and other features of the project in the light of developing experience; in other circumstances it will be concerned to guide the continuing development of a non-objectives curriculum. Furthermore, the aim will be to do this not only in relation to one particular project but to offer illumination for curriculum development as a whole. The holistic approach to curriculum evaluation implies that we do not restrict ourselves to a narrow canvas, in any sense.

Thus curriculum evaluation becomes part of curriculum research. In general, all evaluation procedures see all curriculum planning and approaches as hypotheses to be tested (Taba 1962), but the holistic view sees evaluation as part of a continuous programme of research and development, and recognizes that the curriculum is a dynamic and continuously evolving entity. It thus encourages the adoption of a more sophisticated model not only of curriculum evaluation but also of curriculum planning and one which may be more suited to the notion of education as a process whose ends cannot be seen beyond itself.

Not only is it possible, then, to make an evaluation of a non-objectives curriculum; it also seems to lead to a more fully developed view of the role of evaluation in curriculum development. The procedural principles which we suggested in Chapter 4 provided a better basis for an educational activity than prespecified objectives can and should be monitored, and this monitoring will give us continuous feedback in our efforts constantly to modify and improve our practices. Again, as we also saw in Chapter 4, such a model reflects much more accurately than a simple means–end model what happens in practice when we make an evaluation of any educational activity. For we are seldom content merely to measure outcomes and, when we do, we experience uneasy feelings that we have somehow missed the educational point of the activity. The simple linear model of curriculum evaluation, therefore, may exist only in the minds of theorists.

One final point needs to be made about this approach to curriculum evaluation. We have seen that its concern is not to make decisions but rather to provide information for decision makers. It is thus a highly suitable form of evaluation for school-based curriculum development and equally for the evaluation, and self-evaluation, of the work of individual teachers. In fact, the emergence of these more sophisticated techniques of evaluation has itself contributed much to that shift towards school-based development which we noted in Chapter 5. However, as we also noted there, this is a trend which raises important political questions concerning the control of the curriculum and its decision-making processes. The major thrust of 'process' forms of evaluation is identical with that of school-based forms of curriculum development, since its direction is away from forms of external control and evaluation towards the view that the teachers themselves must have a central involvement in both processes. It thus raises important questions about who should conduct the evaluation procedures and it is to these that we now turn.

The evaluator

The decision as to who should evaluate any particular piece of work or curriculum innovation would seem *prima facie* to hinge on what are considered to be the main purposes of the evaluation process. If we are attempting to obtain data for administrative purposes than one kind of solution to the problem will seem appropriate; if, on the other hand, we are concerned to promote the continued development of the curriculum or to learn something about the problems of curriculum innovation itself as, for example, was the concern of those evaluating the Keele Integrated Studies Project (Shipman 1972), then another answer will be preferred; if we are intending to compare the effects of a project with those of other projects in the same field, a third scheme will be suitable, and so on.

However, we have already noted that our purposes are seldom as clear-cut as this would suggest and in most cases we will be looking to our evaluative procedures for answers to a number of different questions. Furthermore, we have also noted the difficulties which must arise from the fact that different people will have different perceptions and conceptions of any project (Shipman 1972), so that each will emphasize different purposes, look for different kinds of data and make different interpretations of the evidence obtained. In short, we must face the fact that to achieve any kind of objective evaluation of a project will be far from straightforward, whatever the official view of its purposes is.

Clearly, objectivity in evaluation is highly desirable but there are many barriers to its achievement which we should be aware of. At one level, we would expect those people who have been closely involved in a project as administrators or planners or as teachers to have a commitment of some kind to it that is likely to make any kind of objective appraisal very difficult for them. However, as we have just suggested, the problem goes deeper than this, for all of those connected with a project will hold different definitions of it and different views of its nature. As a result, they will conceive the project differently, making different assumptions about its goals and purposes. They will also perceive things differently, since clearly our perceptions are affected by the values we hold; we see what we are looking for. Furthermore, the view an individual takes of the project will itself change continuously as his experience of the work grows.

Such differing views will be held even when the objectives of a piece of work are clearly defined and stated, since there will be ample scope for individual preferences and differences of rank order within and between these objectives, as well as different interpretations of their significance. The problem will be compounded, however, when we attempt to achieve objectivity in our evaluation of a 'process' curriculum, when it is the explicit intention that conceptions of the work and interpretations of it should change as it proceeds and develops.

What we are facing here in the context of curriculum evaluation is the more general problem we referred to briefly in Chapter 2 of whether objectivity is possible in any sphere, since the perceptions and interpretations of each individual are highly personal. Must we accept total subjectivity, as the phenomenologists suggest, or can we reach a definition of objectivity that is worthwhile?

Difficulties arise, as we saw in Chapter 2, when we see the search for objectivity as the pursuit of absolute certain knowledge of a God-given kind. Such knowledge we have already proposed is impossible in any sphere. We have suggested that a more realistic view of knowledge is that which sees it as a system of interrelated hypotheses, each of which fits the evidence we have but is also subject to amendment or rejection in the face of new evidence. The essential ingredients of objectivity are that we recognize the need for evidence, that this evidence should be public and that it should be considered with as much impartiality as is possible.

In short, it may be better to think not so much in terms of achieving objectivity in some absolute sense as of avoiding the most extreme forms of subjectivity and dogmatism that derive from views that are totally idiosyncratic or blindly prejudiced (Hamlyn 1972). This we can best do by recognizing the need to communicate our views, values and interpretations to others, to produce evidence in support of our claims and to be prepared to discuss them with others who may perceive or interpret things differently in as impartial and open a manner as we can achieve. Objectivity comes from recognizing the need to give reasons for our judgements and thus to open them up to rational discussion and debate.

Who should evaluate a curriculum project in order to achieve this kind of objectivity? Again *prima facie* it would seem that we might get closest to it by arranging for external evaluation. This is certainly the feeling of those who advocate the monitoring of standards of achievement in schools by such people as local or government inspectors, and it is also the principle that underlies systems of public examinations. How appropriate is it to the evaluation of a curriculum itself as opposed to the performance of individual pupils engaged on it?

The main difficulty with such an approach to evaluation would seem to stem from the fact we have referred to on several occasions that all curriculum projects are highly complex entities with an intricate interlinking of theoretical and practical elements of a kind that it is unlikely anyone could understand from the outside. External evaluation of this kind therefore would almost certainly lead to an oversimplification which would do violence to the project itself. It is unlikely, for example, that it could go much beyond the assessment of the levels of attainment of individual pupils and we have already referred to the backlash effects of that on curriculum development through systems of public examinations.

To avoid this oversimplification and to achieve the breadth of understanding necessary to make a useful evaluation of the wider aspects of a project, such an outside person would need to get inside the project, to become a specialist evaluator. It is for this reason that in most cases evaluators have been appointed as members of project teams. The point at which the evaluator joins the team varies. In some cases, as with the Science 5–13 Project, he or she has been appointed at the beginning to be involved from the outset in the framing of objectives, purposes or principles (Tawney 1973). In other cases, such as the Cambridge School Classics Project, the evaluator has joined the team at a later stage when much of the groundwork has been completed (Tawney 1973). Whatever the relative merits of these alternatives, they both recognize the need for the evaluator to become involved in the overall planning in order that he should be able to achieve an understanding of the complexities of the project, whether his job is merely to assess its outcomes or to contribute through his skills as an evaluator to the ongoing development of the scheme. In other words, whatever view is taken of the purposes of evaluation and whatever model is adopted, it is recognized that it is desirable and necessary for the evaluator to join the project team at some stage in order to become in a full sense a part of the project.

However, although this kind of practice will ensure that the evaluator has a view of the project that is as close as possible to that of the project team, he will remain, like the other members of that team, external to the schools in which it is being implemented. Furthermore we saw, when we considered the problems of the dissemination of innovation in Chapter 5, that there is always a large and important gap between the conceptions of the planners and the realities of the teacher's work. The teacher's perspective is also, therefore, important and we must examine his role in curriculum evaluation.

There is a further reason why it is important to consider the part that the teacher himself must play in evaluation and that is that much of his work is based on his own planning and not on that of a project team, so that, as we suggested at the beginning of this chapter, discussions of evaluation must concern themselves with the problems of evaluating the work of the individual teacher and not just of attempts at innovation of a large-scale kind.

First of all, then, attention must be drawn to the fact that the teacher is the person who possesses a good deal of the data the evaluator needs so that he or she must be seen as having an important contribution to make to evaluation at that level. Thus, for example, one of the techniques used in the evaluation of the Schools Council's Social Education Project was the recording of interviews with teachers who had worked with the programme. In this way, the teachers' views were canvassed on a range of issues:

1) What do you think of the Social Education Project as it affects the pupils?
2) Do you think they have been given too much or too little responsibility?
3) Has it had any effect on the community round about?
4) What has been the effect of the project on the staff of the school as a whole?
5) How much of the work is new?
6) How would you like the work to develop?
7) Should there be more opportunities for exchange of experiences with teachers in other schools engaged in similar work?
8) Has there been enough discussion and planning among teachers concerned within your own school?
9) How can the work be evaluated?
10) Is there anything you would like to add?

(Schools Council 1974a, pp. 52–53.)

In this way it was hoped that the experience of the teachers could be tapped to provide crucial data for evaluation.

In connection with this kind of process, Wynne Harlen makes an interesting additional point, that any techniques of evaluation that one uses should 'interfere as little as possible with . . . the activities which are going on', and should not be 'arduous or laborious for either children or teachers. It is most important that the evaluation does not interfere, does not reduce enthusiasm, is as unobtrusive as possible and, where it has to be obtrusive, at least enjoyable' (Harlen 1971, p. 132).

However, many have seen the role of the teacher in evaluation as going beyond being a mere provider of data. Again Wynne Harlen has summed this up in saying that 'teachers should be as thoroughly and genuinely involved in the evaluation as they are, or should be, with the development of the material' (op. cit., p. 133). They should not merely be asked to provide data, especially where this is mainly a form-filling exercise, but should be involved in continuous discussion of the questions being asked. The effects of this are two-way. For in the first place the teachers develop the kind of understanding of the problems of evaluation that will make them better at providing appropriate data and, secondly, the evaluators can gain insights that will lead to a better framing of questions. Teachers can and should also be involved in the testing and marking of children where this is included in the evaluation process. Full involvement of teachers in all aspects of the development of a curriculum project is crucial to maximizing its success. 'Improved attitudes of teachers towards evaluation will certainly follow from improved attitudes of evaluators towards teachers' (ibid.).

Serious barriers do exist, however, to the achievement by teachers of anything approaching an objective appraisal of what after all they are responsible for at the coal-face, as some of the work of the Ford Teaching Project has revealed. A key concern of this project was to get teachers to evaluate their own work, to engage in a kind of self-monitoring or self-evaluation process, and it was assumed that this implied the adoption by the teacher of an objective stance. However the whole idea of self-criticism and self-evaluation is threatening to many teachers; the organizational set-up in most schools does not help teachers to engage in this kind of self-appraisal; and many teachers find it difficult to discuss their problems with their colleagues (Elliott and Adelman 1974).

The experience of those engaged in the Ford Teaching Project, however, led them to be 'optimistic about the capacity of the majority of teachers for self-criticism' (Elliott and Adelman 1974, p. 23) and to assume that the barriers to objectivity in such cases are no more than practical difficulties which can be overcome. They also realized that subjectivity of evaluation can in any case be avoided by checking the accounts teachers give of their work by reference to other sources. Thus they developed a procedure they called 'multiple interview' or 'triangulation' in which accounts are obtained not only from the teacher but also from the pupils and an independent observer. There is reason to hope, therefore, that given the right sort of training, preparation and adequate safeguards, teachers should be able to play an increasingly important role in curriculum evaluation, and thus in curriculum development.

In general it does appear that evaluation, like curriculum development itself, is best attained when a variety of talents and points of view are brought to bear on it. Certainly one of the best ways to avoid the worst kind of subjectivity is to encourage a number of people to contribute to the evaluation processes from different points of view. It is probably the case that for a complex undertaking of this kind a skilled specialist evaluator is necessary, but it is equally necessary that all who are involved in the planning and execution of it, including the pupils, should be seen as having a point of view and, therefore, a contribution to make towards its evaluation. That contribution must go beyond merely providing data for the evaluator; it must entail full partnership in the process of evaluation itself.

This is another dimension of the holistic approach to evaluation that we have already discussed. Not only are all kinds of data grist to the evaluator's mill, but also all those involved in the process are to be seen as evaluators. We saw earlier that a holistic approach sees evaluation as an integral part of curriculum development; it represents a form of continuous action-research and feedback. If this is so, and if the desirability of school-based curriculum development is recognized, there is an important role for the teacher in curriculum evaluation as much as in any other aspect of curriculum development. For who needs this continuous feedback more than he does? Without it self-evaluation will be impossible and thus so will any real progress for the teacher and the project.

For self-evaluation is a vital part of the teacher's armoury of professional techniques. Indeed, it might be claimed that in all spheres of human activity improvement can only come from an awareness of one's own previous inadequacies. Such an awareness, however, does not always come from within and there is little doubt that it can and should be augmented and assisted by the observations of those who are in a position to view one's work from different perspectives.

Self-evaluation by teachers, then, is important for the continued development of their work, and the recent attempts by some local authorities in the United Kingdom to encourage teachers to try this kind of self-assessment is to be welcomed. It must be seen, however, as one of several approaches to the evaluation of the work of the school or the teacher, as a necessary but by no means a sufficient condition of effective evaluation. Comment and criticism from all relevant perspectives are needed and must be accepted if we are to ensure a proper coverage and even that limited form of objectivity we suggested earlier was all that is possible.

Lawrence Stenhouse, while largely approving of the general trend of such a development towards a 'democratic' style of evaluation, is concerned about the emergence of the professional evaluator as well as of the professional curriculum developer or at least about the separation of these two roles. He is concerned to promote integrated curriculum research and sees this kind of development as inimical to it. 'Evaluation should, as it were, lead development and be integrated with it. Then the conceptual distinction between development and evaluation is destroyed and the two merge as research' (Stenhouse 1975, p. 122).

The force of this case must be recognized, but several points need to be made in answer to it. In the first place, evaluation must provide continuous feedback into the development of the total curriculum and not only into the work of a particular project (Wilhelms 1971), a point which we saw earlier was one of Barry MacDonald's stated objectives of evaluation. For this reason it must be in the hands of a team that will include others besides the teachers and the planners or designers concerned with a particular project. What is required is essentially a team effort involving cooperation at all stages (Taba 1962).

It is necessary, however, to recognize a problem and perhaps a danger here. For in such a cooperative venture the teacher is likely always to be dependent on those who come from outside, since by definition they are bringing something into the situation that he cannot supply (Elliott and Adelman 1973). Thus the teacher's autonomy is at risk.

This problem may disappear, or at least lose some of its force, if we consider the possibilities of peer-evaluation, the use of fellow-professionals for the external evaluation of one's work. This is a system which has worked effectively for many years in higher education, where every course has its external examiner or examiners whose task it is not merely to check on the standards of the students' performances but to offer comments on the curriculum of the course in order to help in the continuing process of course improvement. Again, it is a device which some local authorities in the United Kingdom are currently exploring, by encouraging the exchange of teachers between schools and inviting the comments of each upon the work of the other. Clearly, this kind of scheme itself presents difficulties. For, just as many teachers find it difficult to take anything other than the most favourable view possible of their own work, so they often find it correspondingly easy to take the most unfavourable view of that of their colleagues, especially those in what might be regarded as 'rival' institutions. It is important, however, that the possibilities of this kind of device are fully explored, since the attainment of a proper level of professional evaluation is vital if evaluation is to promote curriculum development rather than inhibit it.

In fact, what is needed if we are to attain this form of evaluation is the inclusion of as many perspectives as we can obtain, including vitally that of the teacher himself, and this clearly leads us to a consideration of the political dimension of evaluation. For it suggests a particular stance on the issue of the control of the curriculum and points us towards the notion of 'democratic' as opposed to 'autocratic' or 'bureaucratic' evaluation (MacDonald 1975).

These distinctions are offered by Barry MacDonald from a recognition that evaluation is a political activity and the styles he describes represent several different ways in which that activity can be carried out. 'Bureaucratic evaluation is an unconditional service to those government agencies which have major control over the allocation of educational resources. The evaluator accepts the values of those who hold office, and offers information which will help to accomplish their policy objectives' (op. cit., p. 133). 'Autocratic evaluation is a conditional service to those government agencies which have major control over the allocation of educational resources. It offers external validation of policy in exchange for compliance with its recommendations' (ibid.).

'Democratic' evaluation, on the other hand, is defined as 'an information service to the community about the characteristics of an educational programme. It recognises value pluralism and seeks to represent a range of interests in its issue formulation. The basic value is an informed citizenry, and the evaluator acts as a broker in exchanges of information between differing groups . . . the evaluator has no concept of information misuse . . . The key concepts of democratic evaluation are "confidentiality", "negotiation" and "accessibility". The key justificatory concept is "the right to know" ' (op. cit., p. 134).

It will be clear that this is the only form of evaluation that will facilitate that kind of continuous adaptation at the level of the individual school and the individual teacher which this book is concerned to argue is the only route to the proper development of the curriculum. It will also be clear that it is a form of evaluation which requires the fullest participation of the teachers themselves.

It must be recognized, therefore, that what we are discussing here again entails a major change of role for the teacher and one that will make demands on his time that must be acknowledged and reflected in the planning, organization and staffing of schools.

Finally, if teachers are to play this kind of role in the evaluation of their own and/or of their colleagues' work, they need to acquire a range of new skills and to familiarize themselves with a number of techniques which they have hitherto had no need for. We must finally turn to a brief examination of some of the techniques which have been developed by those who have already undertaken the task of curriculum evaluation.

Techniques of evaluation

It is only comparatively recently that the complexities of evaluation processes have come to be recognized and as a result the need for a complex range of evaluation techniques. It is not long since the only technique used was the assessment of the progress of individual pupils so that evaluation was regarded as synonymous with assessment and even with examinations. Thus a good many books that purported to discuss evaluation offered little more than an analysis of assessment techniques.

Two things have happened to change this. In the first place, it has been realized that learning is a highly complex process and that we need a range of sophisticated techniques to measure it properly. Secondly, the complexities of curriculum development and evaluation in themselves have come to be recognized, as we have just seen, so that an awareness has grown that in order to begin to come close to an adequate form of evaluation procedure one must use a variety of techniques to collect relevant data across a wide spectrum.

Unfortunately, although the scope of education has changed and expanded rapidly in recent years, the development of techniques of evaluation has not really proceeded at the same pace. More recently, however, the growing awareness of the need to collect all kinds of data in order to evaluate a curriculum has led to the use of a wider variety of techniques, some of which we have referred to already in other contexts. These include assessments made by independent evaluators and the gathering of evidence of all kinds from teachers, pupils and any other people involved in the work. Thus the Schools Council's Social Education Project, to which we have already referred, lists among the techniques adopted and developed for part of its evaluation processes:

1) teacher interviews;
2) a list of pupils' responses to the concept of social education;
3) interviews with a small but random sample of parents;
4) a test of attitudes to school especially developed for the project;
5) a test of children's accuracy in self-perception and peer-perception;
6) evaluation of constructiveness of contributions to group discussion.

(Schools Council 1974a, p. 51.)

It is clear from this that progress is being made towards the generation of more sophisticated techniques of evaluation to measure the more complex dimensions of recent curriculum development. It will also be clear, perhaps, that the more sophisticated these techniques become the more necessary it will be for the teacher to have the aid of specialists in these techniques in evaluating the curriculum and basing decisions about future changes and innovations on the data they produce.

It is equally apparent, however, that the main focus of evaluation continues to be on the progress of the individual pupil, whether this be defined in terms of his increased knowledge and understanding or, as in the example given, in terms of the development of attitudes or skills of a different kind. The implications for curriculum development of systems of public examinations for the assessment of the progress of individual pupils we must take up in the next chapter where we shall consider several such external influences on curriculum development.

Summary and conclusions

This chapter set out to explore some of the problems of curriculum evaluation. We began by noting the variety of purposes that evaluation procedures may have and the range of possible interpretations of the data they produce. In particular, we stressed the need to maintain a clear distinction between the evaluation of the effectiveness of the programmes adopted to meet the stated aims or principles of any innovation and that of the appropriateness or continued relevance of those aims or principles themselves.

We then went on to suggest ways in which evaluation techniques might be used not only to avoid the worst kinds of inhibiting backlash on the curriculum but actually to promote and contribute to its continuing development. And we noted that those techniques which have developed from attempts to make evaluations without reference to clearly prespecified objectives have been especially helpful in generating the kind of sophisticated procedures which might support the development of the curriculum in this way.

It was argued too that this also necessitates a 'democratic' form of evaluation and that teachers themselves must be involved in the process, so that they can both gain the understanding and enjoy the freedom necessary for the promotion of the continued evolution of the curriculum. We recognized the problems that teachers face in evaluating their own work but noted several developments which suggest that they can be helped to acquire the ability to do this more effectively, both through self-evaluation and through peer-group evaluation. This problem, however, also led us to acknowledge that there continues to be a role for the external specialist evaluator and, indeed, that a proper evaluation will require that a good many perspectives on the teacher's work be obtained.

Several things have emerged as a by-product, as it were, of this discussion of evaluation, and especially of the role that agencies outside the school might have to play in it. One of these is the political dimension of evaluation, its implications for the control of the curriculum and its obvious links with the issue of teacher accountability. A second and related issue is the need to recognize the existence of a range of agencies whose influence on the curriculum may be less overt but is none the less important and significant for curriculum planning. In short, the discussion has led us to an awareness that education, and thus educational planning, have to be seen in their social and their political context.

CHAPTER 7

THE SOCIAL CONTEXT OF CURRICULUM DEVELOPMENT

Up to this point we have discussed curriculum development as though it goes on in a world populated only by teachers and other educationists. We have looked at many of the theoretical and practical difficulties of curriculum planning and the implementation of curriculum innovation, at the theoretical questions that lie behind curriculum planning and some of their practical consequences, as if the intentions of teachers and other curriculum developers were the only factors we need to take account of, as if they were entirely and solely in control of curriculum change.

Our discussion so far, then, has proceeded on the basis of two unwarranted assumptions. The first of these is that influences outside education are not important in affecting what is taught in schools and that curriculum development is entirely a matter of careful planning on the part of the professionals. Secondly, we have assumed that, so long as we take full account of the practical implications of the plans we make for the curriculum, as was suggested in Denis Lawton's model of curriculum planning which we mentioned in Chapter 1, there will be no significant gap between the theory and the practice of curriculum development, between the designing of curriculum programmes and their realization in practice. With these assumptions we have looked at several models of curriculum planning and we have considered some of the theoretical and practical difficulties that arise over the framing of purposes or principles, the choosing of appropriate content and the setting up of adequate procedures of evaluation.

We suggested in Chapter 1, however, that this was only one aspect of curriculum change and development and that there were many other factors at work that we must take full cognisance of. We have also hinted throughout that there is a very wide gap between what is planned and what actually happens, between the official and the actual curriculum, between the ideals and conceptions in the minds of the curriculum planners and the realities of the outcomes of these in the classroom.

We must now, therefore, give due consideration to these two important aspects of curriculum change by looking at the other pressures that are at work, the other influences, both direct and indirect, overt and covert, deliberate and incidental, that play their part in curriculum change and development. We will do this, firstly, by looking at some general sources of constraints both outside and within the school; secondly, by considering in particular the influence of the public examination system; and, finally, by exploring, in Chapter 8, the recent move in the United Kingdom towards more overt political influence on curriculum and towards a greater degree of centralized control.

Influences and constraints

Even in a country such as the United Kingdom, where legal constraints on the curriculum are almost non-existent, it is far from being the case that the control of the curriculum is the sole prerogative of headteachers. For, although the legal responsibility rests with the headteacher of each school, he or she can only exercise the freedom that that responsibility offers within a context of countless pressures, influences and constraints from both within and without the school, so that the most interesting feature of school curricula in the United Kingdom is that, despite the apparent freedom enjoyed in the past by individual schools, they vary extremely little, a fact which makes the recent demands for more centralized control over the curriculum, at least when couched in terms of subject content, appear rather superfluous. It would be difficult to find a school whose curriculum did not include most or all of what might be agreed as constituting such a central or essential core. In short, the headteacher, like all others, defines his role in relation to the expectations of other people who have significance for him and there are many such people and agencies for him to take account of.

We must now consider in detail some of the influences and constraints that affect decisions about the school curriculum.

We must first note the influence of history or tradition that we commented on in Chapter 1. Curriculum development is essentially a matter of changing a curriculum that already exists, and the demands of any entity to be left substantially untouched are always strong. Curriculum change is one aspect of social change so that it shares that tendency of all institutions to resist any attempts to do more than chip away at it and introduce relatively minor modifications.

In the case of curriculum change the reasons for this are not hard to find. Teachers and headteachers have been trained in certain ways, to teach certain subjects or by certain methods, so that there is a strong temptation for them not to want these changed to a degree which will require them to start again from scratch, to learn new techniques or to lose the security of working within a subject or a set of techniques with which they are at home and in which they are confident of their knowledge and ability. The same is true of those who leave the classroom and the school to join the ranks of the inspectorate or other advisory bodies. Too much change in the curriculum or in approaches to teaching and they will know less about what is going on and have less relevant experience than those they are supposed to inspect or advise.

This is one factor in the recent changes that have occurred in the role of the inspectorate and it is well illustrated by the plight of many inspectors and advisers in the face of the recent rapid move in many secondary schools in the United Kingdom towards mixed-ability groupings. This is also one reason why the emphasis in initial training courses for teachers has swung away from mere training towards education, towards developing the kind of professional awareness and understanding that will enable teachers to initiate and adapt to changes. It is also a feature of the current educational scene which makes it imperative that adequate provision be made for the continuing education and training of teachers through in-service courses of all kinds. Tradition, then, does exercise a great constraining influence on curriculum development.

There are a number of different ways in which one can categorize the other influences and constraints to which curriculum development is subject. All of these do, of course, interact with each other but sometimes they also conflict, since often they emanate from groups of people and bodies who view the schools and the curriculum from different perspectives, as parents, for example, or as employers, as teachers or as economists. Some of the confusion that can be discerned in debate about the curriculum, as in the current national debate in the United Kingdom about the common core curriculum, derives from the fact that the several contributors to such debate are approaching it from different standpoints (Warwick 1975). If we are to avoid such confusion ourselves, we must, therefore, distinguish these standpoints at the outset.

To begin with it is worth distinguishing administrative from professional factors (Maclure 1970). Both of these will be sources of influences and constraints on developments in schools and they are also likely to be in conflict with each other more often than not. In particular, financial restrictions will invariably constrain and inhibit professional ambitions for certain kinds of development, such as a reduction in the size of class, improved in-service provision or any other contribution to curriculum development that involves increased financial support. Equally, however, decisions made about the organization of schooling, such as the introduction of comprehensive schools or the raising of the school-leaving age, may conflict with, although they may also on occasion support, certain professional aspirations for curriculum development. It has been suggested that this very conflict of forces provides the right kind of basis for change, since it allows for the interaction of and the development of a balance between these two major influences acting on education and curriculum change (Maclure 1970). It is for this reason that both of these interests are represented on such formal agencies for curriculum change as the Schools Council.

We must also distinguish national from local influences and within the latter those that operate inside the school from those outside it. It may also be important to differentiate between the role of the teacher in curriculum development and that of the headteacher and to recognize that different factors will operate or at least the same factors will operate with different degrees of impact on each. It is this that will result in the gap between the official and the actual curriculum, the ideal and the real, the formal and the operational that we have already referred to several times.

Lastly, it is also likely to be the case that the factors we can identify will be differentially significant at different levels of schooling. The factors that are most influential at primary level are unlikely to be those that have the greatest effect on the curriculum of the secondary school. It is almost certainly the case, for example, that national factors are most in evidence at secondary level while the primary school is more susceptible to local influences.

In all of these cases too, we must remember that these influences are likely at many points to be in conflict with each other, to be pulling in different directions, so that the kind of curriculum change that actually occurs will be the result of these many competing and conflicting forces.

The influence exercised by central government on curriculum development is obviously much greater in those countries where, or at those times in history when, formal decisions about the curriculum are taken centrally or where and when adherence to strict standards is made a requirement for grant aid. Such influence is also very direct. In the United Kingdom this influence has gradually been eroded to the point where, as we shall see when we discuss this issue more fully later, there has recently been a number of moves towards the re-establishment of central control of this kind.

Even where such control is not direct, however, decisions about the organization of the educational system taken centrally will have implications for the curriculum. Again the most obvious example of this is the requirement of the British Government, made known in 1965, that all secondary education in the United Kingdom be organized on comprehensive lines. Such a decision cannot be implemented without far-reaching effects on curriculum development. Nor can a decision such as that to raise the minimum school-leaving age.

This draws our attention to other political influences on the curriculum of a more general kind. In those countries where there is a strong dominant political ideology, as is the case in most Communist countries, for example, that ideology will be reflected massively in the curriculum. In all countries, however, education is in the centre of the political arena, as will be apparent from the most cursory study of the development of education in the United Kingdom during the last fifty years or so. Furthermore, there are political pressure groups other than those associated with national political parties which are formed in order to promote certain kinds of educational reform or to influence educational development generally. Obvious among these are the teachers' unions and professional associations, but there are also bodies such as ACE, CASE and PRISE which have come into being as a result of the desire of groups of interested people to influence the development of education in certain directions (Jenkins and Shipman 1976).

Other bodies, organized for different purposes but having an additional and peripheral interest in education, also join in this national educational debate. The most obvious and influential of such bodies in the United Kingdom are the churches, whose contribution to the original establishment of public education was a great one, and who have, as a result, enjoyed a continuing influence on educational development since that time. Not only do the churches own and control schools and colleges themselves but they also exert a wider influence not least through their contribution to the training of teachers in the many colleges of education they have established, some of which they continue to be responsible for in spite of the recent spate of college mergers and closures.

The influence of a country's economy on the curriculum is also clearly very important. Indeed, to a large extent it is to economic events and factors that one must look for an explanation of the development of most systems of education. Clearly one of the functions of the school system is to produce the manpower a country needs and this is a factor that cannot be ignored in curriculum planning. It would appear, however, that this kind of consideration does not usually lead to demands for increased vocational training in schools. On the contrary, the history, for example, of technical education in the United Kingdom reveals quite clearly that there are no really strong demands for this kind of provision. Nor are the present demands for a core curriculum couched in terms of increased vocational training, in spite of the fact that the needs of a technological society loom very large in the arguments adduced in support of this development. The demand seems rather to be for a good general education, a good grounding in the three Rs (Jenkins and Shipman 1976).

There are at least two reasons for this. The first is that most employers prefer to train their employees themselves. In this way they can provide them with the precise kind of training they need and supervise it themselves. Secondly, there is a need in a rapidly developing technological society for a force of workers who can adapt to changing techniques and this, as we have had cause to notice before, demands that the products of the educational system be educated to think for themselves so that they can adjust to and develop with the evolving technology itself.

However, although these economic influences may not always lead to demands for direct forms of vocational training to be provided by schools, they do result in pressure on schools to emphasize in their curricula those subjects or areas of study that can be seen to have economic or industrial relevance. Thus the pressures on schools, even those catering for the younger child, to emphasize mathematics and science sometimes reach the point where, as in the speech given by James Callaghan as Prime Minister at Ruskin College in 1976, they are linked with overt criticisms of those schools which emphasize the humanities.

Such influences often take a more direct form through decisions taken concerning the allocation of resources, money, materials, equipment and staff, to schools. We have progressed some way from the system of 'payment by results' but economic factors of a similar kind continue to exercise this second form of influence on curriculum planning and development whenever resources are made available for developments in certain areas rather than in others. This is a factor which clearly looms very much larger in a context, like that which applies at present, of great financial stringency.

When we turn to a consideration of local influences on the curriculum, those that come most readily to mind are the influences on the schools exercised by those bodies and people responsible for the running of them. Where, as in the United Kingdom, ultimate responsibility for the financing and administration of schools rests with local government, a good deal of power would seem to reside with local government officers, although we must not forget that most of the money they have to spend on education comes from the central government in the form of a rate support grant.

How far this power extends to direct influence on or control of the curriculum, however, is another matter. Certainly it is the task of the advisory staff to contribute to curriculum development. Equally certainly, as we continually mention, decisions made by those who hold the purse strings will often have important consequences for the curriculum. In practice the balance between professional and administrative interests is most obvious at this local level, the local politicians and education officers working in parallel with the advisers, and the teachers influencing organizational decisions either through their unions or by direct membership of certain advisory bodies.

A good example of the importance of achieving the right kind of balance is to be found in the effects on the curriculum of schools of the recent reduction in the numbers of their pupils. For the way in which a local authority responds to falling roles will not merely influence but will in many cases determine the kind of curriculum a school can offer. Some authorities, for example, may encourage a concentration on a 'core' curriculum by giving priority to the staffing of subjects within this core (Davies 1980), while others may wish to permit schools to continue to offer a range of choices, even where this may necessitate an improvement in the staff – pupil ratio. It is in the face of problems of this kind that the nature of the balance between professional and administrative interests becomes crucial.

An attempt to achieve the same sort of balance can also be seen in the constitution of the governing bodies of individual educational institutions, where again political and professional interests meet. This has been especially true since the recent introduction to many governing bodies of teacher, parent and, sometimes, student members. Technically, these are the bodies responsible for the curriculum of the school. In practice, however, in the United Kingdom they have normally restricted their attentions to the general conduct of the school, leaving responsibility for the curriculum to the headteacher and thus to the school staff. Their power has been, therefore, somewhat limited in its effect but potentially it is great (Jenkins and Shipman 1976), and the addition of more parent, teacher and student members is beginning to unleash this potential force. Certainly, recent events, such as those at the William Tyndale School, which have led to attempts to tighten control over what the schools are doing, seem to be resulting also in a wider exercise of their powers by some governing bodies. Indeed, it was with the intention of promoting this kind of wider sphere of influence that the Taylor Committee (DES 1977a) made its recommendations on the membership of governing bodies. For in suggesting that they should become more truly representative of the community as a whole, the committee also recommended that such bodies should contribute more fully to policy making within the school and exercise a more direct influence on its curriculum.

A major feature of the changes proposed by the Taylor Committee was the increased involvement of parents in school government. In the United Kingdom parents have until recently had little scope for influencing what goes on in schools, in spite of their obvious concern for the standard and kind of education their offsprings are receiving. Parent–teacher associations have tended to operate at the social level only, and even when committees of parents have been organized by local authorities their influence has not been very great (Jenkins and Shipman 1976). In the USA, however, the influence of parents on the curriculum is strong (Jenkins and Shipman 1976); it may well be that now that they have direct access to the governing bodies of many schools in the United Kingdom their influence there will begin to increase. Certainly, if the potential power of the governing bodies is to be realized it is from this direction that the initial impetus is most likely to come.

It is this that gives interest to the proposals of the Taylor Committee, in the United Kingdom, to amend the constitution of governing bodies to make them more 'professional' by including a membership over half of which would be directly elected by parents and school staff, and by insisting that all governors, however elected, should be given a course of training which would include school administration, teaching methods, the curriculum and financial matters. Such a 'professional' governing body would then be given control of the school curriculum.

A development such as this would have the effect not only of giving the parents more 'say' in the affairs of the school and especially in curriculum matters, it would also perhaps put the kind of teeth into the governing body that might enable it to become a more effective factor in curriculum change. It is essential, however, that teachers also be involved at this level, since, as we saw in Chapter 5, in the last analysis they will decide what actually happens in the classroom. The suggestion that if governors are given this kind of control over the curriculum teachers should retain their professional responsibility for methods would seem to acknowledge this fact, but to try to separate the curriculum from the methods used to implement it in this way is to misunderstand totally the nature of the educational process. Teachers must either have autonomy in all aspects of the curriculum or they must be involved with others in all aspects of planning.

Whatever the relationship between teachers and their governing bodies, however, constraints on curriculum development and planning will also arise within the school itself and it is to a brief consideration of some of these that we now turn.

Constraints within the school

The constraints on the curriculum that operate within the school have been well documented by the Schools Council's research into Purpose, Power and Constraint in the Primary School Curriculum (Taylor et al. 1974), and they do to a large extent reflect a detailing of those practical considerations that, as we saw in Chapter 1, form an important element of Denis Lawton's model of curriculum planning.

The research team listed the constraints it regarded as important under three headings: 'Constraints imposed by the human element (personal)', 'Organizational and administrative constraints' and 'Physical constraints' (Taylor et al. 1974). Among the former it included such things as the level of enthusiasm of teachers and their willingness to give time to any project, the level of their initial training and the in-service training provision available to them, the level and quality of support services from cleaning staff, clerical staff and ancillary classroom help. Among the organizational constraints it listed the form of organization in the school, the style of discipline, the form of the timetable, the size of classes, the age of the pupils and their home backgrounds. Finally, it outlined the physical constraints as:

a) size and design of classrooms
b) level of provision of storage space
c) number of classrooms
d) specialist facilities e.g. music room, laboratory, etc.
e) form and style of school architecture.

(Taylor et al. 1974, p. 80).

Most teachers will readily recognize the significance of all of these factors in constraining any ambitions they may have for curriculum development. In addition we should also note how crucial is the availability of suitable resources of all kinds, including teachers with the appropriate skills and talents. There is no point in deciding on the idiosyncratic introduction of, say, Urdu into the curriculum if you have neither relevant resource materials nor a teacher with the necessary knowledge and expertise to teach it.

The curriculum of any given school, then, will be a product of all of these factors operating within the school and outside it at local and national level. The relative strengths of these influences and constraints will clearly vary according to each individual situation but the research project to which we have just referred did attempt to investigate, with interesting results, what teachers regard as being the most and the least influential of them in the primary school.

Among the most important points to emerge from this study were, firstly, the clear evidence that teachers – at least those who work in primary schools – see the in-school and other local influences as having far more bearing on what they do than anything that is done or said about education nationally, the government and the Secretary of State for Education and Science having little or no influence, especially when compared with the influence exercised by such factors as informal meetings of staff within the school. This bears out what has become apparent in other ways, namely the limited influence of most of the projects sponsored by bodies like the Schools Council (MacDonald and Walker 1976). In fact it is clear that when teachers set about curriculum change they do so from considerations of a very practical kind rather than as a result of detailed analysis of the theoretical issues involved (Taylor 1970) or of any national programme or guidelines they are offered. It may well be the case, however, that the increased interest in curriculum which has been evinced at national level during the last few years in the United Kingdom and which we will examine in some detail in Chapter 8, would lead to rather different results if an enquiry of this kind were to be mounted now.

The teacher will view the curriculum, however, from a different perspective from that of others concerned with curriculum development and will use the materials and ideas they produce to achieve his own ends rather than theirs. It is this characteristic of teachers that has contributed to the failure of most nationally developed curriculum projects to 'take' in the schools, and it is this which has led already to a good deal of modification in recent proposals for increased central control of the curriculum, as we shall see. Curriculum theory cannot ignore this.

A second interesting feature of curriculum development to emerge from this study is 'the confirmation that the school and the classroom are separate zones of influence; that the teacher has considerable *de facto* influence in the classroom, and not so much within the school, where the head, with his *de iure* power, has greatest influence' (Taylor et al. 1974, p. 64). The head is outstandingly the most influential factor in the school but the class teacher is regarded as more influential than the head when it comes to what goes on in individual classrooms.

Two further points arise from both of these findings. In the first place, it is clear where the gap is to be found that exists between the ideal and the real, the official and the actual, the formal and the operational curriculum, in other words between the theory and the practice of curriculum development. It will be equally clear, therefore, where effort and attention must be concentrated if this gap is to be closed. Secondly, it is also apparent that effective control of the real curriculum rests still with the teachers and we must recognize the role of the head and especially the classroom teacher in making all effective decisions about the curriculum. Teachers will do their own thing and no curriculum, no matter how carefully planned, will ever reach fruition unless the teachers are committed to it (Barker-Lunn 1970) and unless they understand its implications and the theoretical considerations underlying it. Again we must note the implications of this for a centralized curriculum.

However, one kind of influence on curriculum which teachers have always found difficult to resist and which, in fact, is an influence whose presence and whose force teachers have always recognized is that exerted by the public examination system. It is to an exploration of this that we now turn.

Public examinations and curriculum development

We have already suggested on several occasions that the limitations of the techniques available for evaluation may lead to limitations in the educational goals that teachers set for themselves and their pupils, that the temptation always exists to plan our curriculum according to the techniques of evaluation that are available. It is clear that this is most likely to occur in relation to the certification of individual pupils. Indeed, we have already also referred several times to the degree to which many teachers regard the public examination system as the chief inhibitor of curriculum change. Support for this view can also be found in the obvious backlash effects that the 11+ system of selection for secondary education had on the curriculum of the primary school.

This aspect of the public examination system has been recognized officially for many years. A good deal of evidence of this was offered to the Taunton Commission (1868) and we find it reiterated in similar evidence included in the Beloe Report (Secondary Schools Examinations Council 1960), which records that the committee was told by many people from many different areas of the education service that 'the examination dictates the curriculum and cannot do otherwise; it confines experiment, limits free choice of subject, hampers treatment of subjects, encourages wrong values in the classroom' (op. cit., p. 23, para. 77). It is clear too that this effect is as influential on the methods of teaching which teachers adopt as on the subject content of their work (Pudwell 1980), and that it is 'an influence which extends to age ranges well below the fourth and fifth secondary years' (DES 1981, p. 4).

We also suggested in the last chapter that the assessment of individual pupils remains the major source of data for evaluation, so that, while this continues to be so, the assessment techniques available to us will continue to be a major potential source of limitations on curriculum development. We must begin this discussion of the influences of public examinations on the curriculum, therefore, with a brief consideration of the examining techniques that are available for use, and some attempt to indicate ways in which this kind of assessment may be undertaken without unduly inhibiting curriculum development.

It is not the intention here to raise the interesting questions of how far and in what ways the assessment of individual pupils provides adequate data for evaluating the curriculum itself. Nor is it the intention to look in detail at the present structure of the public examination system in the United Kingdom or elsewhere or to examine the many proposals that are currently under discussion for substantial changes in that structure, fascinating though such a discussion might be. These we will refer to only in so far as they impinge upon or have relevance for our central concern.

That concern will be with the effects of systems of public examinations on curriculum development and the question of whether such effects need to be inhibiting. In other words, we shall consider the claim that curriculum development is inhibited by public examination systems, and we shall try to tease out what factors might be responsible for this and to explore ways in which the worst of these effects might be avoided, ways in which the system might be modified or features of the system that might be promoted in order to resolve some of the problems it creates for teachers and others concerned with curriculum development.

We should perhaps begin by making it clear that what is needed is to find some way in which continuous curriculum development and the demands of the public examination can be reconciled. It is clearly not acceptable, as some extremists seem to think, to abolish examination systems totally in order to free the curriculum from their pressures. What is needed is to devise an acceptable working relationship between the two. For a restricting influence on the curriculum is the *effect* rather than the *purpose* of the public examination system (Pudwell 1980). Its purposes are quite different and we ought not to lose sight of these in the process of considering one of its side-effects, no matter how important that is.

Public examination systems serve several essential purposes. Amongst other things, they contribute more than any other agency to the setting and maintaining of educational and academic standards; they provide incentives to the efforts of both teachers and pupils; they provide useful diagnostic feedback for both; and they fulfil an important administrative function in revealing the talents and abilities of individuals and acting as arbiters of their suitability for certain kinds of career or further educational experiences. The fact that a high degree of inefficiency becomes apparent when one considers the extent to which current procedures do fulfil these administrative functions, of which the errors of the 11 + (Yates and Pidgeon 1957) and the lack of predictive validity of current GCE 'A' level examinations in relation to subsequent achievements in higher education are perhaps the best available examples, should encourage us to look in more detail at the procedures themselves rather than to assume that the only solution is to scrap them altogether.

What is needed is a close consideration of public examination systems to ensure that they both provide those who need it with the right kind of accurate information about the achievements and perhaps also the potential of individual pupils and that they do this without placing undue limitations on curriculum development. 'Examinations must be designed and used to serve the educational process' (DES 1981, p. 4).

Both of these aspects of the problem require that we consider the public examination from two points of view; first of all, from the point of view of the techniques of assessment available to those conducting the examination and, secondly, from the point of view of the way in which the examination procedures are structured and the system organized and administered. For both of these dimensions of the system have been criticized as resulting in the production of the wrong kind of information about pupils while at the same time inhibiting curriculum change in the schools.

Techniques of assessment

It is often claimed that the techniques of assessment available to examiners are so relatively unsophisticated that they cannot properly measure any but the most simple of educational attainments, and that as a result they lead both to the production of unhelpful information for 'consumers' and to the generation of simple curricula and the adoption of simple curriculum models by teachers. The word most commonly used in association with public examinations is 'regurgitation' and the criticism is that the ability to regurgitate largely undigested material (a rather revolting but popular metaphor) is all that most examinations demand, so that their results indicate merely the degree to which pupils can do this – information which is not really very helpful to a potential employer or an institution of further or higher education. Also, this general feature of public examinations invites teachers to aim no higher in their courses than to get pupils to swallow large quantities of information in preparation for regurgitating it at the appropriate time and place. There is the further inference, if we can take this unpleasant metaphor to its equally unpleasant conclusion, that once this material has been regurgitated, then, like the contents of any undigested and regurgitated meal, it is gone for ever. Furthermore, the same is usually true of all taste and liking for that particular kind of sustenance. In this way, it is argued, the examination system inhibits not only the curriculum development but the development of anything that could be described as education.

At a deeper level, what is being argued is that the examination system cannot cope with more complex educational attainments, a point that we considered earlier in relation to evaluation procedures generally. Within the cognitive domain, for example, it is sometimes felt that it cannot measure the higher kinds of cognitive achievement, such as understanding and application, and thus contents itself with the lower levels, such as memorization and rote learning. If this is so, then it must follow that within the affective domain it hardly begins at all, so that teachers may be wasting their own and their pupils' time – in terms of examination results – if they devote too much attention to developing attitudes and feelings in their students towards the subject or material they are dealing with. The methods of assessment will thus decide the nature of the curriculum and how teachers and pupils view it and receive it (Wilhelms 1971).

This may be a caricature of the public examination system but, like all caricatures, it does emphasize a salient feature of its subject and we cannot dismiss this charge with too ready a complacency. Most of those who read this book will have reached a high level in the education system; few will have done so without achieving some of their 'qualifications' by methods not dissimilar to those we have just described. That such things happen is indisputable.

The real question, however, is whether this is how things must be. Can these effects be avoided? There is reason to believe that they can, and recent developments in examination procedures tend to encourage such a view. For the range of techniques used in assessment is gradually being extended and the manner in which each is used is becoming more sophisticated.

In addition to the written essay-type examination paper, which traditionally has been the most common device for assessing pupils' attainment, recent years have seen the arrival or increased use of such techniques as 'open-book' examinations, prior disclosure techniques, the objective test, oral examinations, practical tests, continuous assessment through the examination of course work of many kinds and the use of teacher assessments. This range of techniques increases enormously the scope of assessment procedures to measure a wide variety of achievements in both the cognitive and the affective domains, if we can make best use of it. It also increases the possibility of our being able to obtain accurate and useful data both about the curriculum itself and the performance of individual pupils.

It has also been realized that each of these techniques can be used more subtly to obtain more complex information. The essay-type written examination can test more than factual knowledge and memorization if we frame our questions suitably and even the objective test, whose *prima facie* role would seem to be to test factual knowledge, has been shown to be capable of measuring higher level cognitive attainments too (Vernon 1964). For example, knowledge that goes beyond the mere factual can be measured, as in questions such as the following:

In the view of John Ruskin, the greatest picture is:

a)   that which imitates best
b)   that which teaches us most
c)   that which exhibits the greatest power
d)   that which conveys the greatest number of the greatest ideas.

(Vernon 1964, p. 8.)

So too can comprehension be measured in an objective test, as in: 'Milton! thou shouldst be living at this hour: England hath need of thee; she is a fen of stagnant waters' – Wordsworth. The metaphor, 'she is a fen of stagnant waters', indicates that Wordsworth felt that England was,

a)   largely swampy land.
b)   in a state of turmoil and unrest.
c)   making no progress.
d)   in a generally corrupt condition.

(Vernon 1964, p. 8.)

Furthermore, similar questions can be devised to measure such higher level cognitive skills as application, analysis, synthesis and evaluation.

It would seem inappropriate, therefore, to assume that the examination system need tempt us into settling for simple objectives to our teaching. Both the range of techniques available and the uses that can be made of each of them offer scope for the development of more subtle instruments of examining than were once available to us.

Suspicion of the newer techniques still exists, however, at all levels of education. Teachers like to hold on to their myths as much as any body of people and the view that the written examination paper is the only source of really objective information about pupils dies very hard. Thus other techniques have been slow to achieve acceptance, especially in the more prestigious examinations. In the United Kingdom, for example, the use of course-work assessment procedures was built into the regulations governing the award of the Certificate of Secondary Education (CSE) examinations from their inception but has been very slow to achieve acceptance by the more prestigious and, perhaps, status-conscious General Certificate of Education (GCE) Boards. Indeed, the strange truth is that it has been accepted by the universities themselves for use in their own degree examinations more readily than by the schools examination boards they sponsor.

One reason for this is clearly a real concern people have about the possibilities of plagiarism and other forms of dishonesty in the production of work that is not written under complete supervision. The dangers of this should not be underestimated, although they are not insuperable and should not deter us from adopting a technique that has other manifest advantages.

The objections of some, however, go beyond this, since there are real doubts in the minds of some teachers and educationists about the validity of some of these new and alternative techniques of assessment. As a result, there is a reluctance to adopt some of these techniques because of a concern about their relative validity. It is interesting to note, therefore, that there is some evidence which suggests that the concurrent validity of some of these techniques, especially course-work assessment, is high (Connaughton 1969). In other words, in comparison with other methods of assessment used simultaneously, these techniques appear far more accurate than their critics seem to think.

There is reason to hope, therefore, that the development of increasingly sophisticated techniques for the assessment of pupils' progress, a development which recent years have seen make considerable advances, can result in our being able to establish procedures for public examinations which need not limit our curriculum ambitions and may at the same time provide potential employers and teachers in further and higher educational institutions with information about individuals more suited to their needs. We need to recognize the different functions of these techniques and develop the right combinations of them to provide us with the information we need and to measure all relevant aspects of the activities in which we engage our pupils. One simple truth to cling to is that it is unlikely that the use of only one kind of assessment technique can measure all that we should be concerned with in any educational activity. The use of combinations of techniques, on the other hand, ought to increase quite extensively our scope for the development of the kind of educational curricula we want.

The organization of public examinations

There remains, however, the problem of ensuring that the curriculum can develop continuously. This brings us naturally, therefore, to our second main point – the organization of the public examination systems themselves and especially the role of the individual teacher within them. It is one thing to say that, however complex our curriculum is, the examination system can assess the attainment of pupils within it; it is quite another to devise a system that allows not only for the generation of a complex curriculum but also for its continuing evolution and development. It is this feature of the examination system that has led many teachers to feel that it gives them no scope for change or development or the exercise of individual professional autonomy, even though it does seem essential that the examination system should reflect and follow from the curriculum rather than directing and leading curriculum development.

The first aspect of this problem is the development of examinations for new subjects or areas that are introduced into the curriculum. It will be clear that no curriculum innovation will get beyond the third year of the secondary school or will be made accessible to the more able pupils unless its development is accompanied by the establishment of an accepted public examination.

It is for this reason that most of the curriculum projects designed for use in secondary schools by the Schools Council have been aimed at pupils of average and below-average ability. For their planners have been aware that the demands of the examination system would make it unlikely that schools would be able or willing to adopt new schemes for use with their abler pupils. Thus many curriculum innovations, such as the Humanities Curriculum Project, have more often than not been made available only to those of average and below-average ability and in this way the more able pupils have been deprived of important experiences and debarred from areas of learning or exploration that would seem to have as much value for them as for any other pupils. It is surely not the case, for example, that you do not need a moral or a social education if you can gain seven or eight 'O' level passes in academic subjects.

It is also clear that the existence of public examinations in a subject raises the status of that subject in the eyes of both pupils and parents. Those concerned with a subject like rural studies, for example, while worried about the possibly inhibiting effects of examinations on syllabuses, nevertheless recognize that their subject 'suffers because it does not possess the hallmark stamped upon the older disciplines by the provision of "A" and "O" level examinations' (Schools Council 1969b, p. 22), and that where examinations have been introduced these 'have helped to improve the image of the subject and to give it a certain status in the eyes of the pupils and their parents' (op. cit., p. 12).

Establishing such new examinations is not an easy process but that it can be done has been demonstrated by the use made by individual schools and others of the facilities that exist within the CSE regulations and those of some GCE boards, such as the Associated Examining Board (AEB), for the approval and assessment of school-based projects (Kelly 1974; Smith and Macintosh 1974; Kelly 1975, 1978). If schools are to be able to introduce new areas of study into their curricula they must have procedures for ensuring that the work of the pupils in these areas can be assessed.

The second problem is to ensure continuous development within subject areas. This is perhaps the point at which teachers feel that the public examinations' shoe pinches most. Even if they feel they have good reasons for modifying what they are doing, they will not act on these unless they can be sure that the modifications they make will be reflected in the examinations their pupils are set. Without this they will feel that they are putting their pupils at risk by altering their approach or the content of their teaching. How can these constraints be avoided or minimized without our going to the other extreme of removing external evaluation and checks from the curriculum altogether?

One possible solution to this problem lies in a greater involvement of those responsible for the external examinations in curriculum development itself (Macintosh 1970). That the examining board can use its power not only to inhibit but to promote and direct curriculum development is clear from those instances where this has been done. A look at the history of public examinations in the United Kingdom will reveal the extent to which the procedures of the examination system have influenced the development of the curriculum. The change from a School Certificate requiring evidence of simultaneous achievement in a wide range of subjects to the GCE which can be achieved in one subject only or in a series of subjects examined at different times had a major influence on the development of the curriculum of the secondary schools. It was even claimed in 1971 that 'within the context of any given single subject, CSE and some GCE examinations had brought in new ideas and syllabuses which were an improvement on previous practice' (Schools Council 1971c, p. 16). An example of this to which we have already referred is the major changes brought about in the teaching of handicraft, in fact in its total conversion to Craft, Design and Technology, by the University of London GCE Board of Examiners in the subject (Hicks 1976). This is one extreme way in which an examining board can involve itself in curriculum development.

It should be equally possible, however, for a board to take a less directive role in the development of a curriculum while being effectively involved in decisions about purposes, content and procedures. Unless such involvement can be achieved it will be difficult for others to go very far in effecting significant changes in the curriculum. Examination boards must then be given a new and participatory role in curriculum planning.

One way forward has been indicated by the collaboration that there has been between individual schools and examining boards in those examinations where, as in Mode 3 of the CSE, the development of school-based schemes has been permitted (Macintosh 1970). Quite often these schemes have entailed the use of continuous or course-work assessment techniques and these have the effect of involving teachers themselves in the assessment procedures or at least making it essential that they be involved in discussion with the examiners. The same is also true even where no more than a school-based written paper is to be set.

The possibilities of school-based examinations which can be standardized nationally have been well explored by their use within the CSE and the extension of this facility to all GCE examinations must surely not be far away. This is one way in which the inhibiting effects of the external examination on the curriculum can be minimized. It is clearly especially valuable if we wish our curriculum to be free from the need to begin from a clear specification of its objectives or intended outcomes and if we wish to allow for the fact that in some areas the most significant outcomes are those that defy clear definition in advance (Macintosh 1970).

What is crucial here, however, is not merely that the examination is school-based; it is that, being school-based, it is firmly in the control of the teachers or at least susceptible to their influence. It is often claimed that the public examination system has always been mainly in the hands of teachers. In one sense this is clearly true, since most examination boards have more members drawn from the ranks of teachers than from any other single source. To say that this gives adequate teacher participation in the assessment procedures, however, is to miss the real point. For these teachers will represent only a small proportion of those whose work is affected by the form of the examination and the others will be almost as effectively limited in their work as if all of the examiners came from outer space. What is needed is not that a few representative teachers should be involved in the setting and marking of examinations, but that all teachers who are involved in the development of the teaching of a subject should be involved in or have access to and influence on the actual assessment process (Macintosh 1970).

What this amounts to is that we need an improved 'communications network' between teachers and the examination boards, so that some of the agencies available to support teachers might be activated by the boards themselves (Macintosh and Smith 1974; Pudwell 1980). This would allow teachers 'to move towards a freer curriculum as they see it rather than as others see it for them' (Macintosh and Smith 1974, p. 79). Such a freer curriculum would clearly permit the development of different courses to meet the needs and requirements of individual pupils. It would thus help us to progress away from the inevitable insensitivity of the mass methods of examining too often currently in use (Pudwell 1980).

Safeguards against subjectivity of assessment, halo-effects and the like must, of course, be built into such procedures. That they can be is demonstrated by the experience of those boards which have experimented with school-based examinations and course-work assessment techniques and, indeed, by the well-established procedures of our universities which always examine their own students but at the same time employ external examiners from other universities to advise them, to monitor standards and to ensure as much objectivity as is possible. Similar inter-school and even extra-school moderation can be provided without depriving the teachers themselves of their central role in the assessment of their pupils. Unless they are given that central role, the public examination will continue to be the most effective inhibitor of curriculum development rather than being seen as one aspect of a total programme and itself subject to development in phase with the curriculum it is there to assess.

The existence of strong opposition to this kind of development, however, must also be recognized. Many attempts which have been made by teachers and others, including major agencies such as the Schools Council, in recent years to alter the examinations system in such a way as to make possible changes felt to be desirable in the curricula of the schools, have been hindered and, indeed, in some cases effectively scotched by the response to the proposals by other bodies, especially the central government and universities. Among the most significant examples of this are the lengthy debates over the introduction of a common 16+ examination (Schools Council 1975) and over the changes proposed for examinations at 17+ and 18+ (Schools Council 1978a), debates which have resulted in the rejection of several considered proposals, such as those for Q and F (Qualifying and Further) and N and F (Normal and Further) level examinations, both of which were designed to broaden the curricula of the sixth forms.

This draws our attention to a further respect in which the way in which the system of public examinations is organized and administered can itself exercise a limiting influence on the curriculum. Certainly, the dominant role played by the universities in the United Kingdom in the conduct of schools examinations has been a major factor here. But the most obvious example of this has been the problems created for secondary schools and their pupils by the dual system of examining at 16+, the existence of both CSE and GCE examinations, each with different syllabuses, different modes of examining and different, although overlapping, standards. This has been a major factor in inhibiting the development within secondary schools of mixed-ability groupings, even where these have been felt to be desirable and, indeed, where they have been implemented in the lower school (Kelly 1974, 1975, 1978). But it has also made it difficult for developments to occur even within individual subjects. For it is not easy to contemplate changes and modifications in syllabuses when negotiation must be undertaken with two quite separate organizing bodies, when separate arrangements have to be made within the school for teaching different syllabuses to different groups of pupils and, indeed, when difficult decisions have to be made about the selection of pupils for examinations whose differences are as much a matter of status as of content. Such a situation cannot but limit educational development; yet proposals to replace it with a common system of examining at 16+, which were publicly made as early as 1971 (Schools Council 1971a), have only now achieved acceptance. It is not surprising that one of the objectives of the government in, somewhat belatedly, lending its support to the idea of a single system of examinations at 16+ is stated to be that concern we noted earlier that 'examinations must be designed and used to serve the educational process' (DES 1981, p. 4).

However, the manner in which it has set about the planning and the establishment of this new single system of 16+ examining has already raised some questions about the extent to which this aim is likely to be attained. For this process is to begin with the establishment of agreed guidelines or criteria which all examinations in each subject area must conform to. Each group of GCE and CSE boards will be free to devise its own syllabuses, but these will have to comply with the agreed criteria. Draft proposals of these criteria and questionnaires on each subject have been sent to all the schools concerned, with requests for teachers' comments. Once these have been received, the drafts will be revised by the working parties which produced the originals. Already there are suggestions that these working parties reflect the interests of the examiners rather than those of the teachers and, since it is also planned that the Schools Council and Her Majesty's Inspectorate should express the final views on them, there is a feeling that the teachers' views on how the examination, and thus the curriculum, should be developed will prove to be of least significance. It is also the case that the draft guidelines in some subjects consist merely of detailed statements of course objectives. In short, it begins to appear that, in spite of pious expressions of hopes to the contrary, the new scheme may well be as inhibiting in its effect on the curriculum as the old.

External examinations, then, continue to be a highly cogent form of constraint on curriculum development, and it is clear that they are likely to be so for a long time yet.

One final point needs to be made before we conclude our discussion of examinations and the curriculum. It is clear that some schools permit examinations to exercise an influence over what they do that goes far beyond that necessitated by either the structure of the system or the examining techniques in use. For there are schools which regard examination successes as the central consideration in all their planning. This is an attitude which is naturally more prevalent among schools in the private sector, whose livelihood may appear to depend on their ability to attract customers who are more likely to respond to examination results than to less readily measurable educational merits. It is an attitude which can be seen to result very often in a form of schooling which emphasizes academic attainment to the exclusion of all other considerations. It is thus salutary to be reminded that 'Examination certificates do not purport fully to describe achievements at school even for those pupils who obtain high grades in many subjects' (DES 1981, p. 5). One of the ways of establishing this and of ensuring that all schools see their task in broader terms would be to require schools to provide each pupil with a leaving certificate containing information across a much broader spectrum than that covered by the results of public examinations. This is an area in which the Schools Council has been asked 'to accelerate and expand research and development work . . . on which it has already embarked' (ibid.). It is a development which was proposed as long ago as 1926 by the Hadow Committee, so that such research and development work would seem to be a little overdue. However it is not likely to be forwarded by the requirement that schools should now publish their examination results as an aid to parents in the choice of schools for their children.

Summary and conclusions

The purpose of the present section of this book is to explore some of the many constraints and pressures which constitute the context in which curriculum planning goes on and which thus will affect, if they do not actually determine, the direction and form it takes. This chapter has considered some of the general elements of that background context, the pressures on teachers and other curriculum planners which derive from established traditions, those which are generated by administrative decisions concerning such things as the organization of schools and the allocation and distribution of resources, and those related pressures which are created by the 'consumers', especially by employers and parents. It also attempted to draw attention to some of the pressures which are produced by the school itself through its organizational structure, its facilities, its social climate and, especially, the attitudes adopted by its teachers and headteacher. Lastly, it looked in some detail at the constraining influences of the public examination system and suggested that a more sophisticated approach to assessment could ensure that, while the system continues to fulfil the important function it must perform for society, it might do this in such a way as to minimize its inhibiting effects on the development of the curriculum.

All of these factors are, of course, political, just as in reality they are all closely interrelated and interwoven. Recently, however, as has been noted several times, there has been a major shift in the United Kingdom towards attempts of a more directly political kind to influence the curriculum; developments which are political with a capital 'P'. In short, the focus of the curriculum debate has become overtly political and economic, and thus the context of curriculum change and development has materially altered. It is to an exploration of this change and its implications for the curriculum and for the individual teacher that the next chapter will direct itself.

CHAPTER 8

THE POLITICAL CONTEXT

The last chapter concluded with the suggestion that there is a sense in which the whole social context of curriculum planning can be described as political, but that it is also possible, and indeed necessary, to identify more overt forms of political influence and pressure; in short, to note the point at which such pressure changes from being an influence on curriculum development to being a deliberate attempt to exert control over it. It was also noted that a change of this kind has occurred in the United Kingdom during the last few years.

In this chapter we shall consider this change and its implications for schools and for individual teachers. In effect, therefore, we shall be considering some of the ways in which those general influences which the last chapter discussed have become sharpened up by recent political developments to the point where their impact on education has become more clearly overt, direct and significant and where the degree of autonomy and of responsibility exercised by teachers has become correspondingly more limited. In short, we will be tracing the development of some of these influences into agencies of direct control.

We have seen at various points in our earlier discussions that there have been several changes of emphasis over the years within the curriculum debate. At primary level that debate goes back at least as far as the Hadow Report of 1931, it has throughout been dominated by psychology and it has, both because of its length and its nature, derived from a tradition different from that of other sectors of education, a fact which may go some way towards explaining why the conflict with recent developments appears to be greater here than elsewhere.

At secondary level, the debate dates only from the mid-1950s, there having been little discussion of the curriculum at that level during the first half of this century when, in spite of the attempts of the earlier Hadow Report on *The Education of the Adolescent* to promote such discussion, attention tended to be focused rather on the organization of secondary schooling. Inevitably, the early emphasis, especially in the USA, was again psychological in orientation. In the United Kingdom, however, largely through the work of Richard Peters, there was an early shift towards considerations of a philosophical or epistemological kind, which were only displaced by the advent of 'new directions' in the sociology of education in the late 1960s and early 1970s. This emphasis on the sociology of knowledge as the focus of the curriculum debate has in turn given way to politico-economic forces in the latter half of the 1970s, a development that has been matched by a similar shift within the sociology of education itself.

There are several factors which, with hindsight, one can see have made such a change inevitable. The first of these is the economic recession which recent years have witnessed and which has inevitably led to pressures on schools, and indeed on all parts of the education system, to justify the expenditure of public money on this service. A second is the acceleration of that process of technological, social and cultural change which we noted in Chapter 1. A third is the failure of the education system to respond appropriately from within to these changes.

Thus the present-day student of the curriculum must recognize that, although the other influences persist (and it is the conflicts that result from their persistence that brings complexity to his studies) and have a right to be recognized and acknowledged, the dominant influence at the present time is the political influence, some of the many aspects of which we must now explore.

An attempt will be made in this chapter to identify the major implications of this shift, firstly, by tracing its development and noting its major milestones; secondly, by picking out its major features, notably its demands for increased external control of the curriculum and the greater accountability of teachers; and, thirdly, by drawing attention to some of its major points of impact on the work of the schools. Lastly, we will consider the effects of this development on the individual teacher and suggest some of the things he needs to do if he is to be able to respond appropriately to these new influences, pressures and demands rather than to collapse before them. For it is important to stress that the political focus of the current curriculum debate does not take it beyond either the concern or the reach of the teacher in the classroom but rather renders his contribution to that debate especially important.

The growth of political interest in the curriculum

It is not unreasonable nor unusual for those who hold the purse-strings to have some kind of say in questions of how money shall be spent, as is clear not only from a review of education in other countries but also from the briefest examination of the history of education in Great Britain. For, from the earliest days of state aid, schools in receipt of such aid were required to meet certain conditions concerning the uses made of it, so that some schools were known to refuse badly needed financial assistance in order to retain their control (Davies 1980). With the arrival of state-provided education too, responsibility for the curriculum was in the hands of the School Boards, although usually exercised through curriculum committees or individual governing bodies. The same was true when, as a result of the 1902 Education Act, the county and county boroughs took on responsibility for the schools, and that the ultimate authority for curriculum lay with the local education authorities was reaffirmed by the Education Act of 1944.

However, although this continued and, indeed, continues, to be the legal position, in practice a rather different system had developed. For the Hadow Reports of 1926 and 1931 emphasized the notion of the freedom and responsibility of the teacher in curriculum planning and thus provided a basis for the growth of the idea of teacher autonomy in this area.

It could be argued that the attempt to plan 'education for all' in the United Kingdom effectively began with the Hadow Reports, the main thrust of which was towards the creation of quite separate primary and secondary sectors within the school system. It has already been suggested that this was accompanied by much debate about and deliberate planning of the curriculum in the newly created primary sector. In the secondary sector, however, greater constraints on curriculum change existed, not least in the form of the syllabuses established by Examination Boards, so that little happened there beyond that process of 'unplanned drift' (Hoyle 1969a) to which we drew attention in Chapter 1.

In this context there developed an acceptance of, although at no stage any official concession of, the notion of the autonomy of the teacher in the area of the curriculum. It was generally agreed that that was the sphere of his or her professional expertise and, although the freedom enjoyed there was relative, since, as we saw in Chapter 7, there are always and inevitably a good many indirect external constraints on curriculum planning, the teacher was conceded freedom from direct external control. The cynics might argue that the teacher was allowed this only because he was doing nothing – certainly nothing radical – with it, but, whatever the reason, the fact remains that the official policy was one of *laissez-faire* and the teachers' autonomy in matters of curriculum continued largely unchallenged.

The challenge first came in the mid-1950s along with that felt need for deliberate curriculum planning to which we referred in Chapter 1. As was suggested there, it has been felt not unreasonable to date this from the launching by the Russians of the first space satellite, Sputnik 1, in 1957. There was much concern that the West might be lagging behind in the race for technological advance and, not unreasonably, a prime area for the exploration of that thesis was the education system. It was also, of course, felt that, if the thesis proved to be true, changes in the curriculum would have to occur to correct the trend.

Thus, first in the USA and then in the United Kingdom, money was made available for curriculum research and development, the emphasis of which was naturally on science and technology, although attention was not confined to these areas since there was a parallel stress on 'creativity' which considerably broadened the scope. In the USA, this was accompanied by a good deal of encouragement to senior academics in the universities to interest themselves in the school curriculum and its development.

In the United Kingdom, proposals of a similar kind were viewed by the teachers as a challenge to what they saw as their established autonomy on curriculum matters, so that the attempt by the government to set up in 1961 a Curriculum Study Group, along similar lines to those earlier bodies of that name which had effectively controlled the curriculum in the schools of their day, led to conflict with the teachers' unions and the ultimate creation in 1964 of the Schools Council, a differently constituted, teacher-controlled body. Thus, in 1969, the Minister of Education of the day, Sir David Eccles, had good reason to speak of the curriculum as a 'secret garden' and those people, such as, for example, some intrepid governors of maintained schools, who attempted to trespass there were very firmly warned off.

A new decade has seen considerable inroads made into that garden and it is interesting to speculate on the reasons for this. One reason must be the growing evidence of the relative ineffectiveness of the Schools Council. No one would wish to argue that the work of that body has not generated a good deal of debate about the curriculum and the effects and influence of that debate on the practice of individual teachers and schools is difficult to measure. However, as we saw in Chapter 5, the Council's own evidence of the impact and take-up of its projects (Schools Council 1979a, 1980), along with the growing awareness that the approach it initially adopted of generating projects centrally for dissemination to the periphery, might not in any case be suitable for the task, leaves no doubt as to the relative insignificance of its direct contribution to curriculum change.

A second factor is the growth of public concern over the changes that were taking place in schools. The efforts of several generations of sociologists had combined with the pressures of the Labour party to ensure the spread, which after Circular 10/65 was to become almost total, of comprehensive secondary schools. In many of these, and in most primary schools, there were mixed-ability classes. Furthermore, some of the attempts of the teachers themselves at curriculum change were equally disturbing. 'Modern' or informal methods in primary schools, schemes of integrated studies in secondary schools and other comparable developments were leading to a realization on the part of parents and others that the schools their children were attending were very different from those they had attended themselves. And, instead of recognizing that this was equally true of their homes, their cars, their places of work and their forms of entertainment, they began to get worried at the results of leaving the curriculum to teachers. As so often, autonomy was splendid, so long as no one used it.

These concerns were given articulation in certain publications of the time, notably the series of 'Black Papers' (Cox and Dyson 1969a,b) which, in Jeremiah fashion, inveighed against most forms of educational innovation and assured the world that they were leading to a serious decline in educational standards. Perhaps more seriously, these concerns appeared to be reinforced by the events at the William Tyndale School (ILEA 1976) which were interpreted as evidence not merely of what teacher autonomy can lead to but of what it is likely to result in everywhere.

This growing concern was already well established in certain areas when the effects of that economic recession, to which we have also referred, seemed to make it all the more imperative that some greater external control be exercised over the uses to which teachers put the increasingly scarce resources that were allocated to the school system.

It is this background and growing concern that explains several significant events which occurred during the 1970s. In 1974, there was established the Assessment of Performance Unit (APU) whose task it was to monitor standards of attainment nationally in six major areas of the curriculum: mathematics, language, science, social and personal development, aesthetics and physical development. The intention was not to check on individual schools but, by looking at the records of a range of schools anonymously, to maintain a general watch on national standards.

Then, as we saw earlier, a committee of enquiry was set up under the chairmanship of Thomas Taylor to look into the government of schools. This committee issued its report in 1977 (DES 1977a) and included in that report were certain firm recommendations for increasing the powers of governing bodies, so that, although it was also recommended that teacher representation should be increased, the general effect of these proposals was to reduce the range of the teachers' control of the curriculum.

In the meantime, in the autumn of 1976, James Callaghan, as Prime Minister, speaking at Ruskin College, Oxford, had launched an attack on secondary schools for a number of shortcomings that he claimed were evident in their curricula, notably their failure to ensure that an adequate number of pupils in their VIth forms studied science subjects and thus to provide the force of trained scientists which an advanced technological society requires.

That speech effectively launched the so-called 'Great Debate' which was stage-managed by Mrs Shirley Williams, as Secretary of State for Education and Science, and conducted extensively on TV and through the other media. As a basis for that debate, there was issued a Green Paper, *Education in Schools* (DES 1977b), the first of a spate of official publications which has emerged within a very short space of time.

These publications have included surveys of the major areas of education (DES 1978, 1979), discussion documents prepared by Her Majesty's Inspectorate (DES 1977b,c, 1980a) and resultant sets of proposals or recommendations for change (DES 1980b, 1981). They reflect within themselves a number of the tensions we have identified but their very existence indicates the degree to which the concern over education to which we referred earlier has grown and the extent to which external interest and the desire for external control have increased.

This interest and desire have recently led to several deliberate measures designed to strengthen the external control of the curriculum. In 1980 a new

Education Act was passed, which incorporated several modifications to the Act of 1944. The major feature of this new Act may be said to be an attempt to strengthen external influence on the work of the schools. For, among other detailed provisions, it requires the increased representation of parents on the governing bodies of schools – a proposal which is matched, we ought also to note, by a similar increase in the representation of teachers – and it also attempts to give parents more 'say' in the choice of the schools to which they will send their children. It does not go as far in increasing parental influence as the Taylor Report recommended, but it does represent an important move in that direction. It also devolves more powers to the local authorities and thus might be said to strengthen their control of educational provision and of the curriculum, although in the light of the recent reduction in the Rate Support Grant, many see this as a somewhat hollow gesture. Nevertheless, this new Act does represent a step towards increasing the external control of education.

Subsequently, central government has laid clear charges on local authorities to provide statements of their curriculum policies and these charges have been in turn passed on to the schools and teachers themselves. Thus there is at present fevered activity throughout the schools of the United Kingdom as teachers endeavour to respond suitably to these requests.

Two points need to be made at once about these developments. The first is that they have had the beneficial effect of encouraging discussion of and reflection on curriculum policy in many schools where this has hitherto received little attention. They have also promoted a good deal of self-evaluation in all schools. The second effect, however, is less encouraging. For, the form in which these demands have been made of schools, especially where they have amounted to little more than demands for statements of curriculum objectives, has sometimes resulted in inhibiting rather than promoting curriculum development. It is quite clear that the schemes adopted by some authorities in response to these requests are very much better than those of others. We thus see here the two conflicting faces of external interest in curriculum planning.

It might be worthwhile to pause a moment in order to pick out the major issues that have emerged in the course of the events just described and which are highlighted in the documents to which reference was made earlier.

First of all there is the question of the balance and the content of the curriculum and the related issue of its suitability for an advanced technological society. Secondly, and clearly arising from this, there is the matter of the control of the curriculum and pressures for increased external control and even an increase in centralized control. This has crystallized into several issues of greater substance: pressure for the establishment of a common curriculum, or at least a common core to the curriculum, to be centrally determined; schemes for the monitoring of standards of all kinds; and demands that teachers should be made more accountable for their actions, decisions, judgements and work. Thirdly, important questions have been raised about the role of the major agents of curriculum change, in particular the teachers themselves, the inspectorate at both local and national levels and the Schools Council, whose constitution, as we saw in Chapter 5, has already been modified to reduce the scale of teacher representation and thus control, and whose future role may be said to depend on the results of an enquiry currently being conducted under the direction of Mrs Nancy Trenaman, Principal of St Anne's College, Oxford.

These major points of interest can be summarized as a concern over standards, a consequent desire to reduce the autonomy of teachers by making them more directly accountable for their curriculum decisions and, also consequent on these two, an attempt to establish greater external control over the curriculum. Each of these we must now examine in greater detail.

The monitoring of standards

The most obvious example of the attempt to improve the mechanisms for the monitoring of standards of achievement attained by schools in the United Kingdom is the establishment of the Assessment of Performance Unit (APU). Several events foreshadowed the creation of this unit (Lawton 1980) but it was first announced officially in a Government White Paper in 1974 and effected in the following year. Its terms of reference are 'to promote the development of methods of assessing and monitoring the achievement of children at school, and to seek to identify the incidence of underachievement'. The intention is also to make those findings which result from its investigation available to those responsible both for the work of the schools and the allocation of resources.

It has been stressed, however, from the outset that the role of the APU is to gain and to make known the overall picture of education in the country and not to identify individual pupils or schools or even local education authorities. It is hoped that the provision of this national picture will offer individual schools and authorities a scale against which to measure their own attainments; but the prime task of the unit is to establish a system of monitoring which will clearly indicate trends in performance, so that it can be ascertained whether standards generally are rising or falling.

The areas selected for attention in this exercise, as we indicated earlier, are mathematics, language, science, social and personal development, aesthetics and physical development. The key ages selected for assessment are at present 11 and 15 for mathematics and language, 11, 13 and 15 for science, and 13 only for the first modern language. In each aspect of the curriculum to be monitored, to ensure a representative sample of pupils across the country, it is the intention to involve about 1000 primary and 500 secondary schools in any one year, about 5 percent of schools with 11-year-olds and 10 percent of schools with 15-year-olds. It is claimed that this level of sampling will require the participation of no more than a quarter of all primary schools and a half of all secondary schools each year, even if all the chosen aspects of the curriculum were monitored in the 1980s. Furthermore, it would require that one-fifth of the secondary schools involved might be asked to contribute to the monitoring of two areas of the curriculum. Lastly, if 12 000 pupils were used for each monitoring exercise, any individual pupil would have only a one in four chance of being assessed for this purpose during his school career.

It is important to stress these figures because they constitute the basis for the claim that the activities of this unit will not of themselves exercise any kind of constraining influence or inhibiting effect on the curriculum. For it is quite clear that the architects of this unit have from the outset been aware of the potential dangers of this kind of exercise. In particular, they have been aware of the dangers of restricting the range and nature of work undertaken in schools and of encouraging teachers to 'teach to the tests'. It is in order to meet these problems that they have stressed the scale of their sampling, broadened the range of their interests to include the social/personal, the aesthetic and the physical development of children, attempted to take a 'cross-curricular' rather than a subject-based approach and expressed the intention of using a variety of methods of assessment.

We will consider shortly the question of how far the attempt to perform this kind of function without at the same time influencing the curriculum has been successful. Indeed, we must also ask whether it is possible. It is enough to note here that the dangers have been appreciated and attempts made to avoid them. We must also note, however, that while a certain degree of detached objectivity may be possible at the national level, this has by no means been matched in the attempts of local authorities to monitor the work of their own schools. One effect of the establishment of the APU and, indeed, of the whole movement of which that is a part, has been to exert pressure on local authorities to take a more direct interest in the curriculum of their schools and the standards attained by their pupils. Thus a feature of education in the United Kingdom in recent years has been the growing involvement of the local authorities in the planning and monitoring of school curricula. This has manifested itself in the increased interest which governing bodies have taken and have been encouraged to take, often by the preparation of documents on the curriculum expressly designed for their use, in the curriculum of their schools, and by a noticeable increase in the activities of local authority advisers, who have been demanding from schools and teachers explicit statements of their curricula and detailed records of the attainment of their pupils. It has also resulted, in at least one local authority, in the assumption by the Education Committee itself of direct responsibility for the curriculum of its schools, over the heads not only of the teachers but also of the governing bodies.

This contrast between the style of monitoring adopted at national and local levels is highlighted by the use that has been made by some local authorities of assessment data given in the first reports published by the APU. For, while the APU itself has continued scrupulously to maintain that the evidence it has gleaned will be of significance only when further tests have been made and a basis for comparison thus established, many local authorities have seized upon these first results as a baseline from which to evaluate the standards of their own schools, without always recognizing the need to make due allowance for the inevitable variations that must follow from differences in local conditions. Such a step, as we saw earlier, was foreseen in the setting up of the APU, and must therefore be recognized as an inevitable accompaniment of its procedures, as clear evidence that all forms of external monitoring, no matter how scrupulously conducted with a view to avoiding direct influence on curriculum practice, must in the end have such direct influence.

This, then, is the first and fundamental difficulty of such attempts to monitor educational standards. It cannot be done without adding to those constraints on curriculum planning we have already discussed. It might, of course, be argued by some that that is precisely what is needed and intended. We must pause to consider, however, some of the results of this kind of constraint.

First of all, it is quite clear that this kind of activity, involving as it does a separation of the teaching and the testing processes and the exclusion of the teacher from the latter, must lead to exactly that kind of 'teaching to the tests' which the architects of the APU wished to avoid. In short, its effects cannot be different from those that were clearly associated with 11+ testing when it was in operation and which, as we saw in Chapter 7, are the acknowledged concomitants of the public examination system. If teachers have no involvement in the assessment procedures, they will be forced to concentrate their attention on those things they know are likely to be tested. Indeed, there is already evidence that the knowledge of those aspects of mathematics which are covered by the testing procedures of the APU is influencing the selection of what is taught in individual schools. For, after all, one's own school might be among the 5 percent or 10 percent chosen for sampling. Furthermore, since inevitably such tests only measure the less sophisticated forms of attainment, 'teaching for the tests' will mean a concentration on these.

This narrowing of focus is perhaps most readily seen in the emphasis that usually accompanies, or follows on from, these forms of monitoring on the teaching of what are often called the 'basic skills'. It is these that are most readily tested and assessed and there is a good deal of pressure on teachers, some of it quite overt, to emphasize these in their teaching. The problems resulting from this are threefold. Firstly, there is as yet no clear definition of what a 'basic skill' is, no clear indication of where the line is to be drawn between such skills and more complex forms of teaching and learning. Secondly, it is clear that such a narrow concentration can be positively counterproductive to the achievement of more lasting educational results. It is plain, for example, that many pupils whose scores on reading tests are high by any standards have been brought to that level by methods which have inhibited their love of literature. Thirdly, there is evidence, for example in the recent survey of primary education (DES 1978), that these 'basic skills' themselves are best learnt in a broader educational context. A narrow concentration on them to the exclusion of other, less readily measurable things, then, is fraught with many hidden dangers.

This in turn must lead to a narrowing of the focus and scope of the curriculum itself. Again it is only fair to note the APU's desire to avoid this by including those aspects of education beyond mathematics, language and science, which teachers regard as important, especially personal and social development, aesthetics and physical development. However, the results of the efforts to do this have merely served to emphasize the force of this criticism. For, while the work of the groups concerned with standards in science and mathematics is already well under way, progress in the monitoring of aesthetic development has been much slower, not least because of the difficulties involved in reaching any objective definition of what this is; and many criticisms could be and have been directed at attempts to monitor social and personal development, which can look very like interference with personal liberty and thus ultimately inimical to the very development of a free society. These conclusions in themselves would seem to constitute evidence that this kind of monitoring can only be undertaken on a narrow front, so that it must lead to the emergence of a similarly narrow focus for the curriculum itself. Indeed, it is evidence of the wider problem of defining exactly what is meant by those 'standards' we are concerned to monitor. In general, therefore, the claims that this kind of monitoring will lead to the omission, or at least the diminution, of important areas of the curriculum and a narrowing of the scope of others would seem to be borne out by the evidence of what has occurred already.

There is a further and related problem which perhaps is clearer to recognize in the direct attempts of local authorities to exercise control over the curricula of their own schools. For it is quite clear that this form of external monitoring encourages, always indirectly and sometimes directly, the adoption of simplistic forms of teaching, assessment and curriculum planning and evaluation. Attention has been drawn on several occasions, for example, to the tendency of most forms of assessment or evaluation to encourage the adoption of an objectives planning model for the curriculum. For once one has been encouraged to base one's teaching on what is likely to be externally assessed, teaching to objectives follows automatically. And it is quite clear that many local authority advisers, in requiring more detailed curriculum planning by their schools and teachers, have urged this kind of model upon them, often, sadly, in ignorance of the existence of other, more sophisticated, alternatives. This is perhaps even more clearly apparent in the forms of record-keeping that have been devised in many areas. The difficulties of this form of planning were fully rehearsed in Chapter 4. It is enough to note here that this kind of external monitoring tends to promote the acceptance of this form of planning without always acknowledging its accompanying problems.

Secondly, in spite of those efforts on the part of the APU which we noted earlier to avoid it, this kind of monitoring cannot fail to emphasize the traditional subject divisions of the curriculum. Some of the difficulties of that approach to curriculum planning we noted in Chapters 2 and 3. It is most serious in its likely effects on the work of primary schools, many of which have over the years developed methods of teaching which transcend conventional subject divisions and which see all the six aspects of development listed by the APU, and, indeed, several more, as best prompted by a form of teaching which integrates rather than separates them (Blenkin and Kelly 1981). There is no doubt that attempts to monitor these subjects in isolation from each other must have the effect of discouraging, and of inhibiting, the further development of this important approach to education. Of more immediate concern is the fact that where these attempts take the form of direct requests from the advisory service, which in itself is often subject-based, they will create a direct conflict with the traditional practices and developed approaches of individual schools. They then do not monitor so much as determine, and even in some cases overturn, the curriculum of the school.

This draws our attention to the fundamental problem of this approach to the monitoring of standards, namely the conflict it will inevitably generate between the professional judgement of the teacher and the need he will feel to satisfy testing procedures imposed on him from without. We saw in Chapter 5 the crucial role of the teacher in the development of the curriculum. That his role is crucial is not merely an assertion made by teachers to strengthen their hold on curriculum development; it is a claim that we have seen to be well supported by recent trends. If that claim is accepted, it must be acknowledged as a corollary that teachers cannot fulfil that crucial role in curriculum development if they are constantly looking over their shoulders at external bodies, whether these be Schools Council evaluators, examination boards, local authority advisers or APU testers. Again we must conclude that monitoring, if it is to be effective and non-inhibiting, must, like effective evaluation and effective examining, be in the hands of the teachers themselves. At the very least, they must be centrally involved in the process. The fundamental weakness of existing schemes and models of monitoring is that they imply a rigid separation between the processes of teaching and assessment, when every teacher of any experience knows that the two must go hand-in-hand.

We will find that much the same conclusion has to be drawn from an examination of schemes which have been proposed for the increased accountability of teachers. This is the second of those recent major developments to which we referred earlier, to which we now turn.

Accountability

The first point that needs to be made about teacher accountability is that it must be accepted rather than opposed. It is of the essence of life in a democratic society that no one should be unaccountable for his public actions; that is a privilege enjoyed only by those who hold power in totalitarian states.

Indeed, the need for accountability was recognized by the architects of democratic government, the Athenians of the 5th century BC, as being as crucial, if not more so, than free elections through the ballot box and other forms of participation by the citizenry in the government of the state. The most important element in Athenian democracy was not the free election of government members and officials; in fact, many of these were chosen by lot rather than by election, since the Athenians felt – with some justification one feels – that the gods would make better choices than they would themselves or that anybody could make as good a job of governing as those who thrust themselves forward as self-styled experts or that selection by lot would discourage the attempts of self-seeking individuals to achieve positions of power. Nor did they regard the opportunities for frequent votes on major issues of policy as in themselves adequate to secure completely democratic government, since they well realized that often decisions have to be taken quickly and that a consistent policy cannot always be attained by constant reference to the people as a whole. The most important element in their system was the frequently used arrangement for the accountability of all government members and officials. This is a feature of their democratic procedures which has been too readily overlooked by commentators and by political theorists. For the Athenians believed that true democracy could only be attained if procedures existed, and were used, for calling politicians to account on the completion of their periods of office. Thus quite frequently trials were held, before citizen juries, of politicians whose behaviour had given cause for concern, and, if these juries decided against the defendant, a fine, banishment and even, on some occasions, execution would follow. It is a system whose attractions are enhanced by the actions of many present-day politicians.

A second important point that emerges from this brief excursion into ancient history is that, in addition to being perhaps the most essential ingredient of democracy, accountability is also essentially *post eventum* (Downey and Kelly 1979). It makes neither practical nor logical sense to endeavour to make someone accountable for his actions before he has performed them. A fundamental feature of the concept of accountability is that it comes into play after someone has had the freedom to exercise his judgement and take whatever action he has deemed appropriate. In the context of teaching, therefore, accountability cannot be interpreted as entailing giving in advance an account of what one intends to do, although it has been interpreted by many people in this way and has thus been seen as adding its weight to those demands for the prespecification of teaching objectives.

Indeed, this has been a major feature of those schemes of accountability which have been introduced in many areas of the USA (Hamilton 1976; Atkin 1979) and which have been taken as the model for similar schemes which have recently been advocated in the United Kingdom. By 1974, nearly 40 states in the USA were attempting to establish a legal base for demanding the accountability of teachers (Hamilton 1976) and a major characteristic of their projected schemes was a concern with outcomes or outputs (Atkin 1979), their focus being on 'management by objectives', 'programme budgeting' and even 'performance contracting', a system by which outside agencies are paid to work with teachers to raise the achievement levels of pupils (Atkin 1979). In short, the emphasis has been on achieving increased external control over education by intervention at the beginning, rather than by permitting teachers to exercise their professional judgement and calling them to account when they have done so. Given that these demands for increased control, as we have seen, have resulted from a dissatisfaction with what teachers have been doing, this approach is, of course, understandable. But it must be seen as another aspect of that attempt to provide education in a more business-like way, to make it more 'scientific', particularly through detailed formal planning, the inadequacies of which we discussed fully in Chapter 4.

It is clear, then, that demands for teacher accountability can be interpreted and implemented in a number of quite different ways, so that the crucial question becomes not whether teachers should be accountable for their work but how this is to be achieved. In other words, we must seek for the most suitable model of teacher accountability. Furthermore, a crucial aspect of such a model will be the answer we give to the question of to whom should teachers be accountable and that question also deserves our careful attention. It is equally important also to consider what teachers can reasonably be held accountable for, since there are aspects of the development of pupils which are clearly beyond the scope of their influence. And we need too to ask who else should be held accountable for educational achievement, rather than taking it for granted that the teacher is the only person who can be expected to contribute to this. All of these issues we must consider in a little more detail.

In broad terms, two major models of teacher accountability can be identified as a result of recent practices and debate on this issue. One of these is that instrumental, utilitarian, hierarchical, bureaucratic model that we have just suggested has been widely adopted in the USA. This is the model which Lawrence Stenhouse describes as the 'systematic efficiency model' (1975, p. 185). The second might be described as the intrinsic, democratic or professional model.

The main feature of the first of these models is that it holds the teacher accountable to the public as tax-paying providers of the resources he is expending (Sockett 1976b). It is a crude model, whose major focus is on the economic issues of resource allocation and value for money, and whose central concern is thus with the results obtained for the money spent. It is for this reason that it views the teacher as accountable to those who decide on the allocation of resources, that is the government at local or national level, rather than to parents, pupils, employers or his professional peers. It is also for this reason that it stresses the achievement of prespecified performances and thus adds its support to the adoption of the objectives model of curriculum planning (Atkin 1979). The main means it adopts to assess teacher competence is the setting of tests which are administered but not designed by the teachers concerned (Sockett 1976b), and the future provision of resources is decided by reference to the results of these tests, a system of 'payment by results'. Its main characteristics then are that it is instrumental, economic and political.

The basic assumptions of this model are also worth noting (Elliott 1976). For it assumes, firstly, that teachers are concerned to bring about only a limited range of outcomes; secondly, 'that achievement scores can be used to assess the causal effectiveness of what teachers do in classrooms' (op. cit., p. 49); thirdly, that teachers can be praised or blamed, rewarded or punished, especially through the allocation of resources, on the basis of these causal evaluations; lastly, that the teachers themselves have no rights of participation in such evaluations.

In the light of earlier discussions in this book, it is not difficult to identify the inadequacies of this model. For, to begin with, it trails with it all those difficulties associated with the objectives model of planning which we discussed in Chapter 4. In particular, it encourages the acceptance of simplistic educational goals by suggesting that what cannot be measured cannot be taught (Sockett 1976b). For the model cannot be used to assess educational goals which cannot be defined in behavioural terms or clearly prespecified. It thus threatens to 'destroy schools as places where *education* goes on' (Elliott 1976, p. 51). Secondly, it substitutes teacher-accountablility for teacher-responsibility or, to express this differently, it gives teachers responsibility without freedom (Stenhouse 1975). This in turn has serious effects on teacher morale, as is evidenced by the increasing militancy of teachers' unions (Sockett 1976b). Thirdly, the kind of data that this form of accountability produces does not help in any way with decisions as to how the performance of individual schools or teachers can be improved (Sockett 1976b). In other words, it does not reveal why children have scored badly on the tests, merely that they have. The reasons why they have done badly are quite crucial, since it may be that these would justify the allocation of additional resources to the school, as was once felt to be the case with those schools in the United Kingdom decreed to be in Educational Priority Areas. It is for this reason that it has been claimed that one effect of this model of accountability may be to 'benefit the dominant middle class sectors of society to the disadvantage of minority communities' (Elliott 1976, p. 50), since if a school performs badly, even where this is directly attributable to the social class or ethnic background of its pupils, this scheme will lead to a reduction in its resources, whereas social justice might be felt to require the opposite. In fact, it might be argued that its real purpose is to cut the costs of education rather than to improve its quality.

In contrast, a major characteristic of the intrinsic, democratic, professional model of accountability is that it is 'for adherence to principles of practice rather than for results embodied in pupil performance' (Sockett 1976b, p. 42). It thus eschews all links with curriculum planning by prespecified objectives, and suggests rather, or at least makes possible, the adoption of a 'process' model of planning. For it is a model which is based on a recognition that educational value resides in the teaching-learning process itself rather than in its outcomes (Elliott 1976), so that, whereas the hierarchical model assumes that decisions concerning what is valuable in education are to be taken outside the school, this model recognizes that such decisions must be made within it, as part of the process of education itself. It also acknowledges that teachers have rights as a profession (Elliott 1976) and that they must be regarded as autonomous professional people. Thus it accepts that teachers have a 'right of reply' or of direct involvement themselves in the accountability process, and that any action consequent on the evidence gleaned in that process must be reached after consultation with fellow professionals and not in total independence of their expert opinion. It concedes, therefore, that teachers should be accountable not only to the agencies of government but 'to a variety of "audiences" in society' (Elliott 1976, p. 51), 'to diverse constituencies rather than to the agglomerate constituency of the public alone' (Sockett 1976b, p. 42), and that among this diversity of audiences, or constituencies must be included the teaching profession itself. The form of evaluation it recommends, then, is not the simple summative form of measuring pupil performance associated with the instrumental model, but rather an illuminative form designed to provide information for this diversity of agencies.

The major difficulties with this model clearly stem from its complexity. It has the merit of recognizing that education is a far more sophisticated activity than the advocates of the other, cruder model appear to think, but along with this must be accepted the difficulties of devising suitable and workable schemes for its translation into practice. These difficulties are virtually identical with those associated with the more sophisticated forms of curriculum evaluation which we fully rehearsed in Chapter 6 and focus particularly on the problems of evaluating activities which are concerned with adherence to principles rather than the attainment of outcomes and those concerning the competence of teachers to evaluate each other's work. We must reiterate here what was said there, namely that the solution to these difficulties is to recognize the complexities of education and work towards similarly sophisticated techniques of evaluation and accountability rather than to reduce the work of teachers to the simplistic levels that existing techniques can measure. Schemes of accountability, like all forms of evaluation and assessment, must follow and support the process of education rather than governing and controlling it.

Our discussion of the two major models of accountability has taken us some way towards an answer to the other questions we suggested need to be faced on this issue, particularly that of to whom teachers should be accountable. It could be argued that the debate about forms of accountability merely reflects a wider debate about what education itself is. A plurality of views can legitimately be held on this question, and a major source of the difficulty in reaching agreement on how teachers can be made accountable is that different people have different views about what their task is. This is certainly true and it must be recognized that it is on this basis that one will choose between the models of accountability available. The logic of the position, however, must inexorably take us to the conclusion either that accountability is impossible or that, whatever model is adopted, this diversity of views must be reflected in the involvement of a diversity of agencies in the process. In short, a recognition of differing views in a democratic setting implies not that the view of the dominant group should prevail but that opportunities should be created for a wide involvement which will reflect the plurality of interests to be found in any democratic society. Otherwise accountability comes to represent a struggle for power rather than for educational improvement. Furthermore, the justice of including teachers themselves in that process is indisputable, and the establishment of a General Teaching Council, to fulfil this and other purposes, is long overdue.

A major reason for that claim is that no one knows better than the professional what is within the scope of his professionalism. This brings us to the third question we suggested needed to be examined carefully, that of what teachers can reasonably be held accountable for. Morally, the teacher, like any common criminal, can only be held responsible for what is in his control, and there are important and insuperable limits to and constraints upon the teacher's control of his pupils' learning. It has long been acknowledged that home background, health, psychological security and many other such factors play a crucial role in determining educability. All of these factors will affect pupils' test scores. Yet, for the most part, these are beyond the teacher's control. We noted too in Chapter 7 the degree to which many other external factors, which it is beyond the scope of the individual teacher to affect, will nevertheless constrain his work. The provision and allocation of resources, for example, the reduction of these resources because of general economic stringency, the related effects of falling rolls, not to mention the monolithic syllabuses of the public examination system, all create limitations to the teacher's work. When one takes account of all of these factors, one realizes how difficult it is to define what teachers can be held solely responsible or accountable for, as well as appreciating again the problems of devising appropriate forms of measurement.

This in turn draws our attention to the fact that if there are factors over which the teacher has little or no control, then accountability must be demanded for these from those who have. To make the teacher solely accountable for the educational performance of his pupils, however that is defined, is not only unfair, it is in the extreme naive. As we suggested earlier, in any discussion of teacher-accountability, we must also ask who else should be held accountable for education.

In answering that question we must first of all look to the internal organization of the school. For schools differ markedly in the degree of responsibility which is afforded to the individual teacher and this is clearly an important factor in determining the degree of his accountability. When a headteacher or departmental head retains a large proportion of authority and control, he must accept a larger share of responsibility for what ensues. Headteachers, for example, who themselves take major decisions concerning the allocating of resources within a school must acknowledge that this has to be accompanied by the acceptance of a larger degree of accountability for its work. Teachers must be given and accept a high degree of participation in policy-making within the school, if responsibility and accountability are to be borne equally by all engaged there. It was argued in Chapter 5 that this is crucial for curriculum development itself. What is being said here supports that view.

Secondly, it is clear that local authorities must be accountable to their public and to their teachers for the level of resource provision they make both to the education service within their regions as a whole and to individual schools within it. The standards attained by pupils, however one wishes to define or measure these, will be as much a function of the support provided by the funding authority as of the skill and competence of its teachers. Indeed, it may be argued that the two will go together, for it is apparent that the most supportive authorities attract the most competent teachers. Providing this kind of support, as was suggested earlier, may also mean allocating additional resources to schools whose standards are clearly low rather than penalizing them for this.

Thirdly, the role of the parents in the education of their children has long been acknowledged and the degree of support that they provide will be a critical factor in determining educational attainments. Their share in the process and their accountability for it must also, therefore, be recognized.

Finally, it is worth noting that pupils' attitudes to school, to education, to learning are significantly affected by the general ethos of the society in which they live and are growing up. That ethos is created to a large extent by the combined effects of the communications media and the commercial and industrial concerns often associated with it. The effects of television in particular, through the values implicit both in the kinds of programme it offers and in the advertisements with which they are often punctuated, are indisputable, and they are often such as to undermine rather than to support the work of the schools. A large share of responsibility for the educational development of pupils must be borne by those responsible for that obtrusive aspect of contemporary life and this must be acknowledged in any attempt we make to assess the responsibility or the competence of teachers.

One final point must be made before we leave this discussion of accountability and that is one that places it firmly into the general context of this book. It must be stressed that the form of accountability adopted will be crucial for curriculum development. It will be clear that the nearer one gets to a hierarchical model the more inhibiting its effect will be on the development of the curriculum. We considered in Chapter 5 the evidence that suggests that successful curriculum development can only come when it is school-based. We also saw that this entails a high degree of autonomy for teachers and a freedom from those constraints that limit their scope to modify and change the curriculum. We can now see that, if that process is to be encouraged, we need a model of accountability that will allow for it and such a model must include a high degree of professional involvement. Teacher autonomy need not imply less accountability. Indeed, it might be taken to imply more. What it does imply, however, is that we must get the form and the procedures of accountability right.

Summary and conclusions

An attempt has been made in this chapter to demonstrate that the focus of the curriculum debate has recently shifted towards considerations of a political and economic kind, to trace the development of that process and to pick out its major features. In particular, it has examined recent attempts to monitor the standards of education and to make teachers more accountable for their work.

The main conclusion that has been reached in this discussion is not that this shift of emphasis is necessarily of itself undesirable nor that attempts to improve procedures for the monitoring of standards and for teacher accountability are to be discouraged. Rather it has been that such procedures must be improved, and that this must be done in such a way as to avoid the distortion of education, the loss of valuable elements in it and a further slowing down of the process of curriculum development which this book has argued to be so important. We have seen that these are the effects of some of the measures that have been and are being taken, particularly those which are taken by people outside the teaching profession who lack the kind of understanding of education upon which decisions of this kind must be based. Once again, therefore, our conclusion has been that, if these goals are to be attained, the teachers themselves, both as individuals and as a professional body, must play a major part in their attainment.

It was suggested earlier that this new focus for education has led not only to attempts to improve the means of monitoring standards and of increasing the accountability of teachers but also to proposals to remove the responsibility for curriculum planning from the teachers and locate it in some central agency. Proposals of this kind clearly are in direct conflict with that trend towards the increased responsibility of the teacher for curriculum development which has been a recurring theme of this book. They deserve, therefore, a final chapter to themselves, not least because a consideration of them may also help us to draw together a number of strands of our discussion into something approaching a coherent whole.

CHAPTER 9

THE WHOLE CURRICULUM

It was suggested in the previous chapter that the impact on the work of the schools of the recent increase of political interest in education has been threefold. It has led to demands for a closer monitoring of standards, to pressures for the increased accountability of teachers and to claims that there should be a common curriculum or at least a common core to the curriculum. It is to a consideration of this last issue that we now turn.

This is an issue that has many theoretical implications of a very wide kind and it is certainly one that picks up and links together many of the points that we have endeavoured to examine in earlier chapters of this book. Thus a discussion of the problems and implications of this notion of establishing by central control a common curriculum or a common core to the curriculum will effectively round off our exploration of the theory and practice of curriculum development, since it will draw many threads together and will, as a result, act as a summary to the book as a whole.

There is another reason why this would appear to offer a suitable conclusion to our discussion of the curriculum. For it is beginning to appear that this movement towards increased external control of the curriculum, especially through its associated pressures for the establishment of a common core to the curriculum, has led to a growing concern with the curriculum as a totality. For the evidence of the effects of piecemeal planning by subjects that has emerged from such sources as the survey of secondary education in England and Wales conducted by Her Majesty's Inspectorate (DES 1979), has encouraged many people towards the view that the educational experiences of every individual pupil must be seen and evaluated as a whole. Thus the question of whether there should be a common core to the curriculum or not may be seen to be giving way to that of how far we can ensure that, whether common or not, the actual experiences of the individual pupil add up to a coherent and balanced totality. In short, the desire for external control may be seen either as in part stemming from a concern to ensure some kind of balanced curricular provision or at least as having led to a realization of its desirability, and not merely as the reflection of a desire to attend to the needs of society or of industry. It is thus an issue which picks up for us the idea of planning the curriculum as a whole which we raised in Chapter 1 and several related issues which subsequent chapters have explored.

It is perhaps worth reminding ourselves from the outset that the United Kingdom has been hitherto an exception in allowing its teachers and headteachers the degree of freedom over the curriculum of their schools that they currently enjoy. We have already noted the hidden constraints and influences that they are subject to in this respect and we have commented on the fact that, as a result of these, the most interesting features of the curricula of most schools in the United Kingdom are their similarities rather than their differences. Nevertheless, the fact remains that legally there is no binding requirement on any school to include any particular subject or activity in its curriculum other than a weekly period of religious instruction.

This freedom contrasts most markedly with the procedures in other countries, most of which lay down, in varying degrees of detail, essential requirements for the curriculum of all schools. Thus there is a core curriculum established for the 10-year school in the USSR which sets out the range of subjects to be included for each year group and also lists the number of hours that are to be devoted to each every week. Nor does this requirement leave much scope for the addition of other subjects at the discretion of the individual school, since very little of the working week is left to provide any such latitude. This scheme has provided the basic model for the curriculum of all eastern bloc countries.

A similar approach to curriculum control can be seen also in most Western European countries. There are, of course, variations in the degree of control. Not all countries, for example, specify the number of hours to be devoted to each area; some leave rather more time for optional areas of study; there is some variation in the extent of the control that is exercised in relation to different age-groups of children; and sometimes, as in West Germany, for example, more than one common curriculum is established to cater for children of different intellectual abilities. However, the principle of central control over what are seen as the most important areas of the curriculum is well established and almost unquestioned outside the United Kingdom.

However, in the United Kingdom the tradition has been very different and the idea that there should be a common curriculum for all pupils is a comparatively recent one.

The case for a common core to the curriculum

Broadly speaking, three kinds of argument are produced in favour of the idea of a common curriculum and all of these we have touched upon already. First of all, we have those philosophical or epistemological arguments that base their recommendations for the content of a common curriculum on particular views about the nature of knowledge. Secondly, we have certain social or sociological arguments which base their case on either a sociological assessment of what society and its culture are or certain ideological claims about what they ought to be. Finally, as a kind of subvariant of this, we have the political or economic arguments which claim that the curriculum should be planned in such a way as to ensure that all pupils have the opportunity to develop to a certain standard the skills and knowledge that will enable them to meet the demands of a technological society.

One kind of argument, then, claims that since certain kinds of knowledge have a status and value superior to others they have a prior claim for inclusion in any curriculum that is to be regarded as educational in the full sense. We have already noted the claim of Richard Peters that education is concerned only with those activities which have an intrinsic value (Peters 1965, 1966). To this we might add the theory of Paul Hirst, which we discussed in Chapter 4, that knowledge is to be divided into seven or eight discrete forms of rationality, each distinguishable from the other through its unique logical structure, and of education as the initiation of pupils into all of these forms (Hirst 1965). If this is the view that one takes of education, then it will follow that the curriculum for all pupils must consist of these intrinsically worthwhile activities and of all of these forms of knowledge or understanding (Hirst 1969; Hirst and Peters 1970). On this kind of argument any pupil whose curriculum excludes him from any of these areas of human knowledge and understanding is being offered an educational provision that is by definition inferior or is not receiving an education in the full sense at all.

The sociological version of this same argument is the one we have already noted that is based on the idea that it is the job of the school to transmit the culture of the society and that the curriculum must be designed to convey what is worthwhile in the culture of the society to all pupils.

This is the kind of consideration that has formed the basis of the cases that have been made out hitherto for a common core to the curriculum. These, for example, as we saw in Chapter 2, are John White's major reasons for suggesting that the essential elements of the compulsory curriculum at secondary level should be communication, mathematics, the physical sciences, art appreciation and philosophical thought (White 1973). The same kinds of consideration too underlie Denis Lawton's recommendation that the curriculum should contain six core areas – five disciplines and one interdisciplinary unit. The six areas he suggests are mathematics, the physical and biological sciences, the humanities and social sciences (including history, geography, classical studies, social studies, literature, film and TV and religious studies), the expressive and creative arts, moral education and interdisciplinary work (Lawton 1969, 1973, 1975).

This kind of argument for a common curriculum, then, is based on those particular views of knowledge and of society that we considered earlier in this book and on the belief that it is possible to establish some kind of value system that will enable us to choose what is worthwhile in knowledge and in the culture of the society.

The social arguments for a common curriculum start, as it were, from the opposite end of things. For they begin by considering some of the implications of not offering a common form of education to everyone. They have been prompted by recent attempts to base education on the interests of children, to try to make school-work meaningful and relevant to them by planning it in relation to their experience of their own immediate environment. The suggestion made by the Schools Council's Working Paper No. 11, for example, that we might base the education of pupils in part on the experience to be gained from a study of 'the 97 bus' (Schools Council 1967) was particularly effective in sparking off this kind of reaction. For it is claimed that an approach such as this can lead to a form of social control every bit as sinister as the imposition of one culture or one set of values on all (White 1968, 1973). If a child's experience is to be limited to his own culture, his own environment, what he is already familiar with before he enters school, then there is a real risk that he will be trapped in that cultural environment and given little opportunity of gaining experience outside it.

Furthermore, if we once concede that two or three curricula might be generated to meet two or three broadly different kinds of need, we are almost certainly accepting implicitly the idea that Plato made quite explicit, that education in the full sense is only capable of being achieved by some gifted people and that the rest must be offered something inferior, which can only be some form of indoctrination or 'education in obedience' (White 1968).

This is an idea that has followed in the wake of the wider notion of education for all. There is no logical connection between the idea of education for all and that of a common curriculum, nor do demands for educational equality imply that all must have the same educational diet, since, as the Plowden Report asserted (Central Advisory Council for Education 1967), there is no incompatibility between the idea of equality of educational opportunity and variety of educational provision (Downey and Kelly 1979). Originally, therefore, the ideal of education for all, as it was expressed in the 1944 Education Act, was interpreted as requiring not that all should have the same educational provision but that the content of education should vary according to such considerations as age, aptitude and ability.

This was a natural development of what can be discerned throughout the history of the educational system of the United Kingdom, since this has been characterized from the beginning by the development of two or more separate curricula, those of the grammar and of the elementary schools and later of the grammar, technical (where they existed) and the modern schools. Again we note the dead hand of Plato manipulating us still in the twentieth century and encouraging us to see education as having at least two forms, one for the able and another for the less able.

As a result we find many actually criticizing the work of the secondary modern schools in the 1940s and 1950s on the grounds that they were 'aping the grammar schools' by setting up a curriculum that appeared to be for the most part no more than a watered-down version of the grammar school curriculum. Equally, however, it is not surprising to find them doing this, since the inadequacies and inaccuracies of the selection procedures employed, well documented in many research studies of the time, make it clear that even if the generation of two or more curricula is in itself justified, the practical implementation of these, and especially the matching of pupils to them, is far from clear-cut and easy.

Problems of selection, then, are the focus of the criticisms that have been levelled at the tripartite selective system of secondary education, but these have also been accompanied by charges of unfairness and inequality which have resulted in the ending of selection and the replacement of that system by a pattern of comprehensive secondary education, a movement which would seem to imply a need for some commonality of educational provision. Thus we find the claim now being made that, if justice and fairness are to be attained and the ideal of education for all achieved, all pupils should have access to the same areas or bodies of knowledge and learning.

These social arguments for a common core to the curriculum, then, need to be looked at very closely.

Finally, to these epistemological, sociological and social arguments has recently been added the political and economic case. As we suggested earlier, this movement received its initial impetus from events in several schools where it has been felt that teachers have abused their freedom and autonomy and that as a result their pupils have missed out in certain important respects. This kind of unfortunate occurrence could be avoided, it is felt, if more direct control were exercised over what is done in schools.

Concern over the content of what is taught has been expressed by those who believe that the schools are not producing enough people who have been trained in such a way as to meet the demands of a technological society for scientists and technologists. Too many pupils, it is claimed, are exercising the choices offered them by schools and universities to pursue interests in the humanities or in the social sciences and too few are opting for advanced work in the physical and natural sciences. The only solution that it is felt can be found for this state of affairs is to decree centrally that pupils shall not have such choices and to insist that all have a larger scientific and/or technological component than at present in their curriculum. This, of course, reflects the approach that we have already briefly referred to as adopted in the USSR where there is no doubt that the prime consideration in establishing a central core to the curriculum is the economic needs of society.

All of these arguments appear to have some force, but it will also be apparent that many of them cut across not only most of what has been said earlier in this book but also what we have tried to identify as the whole trend of curriculum development in recent years in the United Kingdom towards an increasingly school-based model and away from this centre–periphery model, the inadequacies of which we attempted to expose in Chapter 5.

We must now consider, therefore, some of the problems and difficulties that this notion of a centralized core curriculum raises.

Problems and difficulties

The first point to be noted here is that the arguments we have just considered, although all leading to the same general conclusion, are derived from very different premises. They are based on different theories of knowledge and different views of education, and they offer different kinds of justificatory argument. The philosophical, epistemological arguments, for example, are based on the notion of the intrinsic value of certain kinds of knowledge, while the political, economic arguments are clearly instrumental and utilitarian. Thus they lead to very different practical proposals and this is a major source of chaos, even where the principle of a common core to the curriculum has been accepted. They lead also to confusion in the minds of some of its advocates, since their views are often based on an amalgam of considerations.

Secondly, in so far as many of the arguments offered in support of the idea of a common curriculum derive from certain views about the nature of knowledge and of values, we need do no more than remind ourselves of the difficulties of this kind of argument which we examined in some detail in Chapter 2, when discussing this same question of the basis upon which we can decide upon the content of the curriculum. For we noted then that there is a variety of positions one can take on this issue of the nature of knowledge and that among the least convincing of these is that which claims some kind of objective status for knowledge. Even less convincing, we claimed, are those arguments which attempt to demonstrate the superiority of certain kinds of knowledge and human activity over others. If we were right to argue there that there is no firm foundation upon which we can establish the prior claims of some areas of human knowledge and activity to be included in the curriculum, then that same argument has even more force in the context of proposals to establish a common curriculum for all pupils.

This becomes immediately apparent when we ask what is to be the content of such a common curriculum and who shall have the right to decide on it. For even if we agree in principle that some of the arguments for a commonality of basic educational provision are strong, such agreement immediately breaks down when we come to decide what such basic provision should consist of and who is to be the arbiter.

Who shall decide? Shall it be the teachers and other educationists? Shall it be the philosophers or the sociologists? Shall it be the politicians or the parents or even the children themselves? It might be argued that in practice all of these groups of people currently contribute to curriculum planning, but to say that any one group or even all of them collectively should decide on the content of a compulsory common curriculum for all pupils is to go far beyond current practice and even, perhaps, beyond common sense. For, as we have just seen, the reasons each of these groups will have for advocating a common curriculum will differ in significant ways.

The same kind of problem emerges when we consider what the content of such a curriculum should be. Again, even if the idea is accepted in principle, further difficulties arise when we undertake the impossible task of reaching agreement on its content. What is it that all pupils should be introduced to as part of their education? Those proposals that have been put forward for the content of such a curriculum are far from indisputable. For they are derived, as we have seen, either from a particular view of the nature of knowledge or from some idea of what is valuable in the culture of society or some attempt at combining both of these considerations (White 1973; Thompson and White 1975; Lawton 1969, 1973, 1975). John White's suggestion, for example, that the compulsory curriculum at secondary level should consist primarily of communication, mathematics, the physical sciences, art appreciation and philosophical thought would hardly have universal acceptance. The idea of compulsory philosophical thought for some of the classes many teachers meet each day in their secondary schools is likely to be particularly productive of wry smiles or even hollow laughter. There is probably no single activity that will have universal support in its claims for inclusion in a common core of the curriculum. Even the teaching of reading has been described and criticized as a subversive activity that schools should not promote (Postman 1970).

The converse of this is also true. For just as there will be minority views opposed to the inclusion even of those things that have almost universal acceptance, there will also be those minority interests that will be vociferously demanding the inclusion of those things that they themselves happen for personal reasons to be committed to. A good example of this is the demand being made at the political level for the inclusion of religious instruction of some kind in the common core. Once the principle of a common core curriculum is accepted, such idiosyncratic demands will proliferate and thus render its implementation almost impossible.

Thus the establishment of a common curriculum must founder on the practical issues of what should be included in it and who shall decide on this.

To these problems that derive from the difficulty, even the impossibility, of establishing any universally accepted criteria for judging the relative worth of different kinds of knowledge, we must add the further difficulties that are raised by the criticisms currently being made of the content of the curriculum by many sociologists (Young 1971). For, as we have seen, their claims that all knowledge must be recognized as being socially constructed lead not only to an awareness of the lack of such objective criteria; they also raise further issues of a more sinister kind concerning the likely results of imposing a common system of knowledge on all pupils.

For, as we saw in Chapter 2, it is argued that knowledge is socially constructed, that culture is impossible to define and that many cultures can be identified in a modern pluralist society. It is also argued that to impose one culture, one set of values on all pupils regardless of their origins, their social class, race or creed is to risk at best offering them a curriculum that is irrelevant, meaningless and alienating and at worst using the educational system as a means of effecting an inhibiting form of social control (Young 1971).

It is claimed, therefore, that such a process results in the attempt to introduce children to areas of knowledge that they find irrelevant to their own lives and meaningless in relation to their own experience and thus encourages them to reject what they are offered, so that it leads not to education but to disaffection and even alienation from both the content of education and society itself. Further, as an attempt to impose a particular value system on pupils, it is difficult to defend such practice even from the charge of indoctrination, so that such a system is not only inefficient and counterproductive, it is also open to criticism on moral grounds.

Further support for such a view has come from the activities of those who have been attempting in practice to develop programmes of work that would be relevant and meaningful to pupils and would as a result encourage in them a fuller and therefore more educational involvement in their work. Thus, as we have already noted, recent years have seen an accelerating movement at all levels of education towards 'progressive', 'pupil-centred' methods, heuristic approaches of all kinds, learning by experience, learning by discovery, learning through interests and so on. The general trend of this movement, as we have seen, has been towards a greater individualization of education. And it is again an example of how a different theory of knowledge will lead to a different view of education and to quite different proposals for educational provision.

Thus we have the strange situation that the idea of a common educational provision which is argued for on grounds of equality, justice and fairness is opposed most vigorously for precisely the same reasons by those who might be regarded as on the 'left wing' of educational debate, those who see the imposition of knowledge as a form of social control and those who even go so far as to advocate total deschooling.

We are, therefore, presented with yet another dilemma, or rather with evidence that we are faced by a debate about means rather than ends. For on both sides we have a commitment to the ideal of educational equality but we are faced with a headlong clash on the question of how such an ideal is to be achieved, whether by insisting that all pupils have access to the same knowledge or by tailoring educational provision to suit their individual needs. This is a point we must return to later.

In the meantime, we must proceed to note that none of these arguments deriving from problems over the nature of knowledge will affect to the slightest degree the political and economic arguments for a common core curriculum. For the case there for the inclusion of certain kinds of knowledge and activity in the curriculum of all pupils is based not on educational or epistemological arguments for the intrinsic value or superiority of these areas of knowledge; it is based entirely on grounds of their social utility and importance. What other grounds could there be for insisting that pupils should be discouraged from spending too much of their time pursuing their interests in the humanities and social sciences and should be required to devote more time to science and technology?

This kind of argument, however, does present some difficulties of its own. In the first place, it raises many issues concerning the rights of individual pupils and parents to choose the content of their education, to decide for themselves or for their children what their interests are and what they wish to spend their time pursuing. We considered in Chapter 2 in some detail the problems and possibilities of basing our curriculum on the interests of pupils. Such a practice clearly will become impossible, except in the limited and perhaps unacceptable sense of using their interests to further the purposes of other people, if we accept that the content of their education is to be decided, even in part, from without. Thus an opportunity to develop an educational provision for each pupil that might be meaningful to him in his own terms will be lost and at the same time his freedom to choose for himself will be infringed beyond any point that can be justified on educational grounds. For it is one thing to attempt to justify requiring pupils to engage in certain kinds of learning activity on the grounds that we believe this will be good for them; it is quite another to justify it as being good for society. Is Plato creeping up on us again?

Secondly, the politicians and the economists are likely to encounter at least as much difficulty in reaching agreement on the content of a common core curriculum as we suggested the educationists, the epistemologists and the culture-theorists would experience. There are several levels at which this will become apparent.

To begin with, as we have already suggested, beyond the need for basic literacy and numeracy, there is likely to be a good deal of disagreement. We have already referred to the attempt by certain politicians to have religious instruction included in the central core as a prime example of the disputes that will immediately follow the acceptance in principle of a common core curriculum. Any list of subjects produced will reflect the personal prefer-ences and values of the person who compiles it. Secondly, even if attention is concentrated on standards in the basic skills, it is difficult to know how a clear standard can be set or what such a standard would mean. Thirdly, there will be further difficulties in determining what is meant by the demand for such things as adequate scientific and technological education. Does this mean theoretical understanding or practical expertise? Does it suggest that we concentrate on developing children's knowledge of what happens and how it can be controlled or of why it happens (Fowler 1977). As Gerry Fowler says, 'Any attempt to determine the content of an accept-able core curriculum by listing subjects is doomed to failure. The list must be either unduly restrictive, or so all-embracing as to tax the wits of the most sophisticated timetabler and the energies of the most dedicated pupil' (op. cit.).

This raises a further point concerning the degree of commonality we should be aiming for. We noted at the beginning of this chapter the variations in this that can be observed in those countries that have a centralized curriculum. How far are we to go in specifying centrally what should be taught in all schools? Is it enough to produce a list of subjects or do we need also to devise central syllabuses? Should there be some central dictation of the methods to be used? Certainly some of the recent events in schools that have acquired national significance have been the result of the methods adopted rather than the subjects being taught. Are we to specify the number of hours each week to be devoted to each subject or even the times of the day when they are to be taught? Are we to prescribe textbooks to be used by all schools in the teaching of these subjects at particular levels and to particular age-groups?

All of these would seem to follow logically upon the demand for common-ality. For if we leave teachers too much scope for individual interpretation then very little that can be described as common will ensue. We have already noted several times the gap that exists between the official and the actual curriculum of any school or individual classroom. That gap will be even greater if there is central dictation of content but latitude for local interpretation of such things as time to be spent on each subject, methods to be employed, approaches to be adopted and textbooks to be used. A consideration of the wide range of interpretation of the present requirement in the United Kingdom for a compulsory period of religious instruction for all pupils will illustrate effectively the point that is being made.

The same kind of difficulty is inherent in the proposal that has recently been under discussion in the United Kingdom for giving school governing bodies control over the curriculum while leaving to the teacher decisions as to the teaching methods to be used, on the grounds that these are his or her professional responsibility. Even if we allow for the fact that the governing bodies would be redesigned to give a majority of members elected by parents and teachers and that all governors would be trained for their task, an arrangement of this kind creates a distinction between content and method which is not only undesirable but also untenable and certainly likely to result in the same gap between the official and the actual curriculum, between theory and practice, that we have just referred to.

To achieve a common curriculum, or any kind of external control over the curriculum, it is not enough to specify only which subjects it must contain. At present, even in the United Kingdom, as we have already mentioned, this is in practice the situation that holds anyway, since all of the subjects likely to be included in any list that might be agreed are already on the curriculum of all schools. If commonality is really to be achieved, much more central direction will be needed than that. It is doubtful if the middle ground is tenable here.

This brings us naturally to a consideration of the major source of prob-lems presented by demands for a common core to the curriculum – those that derive from what we have said so far about the central role of the teacher in curriculum development and, indeed, the trend towards a recognition of this that we have claimed recent years have seen. We must now turn to a consideration of some of the major facets of this.

The implications of a centralized curriculum for curriculum development

As we have just suggested, a further set of problems appears when we consider the consequences for the autonomy of the teacher of the establishment of a compulsory element in the curriculum. One of the most highly prized features of the English educational system in the eyes of many teachers is the degree of autonomy given to individual schools and teachers. This procedure contrasts most markedly, as we have seen, with the practice of many other countries where a common curriculum is decreed by law.

The objection to this in the United Kingdom comes not only from a desire for the freedom and autonomy that individual schools and teachers enjoy, nor even from an abhorrence of basing educational decisions on economic considerations, but also from the conviction, mentioned already several times, that there can be no satisfactory curriculum development unless this takes place at the coal-face of the individual school and classroom. We have already noted that this would almost certainly result in an individual interpretation of any common centralized curriculum by each school. It also makes the notion of such central dictation not only unacceptable but also perhaps incompatible with the idea of curriculum development in its full sense. Thus many people who accept the full force of the arguments we listed earlier in favour of attempting to offer all pupils a common range of educationally extending experiences would be loathe to accept that this should be done by some kind of central dictation of the content of the curriculum.

We must now look in more detail at some of the facets of this problem. To a large extent we must do this by reiterating many of the points we have made earlier in this book and especially in Chapters 5 and 6 about the role of the teacher in curriculum development. For we have assigned him a central role and the proposals for a common curriculum will have the effect of pushing him back towards the periphery.

To begin with, as we suggested earlier, to achieve anything describable as commonality in the curriculum we must reduce the latitude for individual interpretation by the teacher to an absolute minimum. We suggested that it would not make sense to decide on common subjects and leave the choice of methods, approaches, textbooks and so on to the teacher. Thus, within the context of any real attempt to establish a common curriculum, his role must be reduced to that of a puppet, operated by remote control and able to exercise professional judgement only in the very limited sphere of immediate methodology, if it is possible even there. If we do not accept that this is a proper role for teachers, we cannot accept the idea of a common curriculum, since, as we have tried to show, both logically and practically the two things go together.

One might, of course, react to this point by saying 'So what?' In other words, it might appear to some that teachers should not be given scope for exercising professional judgement of a wider kind. On the other hand, the central theme of this book has been that the task of the teacher cannot be defined in the kind of mechanistic terms that such a view implies, that education in the full sense can only proceed if teachers are able to make judgements on a much larger scale and that any attempt to inhibit them in exercising this kind of judgement is likely to redound to the disadvantage both of education and of their pupils. One of the strongest arguments for the autonomy of the school and the teacher is that only those on the spot can devise a programme suited to their particular school and its pupils. The experts from outside not only lack this local knowledge, they are also usually people whose expertise is too narrow to enable them to make the kind of holistic judgement that is needed for decisions of practical policy (Dearden 1976). Such holistic judgements only teachers can be expected to make.

Furthermore, we have also argued that it is only through the exercise of this kind of judgement that curriculum development of any meaningful kind can proceed. We examined in Chapter 5 some of the problems of adopting a centre–periphery model for the dissemination of curriculum innovation. We saw the variety of response that there always is from teachers to any curriculum project. We saw the difficulties of getting a project to 'take' in a school and suggested that this could only be achieved if the teachers responsible for implementing it both had a deep understanding of its import and were committed to its ideology, since teachers will only work effectively if they understand what they are about and believe in it. We also suggested that they are most likely to have this kind of understanding and commitment if they have themselves recognized the need for change and have been involved in the planning, the decision making and the development of the project generally. We further illustrated this point by reference to the disastrous effects that often follow when attempts are made to impose particular innovations or methods, such as mixed-ability groupings, on teachers who are opposed to them.

All of this, if true, reinforces what we have already said about the variations in interpretation that there will be of any curriculum imposed from outside; it suggests too that such an approach will bring out the saboteurs; it raises the question of whether, as a result, the imposition of a common curriculum is not likely to lead to less efficient rather than more efficient teaching; it also must cause us to reflect that if the central factor in curriculum development is thus rendered largely ineffective, the overall effect will be the ossification of the curriculum.

We noted in Chapter 5 that an awareness of this had led to the recent move towards school-based curriculum development, and we suggested that this shift implies an acceptance of the view that it is the needs of the child rather than those of society that must be accorded priority in curriculum planning.

We are thus faced with a serious dilemma. One solution to this might be to press a distinction we made earlier between central dictation of content and a monitoring of standards. It may be that if we content ourselves with attempting to ensure that certain standards are being attained rather than with specifying in great detail what should be going on in schools, we may be able to exercise the control that some feel to be desirable without unduly inhibiting the teacher in his roles as educator and as curriculum developer. However, we also argued in Chapter 6 that processes of evaluation and assessment themselves have a 'make or break' role in curriculum development. We must now look at this in relation to the idea of a common curriculum.

Evaluation, accountability and the centralized curriculum

It has been suggested that there are three types of decision for which the data produced by evaluative procedures are used – course improvement, decisions about individual pupils, and administrative regulation (Cronbach 1963). Where decisions about the curriculum are made by the headteacher and others in the individual school, as at present is the case in the United Kingdom, all three of these aspects of curriculum planning can be and usually are taken together (Stenhouse 1975), and the demands of each, perhaps sometimes conflicting, can be weighed against each other. It must also be noted, however, that where decisions about the curriculum are taken centrally, by school boards, by the state or by central government, as, for example, in the USA and Sweden, the facility to balance these aspects of curriculum development and evaluation against each other seems to disappear. The emphasis, in this case, tends to swing very much towards the use of evaluative procedures for administrative purposes, to assess the worth of individual teachers, schools or even the school system itself and to measure curricular innovations in terms of what can be recommended to schools as a whole rather than in terms of what seems to be appropriate to the development of the curriculum in any particular school.

Such a change of emphasis must be expected to follow the introduction of any kind of centralized control over the curriculum in the United Kingdom, at least in those areas of the curriculum that become subject to such control. It has several facets.

In the first place, such an approach is clearly likely to lead us back to an objectives model both for the curriculum and for our evaluation procedures. For if we want to know for administrative purposes of the kind we have briefly referred to whether a curriculum works or not, we are inevitably going to begin by stating clearly what that curriculum is supposed to achieve. Thus the pronouncements of politicians on this issue of centralized control over the content of the curriculum and the monitoring of standards of achievement are always couched in terms of their expectations of the output of educational institutions – more scientists, better trained technologists and people who are basically literate and numerate so that they can read the material and do the sums that the jobs they subsequently take up will require of them (but not, one presumes, those that reveal the state of the economy). While admitting the desirability of training a few politicians who were literate and numerate or at least some who could take on the task of getting the state's finances right, we must draw attention to the means/end view of the school's role that is implicit in such statements, some of the dangers of which we examined in our discussion of objectives in Chapter 4 and in our more detailed discussion of evaluation in Chapter 6. It is quite clear that it is this simple model of both the curriculum and of evaluation that we are brought to by the adoption of a system of centralized monitoring of the curriculum.

The second aspect of this is that it raises the whole question of who should undertake the task of evaluation. For the whole thrust of any decision to centralize control of curriculum development is towards an external monitoring of the work and the standards of individual schools or groups of schools. If the results of evaluation are to be used by administrators to help them to organize the work of the schools then clearly they will want to or will be forced to undertake the task of evaluation themselves and to set up their procedures in such a way as to ensure that they obtain the most suitable kind of data from them.

But who is competent to make this kind of judgement from outside the school? We saw in Chapter 7 that the role of the inspector has changed, primarily because of his inability to keep up with the pace of curriculum development in the schools and the difficulties of gaining from the outside the kinds of insight and understanding needed to make a proper evaluation of it. This is still a valid point.

We also suggested that to make it possible for any outsider to do the job we must accept a very simple and unsophisticated view of the curriculum and this is borne out by what is happening as a result of the attempts to establish this kind of accountability in the USA. So many of the dangers which throughout this book we have suggested should be avoided in curriculum planning reappear once external monitoring becomes a central feature of the school system – a clear prespecification not only of behavioural objectives but of those simple objectives that can readily be measured by objective-referenced tests; a reduced 'say' for teachers in the content of the curriculum and in the methods they will adopt; a similarly reduced 'say' for pupils, introducing again the dangers of irrelevance and alienation; the inhibitions on any real educational development that come from having to accept external dictation and external checks on the curriculum; in short, an erosion of the kind of teacher autonomy that we have suggested throughout this book is vital to real curriculum development and educational progress.

The implications for curriculum development of this approach to evaluation were examined at some length in Chapter 6. It should, therefore, be sufficient to note here that this will represent a move away from what we described there as a 'democratic' style of evaluation towards a style that is better described as 'autocratic', or even 'bureaucratic'. We noted before that these distinctions are made by Barry MacDonald from a recognition that evaluation is a political activity. However, the styles described do represent very different ways in which this political activity can be carried out. 'Bureaucratic evaluation is an unconditional service to those government agencies which have major control over the allocation of educational resources. The evaluator accepts the values of those who hold office, and offers information which will help to accomplish their policy objectives' (MacDonald 1975, p. 133). 'Autocratic evaluation is a conditional service to those government agencies which have major control over the allocation of educational resources. It offers external validation of policy in exchange for compliance with its recommendations' (ibid.). It will be plain from these definitions that they approximate more to the style of evaluation that the external monitoring of a common core curriculum will require than does the 'democratic' style.

That style we have noted is defined as 'an information service to the whole community' (op. cit., p. 134) and its central concerns are to encourage negotiation between all groups who have an interest in a particular aspect of curriculum development and to leave it to the consumers to decide what they will do as a result of the information they have been given; 'the evaluator has no concept of information misuse' (ibid.).

It was within the context of this style of evaluation that we made out a case in Chapter 6 for the teacher as evaluator and suggested that, if the teacher were thus involved both as evaluator himself and as the recipient of information from other evaluators, evaluation could be seen as a central feature of school-based curriculum development, in fact as the kind of action-research that we suggested was implied by that model of curriculum development that sees evaluation as 'formative' or 'illuminative' rather than 'summative'. Such continuous action-research and feedback, allied to the autonomy of schools and teachers to modify their curricula in the light of such information gained or received, was, we claimed, central to any kind of effective and continuous curriculum development.

It will be clear from the preceding discussion that such continuous development will not be possible if the monitoring is done from the outside and if the schools in any case lack the autonomy to change their curricula in the light of what is learnt from it.

The implications of external monitoring, then, for curriculum development are as inhibiting as were those that derived from the external dictation of content. The dilemma remains. Are we to leave everything entirely in the hands of the teachers and risk the occasional disaster when they abuse the freedom this gives them? Or are we to remove this freedom and risk not only inefficiency of teaching and inadequacies of educational provision but also the charge of attempting either to indoctrinate children with a particular system of values or of using them to serve the ends of the state?

One solution to this dilemma may lie in the way we interpret the notion of accountability. Perhaps we can, as in the Athenian democracy of old, organize things in such a way as to provide autonomy of action but follow it up with some demands that a reckoning be given, that a justification be offered and an account rendered for how that autonomy has been used.

We saw in Chapter 8 that there are dangers at a number of levels in accepting a hierarchical model of accountability as accountability to those central and local government bodies that exercise control over the finances of education. What is fundamentally wrong with the hierarchical model of accountability is that it attempts to make teachers accountable to only one of the agencies that have an interest in education, or it assumes that governmental bodies can act on behalf of all interested parties. This is clearly not so and the only acceptable form of teacher accountability will be one which makes him clearly accountable to all those people and bodies that have a stake in what he is doing.

Teachers are professionally responsible to a number of different bodies in society and it is to all of these bodies that they should be accountable. Awareness of this, as we saw in Chapter 8, leads to what has been called a 'democratic' model of accountability (Elliott 1976). It has also been argued that the very fact that the teacher is accountable in this way gives him the right to participate himself in the process of evaluation to which his work is thus subject (Elliott 1976). He has a right of reply, even if one is not to put it higher than that, a right that the hierarchical model of external monitoring by government agencies would seem to deny him. Thus we have a model of accountability as a two-way process between the teacher and all of those outside agencies who have a stake in his work. Only thus, it is argued, can we have a genuine system of classroom accountability.

Such a system of accountability acknowledges the central role of the teacher in curriculum development. At the same time, however, it also introduces the idea of the involvement of other interested parties in curriculum development, not only in the evaluation of the curriculum but in the planning that ensues from such evaluation. It requires of teachers that in exercising their central role they take full cognisance of all of those pressures and influences we discussed in Chapter 7 and recognize the rights of other people both to contribute their views on the methods and content of the curriculum and to join in the evaluation processes, provided that this is done in collaboration with and with the full participation of the teachers themselves.

It is in this direction, perhaps, that we must look not only for an adequate scheme of teacher accountability, but also for the only sound basis for true curriculum development.

It is clear, however, that the demand for greater external control and the pressures it has generated have already begun to have the effect of distorting the work of many schools and teachers. The work of individual teachers has in many cases been inhibited by requests that they produce plans or records of their work in a form or according to a curriculum model which conflicts with rather than matches their own style of teaching. Schools have shown a greater reluctance than ever to embark on new ventures and, if doing so, have often experienced similar conflicts of style. And in general there has resulted a slowing down rather than an acceleration of curriculum development.

It has also become apparent that, for the reasons we have just listed, this is inevitable and that, for the reasons we listed earlier, especially in Chapter 5, if there is to be real curriculum development, a climate must be created in which schools and teachers can promote it from within their classrooms, that local initiatives offer a sounder base than national directives for educational advance.

Hence one can detect another recent shift of focus in the curriculum debate, a shift towards offering guidelines rather than directives to schools. This is reflected in a change of terminology, so that we have heard less of late about a common curriculum and rather more about the 'essential' curriculum, about the 'balanced' curriculum, about the 'total' curriculum. And there is substantial evidence for such a shift in the withdrawal of the Department of Education and Science's pamphlet *A Framework for the School Curriculum* (DES 1980b), whose attempt to establish a common core curriculum made evident the gross inadequacies of that approach, and its replacement with *The School Curriculum* (DES 1981), which adopts a less assured and more tentative tone and offers advice rather than directives, general guidelines rather than specific injunctions.

It is along these lines that a solution to the problem must be sought.

The balanced curriculum

Several important implications can be seen in the trend we have just identified. What these are, however, is not clear without further analysis.

For, without such closer examination, the use of terms like 'essential' and 'balance' will appear to bring with them those connotations of scientific exactitude which we have seen on other occasions to be spurious and misleading in educational contexts. The notion of balance in physics is precise and can be expressed as a mathematical formula. For it is a function of the weight of the objects in balance in relation to the distance of the forces they exert from the fulcrum around which they exert them. It would clearly be a mistake to look for this kind of precision in any educational context and we must recognize that the use of such terms in education is figurative and that any promise of exactitude they seem to offer is spurious. Like all other such notions, that of balance in education must be recognized as relative, taking its meaning almost entirely from the value system of the person using it. In short, we will all have our own views of what constitutes a balanced curriculum and what that view is will in turn depend on what we see as the fundamental principles of education. We must begin, therefore, by recognizing this and noting once again, as we did in Chapter 2, the essential and problematic value element in all educational debate.

This notion does bring several elements into the debate, however, which take us a good way beyond the idea of a common curriculum. For, in the first place, the demand that the curriculum be balanced requires that we view it and plan it as a totality and not in the piecemeal fashion hitherto adopted. The dangers of the piecemeal approach to curriculum planning within subjects emerged clearly and disturbingly from the survey of secondary education in England conducted recently by Her Majesty's Inspectorate (DES 1979). It became apparent from that survey that the 'options' system employed by most secondary schools for their fourth- and fifth-year pupils has resulted often in a curriculum for some individual pupils which few would or could describe as balanced, whatever their notion of education.

> Something would seem to have been wrong with guidance when, for example, a boy was found with a programme of English, mathematics, religious education, physical education, physics, chemistry, computer studies, geology and metalwork, and a girl with a course which consisted of English, mathematics, religious education, physical education, home economics, careers, typing, shorthand and commerce. It could indeed be argued that each of these programmes exhibited a degree of coherence but it will be noted that both pupils had discontinued history, geography, all aesthetic subjects and modern languages; the girl had also dropped science altogether. What was lacking was breadth in that important areas of the curriculum were excluded, wholly or almost wholly, from the programme of both pupils. The loss of some subjects reduced the range of opportunities, whether for employment or for continued education, open to these pupils at the end of their fifth year. The loss of other subjects removed opportunities to enlarge experience and understanding in ways potentially valuable for the future quality of their lives as adults and citizens. (op. cit., p. 41).

The survey goes on to argue on the basis of this kind of evidence that 'teachers need a view of the school curriculum as a whole . . . if they are to coordinate their pupils' learning and provide them with some sense of coherence in their programmes' (op. cit., p. 42).

One important element, then, which the notion of curriculum balance introduces into the curriculum debate is the need to plan the curriculum as a totality if we are to ensure a balanced educational diet for all pupils.

A second element, which also emerges from the examples quoted above, is that the need for balance must be recognized not only within education but also between education and the other demands that the schools must respond to. For the criticism offered of the two programmes described above is not only based on the fact that they represent an imbalance in educational terms, by losing opportunities, for example, 'to enlarge experience and understanding', but also that they fail to achieve a balance between educational and vocational considerations. This suggests, therefore, a further dimension to the notion of curriculum balance, that in planning the curriculum we should be looking not only for a balance of educational experiences for each individual, but that we must also be aiming for a balanced response to the conflicting claims of the interests of the individual and those of society, of the needs of the individual for both personal and vocational preparation. Among the wiser and more wholesome sayings of Confucius there is the very sound advice that if one has twopence to spend one should spend one penny on bread and the other on a flower – the bread to enable one to live, the flower to make life worth living. This provides a perspective on education that is too often ignored. The notion of curriculum balance encourages us to be mindful of it. It suggests too that we must strive for balance between demands for the development of the pupil's capacities and those for the learning of certain necessary bodies of knowledge, and between the need for specialization and that for breadth of study and experience. The balance we are looking for, then, is that of the juggler rather than that of the scientist, the engineer or the architect.

In fact, it is more delicate a notion than that, since the juggler, although needing to keep many balls in the air at one time, must achieve this by adherence to certain scientific and mathematical principles. These are not the principles that apply to calculations of educational balance. For here 'balance should not . . . be thought of in terms of equal quantities; the balance referred to here is a judicial balance rather than a mathematical one' (Schools Council 1975c, p. 27).

Again, therefore, we must remind ourselves that the notion of balance in education must be loose, flexible and relative. If we do so, we can recognize that it not only introduces into the debate an acceptance of the existence of competing interests whose demands have to be accommodated to each other. It also introduces the idea of the need for individual interpretation and reveals precisely why we have to concede a good deal of freedom in curriculum matters to local authorities, to schools, to teachers and even to individual pupils. For it makes clear that successful educational planning must always be of an *à la carte* rather than a *table d'hôte* kind, and that a balanced education, like a balanced diet, must be suited to the needs of the individual organism.

It suggests too the need to be tentative rather than dogmatic in educational planning, and thus illustrates what is the root inadequacy of the plan to establish a common core to the curriculum. For, in a somewhat paradoxical manner, the introduction of the apparently precise term 'balance' into the educational debate brings connotations of inexactitude, imprecision and the need for individual interpretation. For a common curriculum would in practice result in a very unbalanced curriculum for a majority of pupils, as we suggested earlier.

External guidance, then, should take the form not of directives or specific statements of subjects or subject content, but rather of broad principles or guidelines. And it is this that points us towards the desirability of adopting that 'process' approach to curriculum planning which we discussed in Chapter 4. For it suggests that the basis of educational planning should be certain broad principles which are susceptible to individual interpretation rather than lists of subjects or lists of goals or aims to be translated into step-by-step hierarchies of objectives. 'The true balancing agent lies not in the subject content but in the methods and approaches of the teacher and his inter-reaction with the pupils' (Petter 1970, p. 43; Schools Council 1975a, p. 18).

For the major error committed by the advocates of a common core curriculum is one that can be detected also in the work of most educational theorists. For almost all of them, from Plato onwards, having set out their educational principles, have immediately translated these into prescriptions for subject content, and have thus failed to recognize the simple truth that education consists of learning *through* subjects rather than the learning *of* subjects. A number of problems follow from this kind of misconception, some of which we noted in Chapters 2 and 3, but the major difficulty it presents is that it denies the possibility of interpretation and adaptation to individual needs and circumstances.

If we are to make this possible, and thus to resolve the problem we noted earlier of the conflict between pressures for external control and the requirements of internal development, we have to recognize that what is or should be common to everyone's education, what is essential to it, what constitutes a balanced educational diet cannot be defined by listing subjects but only by listing broad procedural principles. In the same way, and for the same reasons, what constitutes a proper nutritional diet cannot be defined merely by listing foodstuffs but only by establishing broad dietary principles to be translated into individual prescriptions to suit the requirements of each separate and unique physical constitution. We would rightly look with some suspicion on a doctor who prescribed the same diet or medicines for all of his patients; we must begin to view educational prescriptions in a similar light.

Broad procedural principles, then, are the only basis for curriculum planning, as some exponents of the primary school curriculum suggested a long time ago (Hadow Report 1931). For it is by reference to these that choice of subjects and of content is made; it is by reference to these that objectives are chosen when they are chosen; it is by reference to these that those objectives are modified and changed; it is by reference to these that the value of 'unintended learning outcomes' is gauged; and it is by reference to these that the content of education can be varied to meet the needs of individual schools, teachers and pupils, with no loss of educational value or validity.

We are likely to find too that agreement is easier to attain at this level than at that of subjects or subject content. For the question to be asked is what it means to be educated and few would wish to argue against the propositions that it means, for example, to have learned to value some activities for their own sake, to have learned to think for oneself, to have developed the ability to view the world critically, to have acquired understanding, to have achieved this in a number of fields, to have gained insight into several areas of human experience, to have been assisted to develop emotionally, aesthetically and physically as well as intellectually and, in general, to have developed capacities and competences of a number of kinds. Few would want to argue too against the proposition that education must prepare the individual to take his place in society with all that that entails. For these reasons, few have raised serious objections to the eight adjectives which Her

Majesty's Inspectorate have offered to 'identify 8 broad areas of experience that are considered to be important for all pupils' – aesthetic/creative, ethical, linguistic, mathematical, physical, scientific, social/political and spiritual (DES 1977c).

It is at this level, then, that we can hope to achieve some kind of agreement about what should be common to the curriculum of all pupils. We must, however, resist the temptation to translate these immediately into subjects, since it is this that creates not only controversy but also some of the confusions and resultant inadequacies, as we noted earlier. The pressures to do so are, of course, strong. The organizational structure of universities and secondary schools, the related system of public examinations, the traditional view of schooling adopted by parents and pupils, the basis of the Inspectorate at both local and national levels, the shape of courses of training for teachers, the constitution of the Schools Council and its early approach to curriculum development, along with many other factors, which we have noted in earlier chapters, all combine to tempt us in this direction. But, for all the reasons given throughout this book, they must be resisted and, indeed, reformed. Unfortunately, there is some evidence that the opposite is in fact happening and that these influences are beginning to extend even into the primary schools, some of which have hitherto been able to develop a 'process' approach to education because they have been free of such constraints (Blenkin and Kelly 1981; Kelly 1981), but it is to be hoped that, in the war between these two approaches, the latter will prevail, because it is only in that direction that we can hope to attain a balance between the demands for external control of education and the need to allow for the free development of the curriculum inside the schools.

Agreement on broad principles, then, should be the aim. The interpretation of these principles and decisions as to how they apply to individual schools and individual pupils must be left to the individuals concerned.

We must also resist the temptation to see these principles as aims and to translate them into hierarchies of curriculum objectives. For we must remember that, as was stressed in Chapter 4, the distinction between principles and aims in curriculum planning is very much more than a semantic one. It is quite fundamental. And it is the failure to recognize this that bedevils attempts, such as that of the Schools Council's Working Paper 70, *The Practical Curriculum* (Schools Council 1981), to solve the problem we have been discussing. For, although it begins with statements of the underlying principles of the curriculum and recognizes that the 'most important of the practical arguments for agreeing underlying principles, and basing action on them, is that this may be the only way of guaranteeing an effective curriculum for every child' (op. cit., p. 13), it quickly reverts to calling these 'aims' and, in no time at all, is deducing from these 'more specific aims' and thus leading us back into the whole hierarchy of linear, objectives-based approaches to learning, the problems of which were elucidated at some length in Chapter 4.

It is important, then, to treat principles as principles, to recognize that they are fundamental to planning that is to be educational in the full sense, to acknowledge that, while permitting a degree of centralized control, they also invite that complementary degree of local interpretation which we have seen is essential not only for the satisfactory education of every pupil but also for the continuing evolution of the curriculum itself.

Summary and conclusions

This chapter has attempted to show what the book itself has revealed, namely that curriculum development can only be effective if in a real sense it begins within the school, that any attempt to exercise complete control from without can only be successful if predicated on a very narrow definition of the curriculum as a collection of subjects or bodies of knowledge-content – a definition which does not bear too close a scrutiny in the light of any reasonable analysis of the concept of education. On the other hand, it has also revealed, as the book too has done, the legitimacy of the claims of outsiders for some control of what goes on in the nation's schools.

An attempt has, therefore, been made to explore the question of how these two apparently conflicting conclusions may be reconciled, how we may hope to achieve a proper measure of external control without *ipso facto* inhibiting the natural and essential evolution of the curriculum from within. This exploration appears to have revealed that such a reconciliation will only be achieved if we rethink a number of traditional views of education. We must begin by recognizing that in a real sense education must be development of a highly individual kind and that it cannot be a process of offering the same diet to all pupils and attempting to ensure that as far as is possible they should be homogenized. We must, secondly, appreciate that education is not a process of assimilating certain chosen bodies of knowledge but it is a matter of developing certain capacities, the route to which will be different for different people. This must lead to an appreciation of the undesirability and, indeed the impossibility, of controlling education from the outside by the imposition of requirements couched in terms of subjects or of aims and objectives; effective central control can only be exercised through the framing of broad principles of a kind that will promote rather than inhibit the processes of education and assist rather than retard the progress of curriculum development. The corollary of that assertion is that a good deal of scope must be given to individual schools, teachers and pupils to interpret these principles and apply them in such a way as to ensure an effective and balanced curriculum for every pupil.

We are left, therefore, with an awareness of the central role that the teacher must play both in the education of pupils and in the evolution of the curriculum. This may appear to some to be a ridiculous mouse to have emerged from such a mountain of verbiage and, indeed, it is strange to have to argue at such length for what may seem to some the very obvious proposition that the quality of education and of curriculum development must crucially hinge on the quality of the teacher. Yet the case has had to be made because there are so many who seem to wish to take on this responsibility themselves. It would seem clear that outside the school there are no proper opportunities to do this.

It should also be the case that those who have not had the professional preparation of the teacher will lack the expertise to meet the needs either of the education of pupils or of the development of the curriculum. And this brings us to the final point that must be made in conclusion not only of this chapter but also of this book. It is something of a truism to say that all curriculum development is teacher development, but that is the message of this excursion into the theory and practice of curriculum planning and development. For, if we are right to claim that curriculum development must in the last analysis rest in the hands of the teacher, we must conclude by urging that teachers be provided with the expertise to meet the demands which this makes of them, and with conditions of work which will enable them to respond to this new and more complex role. Some must also be provided with opportunities to acquire special expertise in the area of the management of curriculum development. For, as we have seen, there is a need for change-agents within the school, whose task must include at the very least the encouragement of staff to debate curriculum issues with each other and thus collectively achieve an overview of the total curriculum the school is offering to its pupils.

Our present system of preparing teachers falls far short of performing these functions. There is still a major emphasis in almost all courses of teacher education on subject-content as the major need. An increasing number of teachers in the United Kingdom are being prepared to work with children of all ages by a period of eight or nine months of training, following three years of study of a subject or subjects; and, quite often, these short courses of training in themselves place a heavy emphasis on continued involvement in the subject. In the period immediately following the Second World War, training periods of this length were described as 'emergency training courses'; they are now becoming the norm.

It does a grave injustice and, indeed, untold violence to the quality of education and of curriculum development that they rest in the hands of people most of whom have had a minimal preparation for these responsibilities, and most of whom will have few opportunities to improve their competence and skills through in-service courses. The length, the scope and thus the quality of the initial and in-service education of teachers must be improved if we are to be able to leave education and curriculum development to them with an easy mind. It is to that end that those who wish to raise standards and maintain quality-control in education need to direct their energies. A proper system of education based on a continuously evolving curriculum will only be attained when we have teachers capable of taking responsibility for it themselves rather than attempting to act on the dictates of others.

This book is offered as a small contribution towards the development of that capability.

BIBLIOGRAPHY

Adams, A. (1976) *The Humanities Jungle*. London: Ward Lock Educational.

Archambault, R.D. (ed.) (1965) *Philosophical Analysis and Education*. London: Routledge and Kegan Paul.

Ashton, P., Kneen, P. and Davies, F. (1975) *Aims into Practice in the Primary School*. London: University of London Press.

Atkin, J. Myron (1979) Educational accountability in the United States. 5–22 in Stenhouse, L. (ed.) (1979).

Ayer, A.J. (1936; 2nd edition 1946) *Language, Truth and Logic*. London: Gollancz.

Ball, Elaine (1981) *School Focused Curriculum Development: Constraints and Possibilities*. Unpublished MA thesis, University of London.

Bantock, G.H. (1968) *Culture, Industrialisation and Education*. London: Routledge and Kegan Paul.

Bantock, G.H. (1971) Towards a theory of popular education. 251–264 in Hooper (1971).

Barker-Lunn, J.C. (1970) *Streaming in the Primary School*. Slough: National Foundation for Educational Research.

Barnes, D. (1976) *From Communication to Curriculum*. Harmondsworth: Penguin Books.

Becher, T. and Maclure, S. (1978) *The Politics of Curriculum Change*. London: Hutchinson.

Bell, R., Fowler, G. and Little, K. (eds.) (1973) *Education in Great Britain and Ireland*. London and Boston: Routledge and Kegan Paul with the Open University Press.

Bernstein, B. (1967) Open schools, open society?, *New Society*, 14 September.

Bernstein, B. (1971) On the classification and framing of educational knowledge. 47–69 in Young (ed.) (1971).

Blenkin, G. (1980) The influence of initial styles of curriculum development. 45–64 in Kelly (ed.) (1980).

Blenkin, G.M. and Kelly, A.V. (1981) *The Primary Curriculum*. London: Harper and Row.

Bloom, B.S. et al. (1956) *Taxonomy of Educational Objectives. I: Cognitive Domain*. London: Longmans.

Blum, A.F. (1971) The corpus of knowledge as a normative order: intellectual critique of the social order of knowledge and commonsense features of bodies of knowledge. 117–132 in Young (ed.) (1971).

Blyth, W.A.L. (1974) One development project's awkward thinking about objectives. *Journal of Curriculum Studies* **6**, 99–111.

Bobbitt, F. (1918) *The Curriculum*. Boston: Houghton Mifflin.

Bolam, D. (1971) Integrating the curriculum: a case study in the Humanities. *Paedagogica Europaea* **6**, 157–171.

Charters, W.W. (1924) *Curriculum Construction*. New York: Macmillan.

Connaughton, I.M. (1969) The validity of examinations at 16-plus. *Educational Research* **11**, 163–178.

Cooksey, G. (1972) Stantonbury Campus – Milton Keynes. *Ideas* **23**, 28–33.

Cooksey, G. (1976a) The scope of education and its opportunities in the 80s. 4–13 in Kelly (ed.) (1976).

Cooksey, G. (1976b) Stantonbury Campus: the idea develops – December 1975. *Ideas* **32**, 58–63.

Cox, C.B. and Dyson, A.E. (eds) (1969a) *Fight for Education: A Black Paper*. Manchester: Critical Quarterly Society.

Cox, C.B. and Dyson, A.E. (eds) (1969b) *Black Paper Two: The Crisis in Education*. Manchester: Critical Quarterly Society.

Cronbach, L. (1963) Course improvements through evaluation. *Teachers' College Record* **64**, 672–683.

Davies, I.K. (1976) *Objectives in Curriculum Design*. Maidenhead: McGraw-Hill.

Davies, W. (1980) Administrative and historical aspects. 111–132 in Kelly (ed.) (1980).

Dearden, R.F. (1968) *The Philosophy of Primary Education*. London: Routledge and Kegan Paul.

Dearden, R.F. (1976) *Problems in Primary Education*. London: Routledge and Kegan Paul.

Dearden, R.F., Hirst, P.H. and Peters, R.S. (1972) *Education and the Development of Reason*. London: Routledge and Kegan Paul.

Dewey, J. (1938) *Experience and Education*. New York: Collier-Macmillan.

Downey, M.E. and Kelly, A.V. (1979) *Theory and Practice of Education: An Introduction*. Second edition. London: Harper and Row.

Eisner, E.W. (1969) Instructional and expressive educational objectives: their formulation and use in curriculum. 1–8 in Popham et al. (1969).

Eliot, T.S. (1948) *Notes Towards a Definition of Culture*. London: Faber and Faber.

Elliott, J. (1976) Preparing teachers for classroom accountability. *Education for Teaching* **100**, 49–71.

Elliott, J. and Adelman, C. (1973) Reflecting where the action is. *Education for Teaching* **92**, 8–20.

Elliott, J. and Adelman, C. (1974) *Innovation in Teaching and Action-Research*. Norwich: Centre for Applied Research in Education.

Fowler, G. (1977) Uncommonly hard road to the core. *Times Educational Supplement*, 4 February.

Freeman, J. (1969) *Team Teaching in Britain*. London: Ward Lock.

Freire, P. (1972) *Pedagogy of the Oppressed*. Harmondsworth: Penguin Books.

Goldsmiths' College (1965) *Report of the First Pilot Course for Experienced Teachers: The Role of the School in a Changing Society*. London: Goldsmiths' College.

Gribble, J.H. (1970) Pandora's box: the affective domain of educational objectives. *Journal of Curriculum Studies* **2**, 11–24.

Gross, N., Giacquinta, J.B. and Bernstein, M. (1971) *Implementing Organizational Innovations: a Sociological Analysis of Planned Change*. New York: Harper and Row.

Halpin, A.W. (1966) *Theory and Research in Educational Administration*. New York: Macmillan.

Halpin, A.W. (1967) Change and organizational climate. *Journal of Educational Administration* **5**.

Hamilton, D. (1976) *Curriculum Evaluation*. London: Open Books.

Hamingson, D. (ed.) (1973) *Towards Judgement: the Publications of the Evaluation Unit of the Humanities Curriculum Project 1970–1972*. Norwich: Centre for Applied Research in Education, Occasional Publications No. 1.

Hamlyn, D.W. (1972) Objectivity. 96–109 in Part 2 of Dearden et al. (1972).

Hargreaves, D.H. (1972) *Interpersonal Relations in Education*. London: Routledge and Kegan Paul.

Harlen, W. (1971) Some practical points in favour of curriculum evaluation. *Journal of Curriculum Studies* 3, 128–134.

Harlen, W. (1973) Science 5–13 Project. 16–35 in Schools Council (1973).

Harris, C.W. (1963) Some issues in evaluation. *The Speech Teacher* 12, 191–199.

Havelock, R.G. (1971) *Planning for Innovation through the Dissemination and Utilization of Knowledge*. Ann Arbor, Michigan: Centre for Research and Utilization of Knowledge.

Hicks, G. (1976) *Design Studies in Education*. Unpublished M.Phil. thesis, University of London.

Hirst, P.H. (1965) Liberal education and the nature of knowledge. 113–138 in Archambault (ed.) (1965). Also 87–111 in Peters (1973b).

Hirst, P.H. (1969) The logic of the curriculum. *Journal of Curriculum Studies* 1, 142–158. Also 232–250 in Hooper (1971).

Hirst, P.H. (1975) The curriculum and its objectives – a defence of piecemeal rational planning. 9–21 in *Studies in Education 2. The Curriculum. The Doris Lee Lectures*. London: University of London Institute of Education.

Hirst, P.H. and Peters, R.S. (1970) *The Logic of Education*. London: Routledge and Kegan Paul.

Hogben, D. (1972) The behavioural objectives approach: some problems and some dangers. *Journal of Curriculum Studies* 4, 42–50.

Hollins, T.H.B. (ed.) (1964) *Aims in Education: The Philosophic Approach*. Manchester: Manchester University Press.

Holly, D. (1973) *Beyond Curriculum*. St Albans: Hart-Davis, MacGibbon.

Hooper, R. (ed.) (1971) *The Curriculum: Context, Design and Development*. Edinburgh: Oliver and Boyd in association with the Open University Press.

House, E.R. (ed.) (1973) *School Evaluation: the Politics and Process*. Berkeley: McCutchan Publishing Corporation.

House, E. (1974) *The Politics of Educational Innovation*. Berkeley: McCutchan Publishing Corporation.

Hoyle, E. (1969a) How does the curriculum change? 1. A proposal for inquiries. *Journal of Curriculum Studies* 1, 132–141. Also 375–385 in Hooper (1971).

Hoyle, E. (1969b) How does the curriculum change? 2. Systems and strategies. *Journal of Curriculum Studies* **1**, 230–239. Also 385–395 in Hooper (1971).

Illich, I.D. (1971) *Deschooling Society*. London: Calder.

James, C.M. (1968) *Young Lives at Stake*. London: Collins.

Jenkins, D. (1973) Integrated Studies Project. 70–79 in Schools Council (1973).

Jenkins, D. and Shipman, M.D. (1976) *Curriculum: an Introduction*. London: Open Books.

Keddie, N. (1971) Classroom Knowledge. 133–160 in Young (ed.) (1971).

Keddie, N. (ed.) (1973) *Tinker, Tailor: The Myth of Cultural Deprivation*. Harmondsworth: Penguin Books.

Kelly, A.V. (1973) Professional tutors. *Education for Teaching* **92**, 2–7.

Kelly, A.V. (1974) *Teaching Mixed Ability Classes*. London: Harper and Row.

Kelly, A.V. (ed.) (1975) *Case Studies in Mixed Ability Teaching*. London: Harper and Row.

Kelly, A.V. (ed.) (1976) *The Scope of Education: Opportunities for the Teacher*, Report of a Conference at Goldsmiths' College, London.

Kelly, A.V. (1978) *Mixed Ability Grouping: Theory and Practice*. London: Harper and Row.

Kelly, A.V. (1980) Ideological constraints on curriculum planning. 7–30 in Kelly (ed.) (1980).

Kelly, A.V. (ed.) (1980) *Curriculum Context*. London: Harper and Row.

Kelly, A.V. (1981) Research and the primary curriculum. *Journal of Curriculum Studies* **13**, 215–225.

Kelly, P.J. (1973) Nuffield 'A' level biological science project. 91–109 in Schools Council (1973).

Kerr, J.F. (ed.) (1968) *Changing the Curriculum*. London: University of London Press.

Kratwohl, D.R. (1965) Stating objectives appropriately for program, for curriculum, and for instructional materials development. *Journal of Teacher Education* **16**, 83–92.

Kratwohl, D.R. et al. (1964) *Taxonomy of Educational Objectives. II. Affective Domain*. London: Longmans.

Lawton, D. (1969) The idea of an integrated curriculum. *University of London Institute of Education Bulletin* **19**, 5–11.

Lawton, D. (1973) *Social Change, Educational Theory and Curriculum Planning*. London: University of London Press.

Lawton, D. (1975) *Class, Culture and the Curriculum*. London: Routledge and Kegan Paul.

Lawton, D. (1980) *The Politics of the School Curriculum*. London: Routledge and Kegan Paul.

Lee, S.G. (1977) *The Role of the Change Agent in the Cooperative Model of Curriculum Innovation*. Unpublished MA thesis, University of London.

Lovell, K. (1967) *Team Teaching*. Leeds: University of Leeds Press.

MacDonald, B. (1971) Briefing Decision Makers. Internal paper, Evaluation Unit of the Humanities Curriculum Project, later reprinted in Hamingson (ed.) (1973), House (ed.) (1973) and Schools Council (1974b).

MacDonald, B. (1973) Humanities Curriculum Project. 80–90 in Schools Council (1973).

MacDonald, B. (1975) Evaluation and the control of education. 125–136 in Tawney (1975).

MacDonald, B. and Rudduck, J. (1971) Curriculum research and development projects: barriers to success. *British Journal of Educational Psychology* **41**, 148–154.

MacDonald, B. and Walker, R. (1976) *Changing the Curriculum*. London: Open Books.

Macintosh, H.C. (1970) A constructive role for examining boards in curriculum development. *Journal of Curriculum Studies* 2, 32–39.

MacIntyre, A.C. (1964) Against utilitarianism. 1–23 in Hollins (ed.) (1964).

Maclure, J.S. (1970) The control of education. *History of Education Society Studies in the Government and Control of Education since 1860*. London: Methuen.

Mager, R.F. (1962) *Preparing Instructional Objectives*. Palo Alto, California: Fearon.

Maslow, A.H. (1954) *Motivation and Personality*. New York: Harper and Row.

Musgrove, F. (1973) Power and the integrated curriculum. *Journal of Curriculum Studies* 5, 3–12.

Parlett, M. and Hamilton, D. (1975) Evaluation as illumination. 84–101 in Tawney (1975).

Peters, R.S. (1965) Education as initiation. 87–111 in Archambault (ed.) (1965).

Peters, R.S. (1966) *Ethics and Education*. London: George Allen and Unwin.

Peters, R.S. (1967a) In defence of Bingo: a rejoinder. *British Journal of*

Educational Studies 15, 188–194.

Peters, R.S. (1967b) What is an educational process? 1–23 in Peters (ed.) (1967c). •

Peters, R.S. (ed.) (1967c) *The Concept of Education*. London: Routledge and Kegan Paul.

Peters, R.S. (ed.) (1969) *Perspectives on Plowden*. London: Routledge and Kegan Paul.

Peters, R.S. (1973a) Aims of education: a conceptual inquiry. 11–29 in Peters (1973b).

Peters, R.S. (1973b) *The Philosophy of Education*. Oxford: Oxford University Press.

Petter, G.S.V. (1970) Coherent secondary education. *Trends in Education* 19, 38–43.

Phenix, P.H. (1964) *Realms of Meaning*. New York: McGraw-Hill.

Pirsig, R. (1974) *Zen and the Art of Motorcycle Maintenance*. London: The Bodley Head.

Popham, W.J. (1969) Objectives and instruction. 32–52 in Popham et al. (1969).

Popham, W.J., Eisner, E.W., Sullivan, H.J. and Tyler, L.L. (1969) *Instructional Objectives*. American Educational Research Association Monograph Series on Curriculum Evaluation No. 3. Chicago: Rand McNally.

Postman, N. (1970) The politics of reading. *Harvard Educational Review* 40, 244–252. Also 86–95 in Keddie (ed.) (1973).

Pring, R. (1971a) Bloom's Taxonomy: a philosophical critique (2). *Cambridge Journal of Education* 2, 83–91.

Pring, R. (1971b) Curriculum integration. *Proceedings of the Philosophy of Education Society of Great Britain*, 170–200.

Pring, R. (1973) Objectives and innovation: the irrelevance of theory. *London Educational Review* 2, 46–54.

Pudwell, C. (1980) Examinations and the school curriculum. 83–110 in Kelly (ed.) (1980).

Purcell, F.A. (1981) *The Role of the Change Agent in Curriculum Development*. Unpublished MA thesis, University of London.

Richards, R. (1979) Learning through science. *Schools Council Newsletter* 30, 5–7.

Rudduck, J. (1976) *Dissemination of Innovation: the Humanities Curriculum Project*. Schools Council Working Paper 56. London: Evans/Methuen Educational for the Schools Council.

Russell, B. (1950) *Unpopular Essays*. London: Allen and Unwin.

Scheffler, I. (1960) *The Language of Education*. Springfield, Illinois: C.C. Thomas.

Schon, D.A. (1971) *Beyond the Stable State*. London: Temple-Smith.

Schools Council (1967) *Society and the Young School Leaver*. Working Paper 11. London: Her Majesty's Stationery Office.

Schools Council (1969a) *Education through the Use of Materials*. Working Paper 26. London: Evans/Methuen Educational for the Schools Council.

Schools Council (1969b) *Rural Studies in Secondary Schools*. Working Paper 24. London: Evans/Methuen Educational for the Schools Council.

Schools Council (1970) *The Humanities Project: An Introduction*. London: Heinemann.

Schools Council (1971a) *A Common System of Examining at 16+*. Examinations Bulletin 23. London: Evans/Methuen Educational for the Schools Council.

Schools Council (1971b) *Home Economics Teaching*. Curriculum Bulletin 4. London: Evans/Methuen Educational for the Schools Council.

Schools Council (1971c) *Choosing a Curriculum for the Young School Leaver*. Working Paper 33. London: Evans/Methuen Educational for the Schools Council.

Schools Council (1972a) *With Objectives in Mind: Guide to Science 5–13*. London: Macdonald Educational for the Schools Council.

Schools Council (1972b) *Exploration Man: An Introduction to Integrated Studies*. Oxford: Oxford University Press for the Schools Council.

Schools Council (1973) *Evaluation in Curriculum Development: Twelve Case Studies*. Schools Council Research Studies. London: Macmillan Education for the Schools Council.

Schools Council (1974a) *Social Education: an Experiment in Four Secondary Schools*. Working Paper 51. London: Evans/Methuen Educational for the Schools Council.

Schools Council (1974b) *Dissemination and In-Service Training: Report of the Schools Council Working Party on Dissemination (1972–1973)*. Schools Council Pamphlet 14. London: Schools Council.

Schools Council (1975a) *The Whole Curriculum 13–16*. Working Paper 53. London: Evans/Methuen Educational for the Schools Council.

Schools Council (1975b) *Examinations at 16+: Proposals for the Future*. Examination Bulletin 23. London: Evans/Methuen Educational for the Schools Council.

Schools Council (1975c) *The Curriculum in the Middle Years*. Working Paper

55. London: Evans/Methuen Educational for the Schools Council.

Schools Council (1978a) *Examinations at 18 + : the N and F Studies.* Working Paper 60. London: Evans/Methuen Educational for the Schools Council.

Schools Council (1978b) *Impact and Take-up Project. A First Interim Report.* London: Schools Council.

Schools Council (1979) *Examinations at 18 + : Report on the N and F Debate.* Working Paper 66. London: Methuen Educational for the Schools Council.

Schools Council (1980) *Impact and Take-up Project. A Condensed Interim Report on Secondary Schools.* London: Schools Council.

Schools Council (1981) *The Practical Curriculum.* Working Paper 70. London: Methuen Educational for the Schools Council.

Scriven, M. (1967) The methodology of evaluation. 39–89 in Stake (ed.) (1967).

Shipman, M.D. (1972) Contrasting views of a curriculum project. *Journal of Curriculum Studies* **4**, 145–153.

Shipman, M.D. (1973) The impact of a curriculum project. *Journal of Curriculum Studies* **5**, 47–57.

Skilbeck, M. (1973) Openness and structure in the curriculum. 116–124 in Taylor and Walton (eds.) (1973).

Skilbeck, M. (1976) School-based curriculum development. 90–102 in Open University Course 203, Unit 26. Milton Keynes: The Open University Press.

Smith, L.A. and Macintosh, H.G. (1974) *Towards a Freer Curriculum.* London: University of London Press.

Sockett, H. (1976a) *Designing the Curriculum.* London: Open Books.

Sockett, H. (1976b) Teacher accountability. *Proceedings of the Philosophy of Education Society*, July 1976, 34–57.

Stake, R.E. (ed.) (1967) *Perspectives of Curriculum Evaluation.* American Educational Research Association, Monograph Series on Curriculum Evaluation No. 1. Chicago: Rand McNally.

Stake, R. (1972) Analysis and Portrayal. Paper originally written for AERA Annual Meeting presentation 1972. Republished as Responsive Education in *New Trends in Education* No. 35 (1975) Institute of Education, University of Göteborg.

Stenhouse, L., (1969) The humanities curriculum project. *Journal of Curriculum Studies* **1**, 26–33. Also 336–344 in Hooper (1971).

Stenhouse, L. (1970) Some limitations of the use of objectives in curriculum research and planning. *Paedagogica Europaea* **6**, 73–83.

Stenhouse, L. (1975) *An Introduction to Curriculum Research and Development*. London: Heinemann.

Stenhouse, L. (ed.) (1979) *Educational Analysis*, Vol. 1, No. 1. Lewes: Falmer.

Taba, H. (1962) *Curriculum Development: Theory and Practice*. New York: Harcourt, Brace and World.

Tawney, D. (1973) Evaluation and curriculum development. 4–15 in Schools Council (1973).

Tawney, D. (ed.) (1975) *Curriculum Evaluation Today: Trends and Implications*. Schools Council Research Studies. London: Macmillan Education.

Taylor, P.H. (1970) *How Teachers Plan their Courses*. Slough: National Foundation for Educational Research.

Taylor, P.H. and Walton, J. (eds.) (1963) *The Curriculum: Research, Innovation and Change*. London: Ward Lock Educational.

Taylor, P.H., Reid, W.A., Holley, B.J. and Exon, G. (1974) *Purpose, Power and Constraint in the Primary School Curriculum*. London: Macmillan.

Thompson, K. and White, J. (1975) *Curriculum Development: A Dialogue*. London: Pitman.

Tyler, R.W. (1932) *The Construction of Examinations in Botany and Zoology. Service Studies in Higher Education*. Ohio State University, Bureau of Educational Research Monographs, No. 15, 49–50.

Tyler, R.W. (1949) *Basic Principles of Curriculum and Instruction*. Chicago: University of Chicago Press.

Vernon, P.E. (1964) *The Certificate of Secondary Education: An Introduction to Objective-type Examinations*. Secondary Schools Examinations Council, Examinations Bulletin No. 4. London: Her Majesty's Stationery Office.

Warnock, M. (1977) *Schools of Thought*. London: Faber and Faber.

Warwick, D. (1971) *Team Teaching*. London: University of London Press.

Warwick, D. (ed.) (1973) *Integrated Studies in the Secondary School*. London: University of London Press.

Warwick, D. (1975) *Curriculum Structure and Design*. London: University of London Press.

Weiss, R.S. and Rein, M. (1969) The evaluation of broad aim programmes: a cautionary tale and a moral. *Annals of the American Academy of Political and Social Science* **385**, 133–142.

West, E.G. (1965) Liberty and education: John Stuart Mill's dilemma. *Philosophy* **XL**, 129–142.

Wheeler, D.K. (1967) *Curriculum Process*. London: University of London Press.

White, A.R. (1964) *Attention*. Oxford: Blackwell.

White, A.R. (1967) *The Philosophy of Mind*. New York: Random House.

White, J.P. (1968) Education in obedience. *New Society*, 2 May.

White, J.P. (1971) The concept of curriculum evaluation. *Journal of Curriculum Studies* **3**, 101–112.

White, J.P. (1973) *Towards a Compulsory Curriculum*. London: Routledge and Kegan Paul.

Whitehead, A.N. (1932) *The Aims of Education*. London: Williams and Norgate.

Wiley, D.E. (1970) Design and analysis of evaluation studies. 259–269 in Wittrock and Wiley (1970).

Wilhelms, F.T. (1971) Evaluation as feedback. 320–335 in Hooper (ed.) (1971).

Wilson, P.S. (1967) In defence of Bingo. *British Journal of Educational Studies* **15**, 5–27.

Wilson, P.S. (1971) *Interest and Discipline in Education*. London: Routledge and Kegan Paul.

Wittrock, M.C. and Wiley, D.E. (1970) *The Evaluation of Instruction: Issues and Problems*. New York: Holt, Rinehart and Winston.

Yates, A. and Pidgeon, D.A. (1957) *Admission to Grammar Schools*. London: Newnes.

Young, M.F.D. (ed.) (1971) *Knowledge and Control*. London: Collier-Macmillan.

Young, M.F.D. (1973) On the politics of educational knowledge: some preliminary considerations with particular reference to the Schools Council. 70–81 in Bell et al. (eds.) (1973).

Government reports and other official publications referred to in the text and listed in chronological order:

Report of the Schools Inquiry Commission (The Taunton Report) (1868).

Board of Education (1926) *The Education of the Adolescent* (The Hadow Report on Secondary Education). London: Her Majesty's Stationery Office.

Board of Education (1931) *Primary Education* (The Hadow Report on

Primary Education). London: Her Majesty's Stationery Office.

Central Advisory Council For Education (1959) *15 to 18* (The Crowther Report). London: Her Majesty's Stationery Office.

Secondary Schools Examinations Council (1960) *Secondary School Examinations other than the GCE* (The Beloe Report). London: Her Majesty's Stationery Office.

Central Advisory Council for Education (1963) *Half Our Future* (The Newsom Report). London: Her Majesty's Stationery Office.

Central Advisory Council for Education (1967) *Children and Their Primary Schools* (The Plowden Report). London: Her Majesty's Stationery Office.

Department of Education and Science (1972) *Teacher Education and Training* (The James Report). London: Her Majesty's Stationery Office.

Department of Education and Science (1975) *A Language for Life* (The Bullock Report). London: Her Majesty's Stationery Office.

Inner London Education Committee (1976) *Report of the Public Enquiry into Teaching, Organisation and Management of William Tyndale Junior and Infant Schools* (The Auld Report). London: ILEA.

Department of Education and Science (1977a) *A New Partnership for our Schools* (The Taylor Report). London: Her Majesty's Stationery Office.

Department of Education and Science and the Welsh Office (1977b) *Education in Schools: A Consultative Document* (Green Paper). Cmnd. 6869. London: Her Majesty's Stationery Office.

Department of Education and Science (1977c) *Curriculum 11–16*. London: Her Majesty's Stationery Office.

Department of Education and Science (1978) *Primary Education in England: A Survey by HM Inspectors of Schools*. London: Her Majesty's Stationery Office.

Department of Education and Science (1979) *Aspects of Secondary Education in England: A Survey by HM Inspectors of Schools*. London: Her Majesty's Stationery Office.

Department of Education and Science (1980a) *A View of the Curriculum*. HMI Series, *Matters for Discussion* No. 11. London: Her Majesty's Stationery Office.

Department of Education and Science and the Welsh Office (1980b) *A Framework for the School Curriculum*. London: Her Majesty's Stationery Office.

Department of Education and Science and the Welsh Office (1981) *The School Curriculum*. London: Her Majesty's Stationery Office.

Index of Names

Index of Subjects